ZERO HOUR

ZERO HOUR

Turn the Greatest Political and Financial
Upheaval in Modern History to Your Advantage

HARRY S. DENT, JR.
WITH ANDREW PANCHOLI

Edited by Teresa van den Barselaar

PORTFOLIO/PENGUIN

Portfolio / Penguin
An imprint of Penguin Random House LLC
375 Hudson Street
New York, New York 10014

Most Portfolio books are available at a discount when purchased in quantity for sales promotions or corporate use. Special editions, which include personalized covers, excerpts, and corporate imprints, can be created when purchased in large quantities. For more information, please call (212) 572-2232 or e-mail specialmarkets@penguinrandomhouse.com. Your local bookstore can also assist with discounted bulk purchases using the Penguin Random House corporate Business-to-Business program. For assistance in locating a participating retailer, e-mail B2B@penguinrandomhouse.com.

ISBN: 9780525536055 (hardcover)
ISBN: 9780525536062 (e-book)

Printed in the United States of America
1   3   5   7   9   10   8   6   4   2

To my wife, Jean-ne, the love of my life, and the person that has stood by me the most, through all my trials and tribulations.

To my deceased father, Harry S. Dent, Sr., who was a brave and visionary political strategist that thrust the South into the political mainstream by electing Nixon through the swing vote in 1968. He became known for his "southern strategy." He's the best politician I know and I learned much from him. He was the greatest role model a son could have.

—Harry Dent

To my father, Vijay, who is no longer with us, and my mother, Nila— both of whom always encouraged the gathering of knowledge. To Karen, Chanteyhl, and Jake for their never-ending support.

—Andrew Pancholi

CONTENTS

PART III
How to Profit from the Greatest Revolution and Financial Crisis since the Late 1700s

ZERO HOUR

PREFACE

What the Politicians Don't Know

Trump and Brexit are only the beginning of a monumental revolution in politics, economics . . . everything.

Harry Dent

THERE MAY NOT BE JACOBITES running through the streets, kilts flapping around hairy knees, wielding swords while screaming like madmen. . . .

There may not be royal heads thudding into blood-soaked baskets as sunlight glints off the sharp edge of the rising guillotine. . . .

There may not be millions of starved and emaciated Russian protesters clashing with police around the capital.

But mark my words: we are now witnesses to the greatest revolution since the rise of democracy, in the late 1700s . . . the emergence of free-market capitalism . . . and the Industrial Revolution.

How many people have you met who can say that?!

And while we don't have Jacobites or dead royal Frenchmen or desperate Petrograd workers, what we have is equally serious and volatile.

Demonstrators are making their causes heard in streets around the world. Terrorists are an even more nefarious threat than ever. The frequency and numbers involved have grown steadily since 2001.

Black Lives Matter.

Brexit.

November 2016 presidential campaign protests in Chicago, Los Angeles, and New York.

The Women's March on Washington, D.C. (and across the globe), after President Donald Trump's inauguration.

The South African protests against President Jacob Zuma and his cronies.

Protests and all-out civil war in Syria.

Egypt and the Arab Spring.

Macedonia.

Ethiopia.

Brazil.

Moldova.

The Congo.

South Korea.

Poland.

Venezuela.

I can't think of many (if any) countries that *haven't* seen an uprising of the citizenry against the establishment.

The thing is, all of this was inevitable and predictable. Not, of course, the specific details of each of the uprisings we've seen and will continue to see until this 21st-century revolution has run its course. Rather, the revolution itself was predictable.

That's because revolutions are cyclical. They run on a very specific timetable.

But then, so does EVERYTHING.

Yet the presidents and their men and women miss it every time, because they're blind to cycles. (I could list all the other things they're blind to, but I'll let you have fun with that one after you've put this book down.)

Unfortunately, this cycle-blindness extends to most people. And that's why I've written this book.

Your life could be so much easier, happier, healthier, and wealthier if you grasped the powerful cycles that influence everything you do and touch. Rather than deny or fight against them, if you embraced the cycles in your life and the world, you'd accomplish more and be less stressed.

(Your life could be so much easier, happier, healthier, and wealthier if politicians and governments—presidents and their posses—appreciated and understood cycles as well!)

Take technology, for example.

It's constantly evolving, automating old jobs and ways of doing business. Yet, despite its continually improving our quality of life on a regular cycle, people still resist progress.

I understand why.

When people lose their jobs to industrial machines or computers or robots, it hurts. But to think that automation is a bad thing is to think too short-term. In the long run, it creates better jobs and a more affluent society—every time.

Think about it. Our society consisted mostly of farmers in the late 1800s. Now only 1.5 percent of our population produces all the food we need (and then some, for export). This has freed us up to become doctors, lawyers, managers, and technicians.

Besides, if more people understood the cycles, they wouldn't be so worried about automation destroying working-class jobs. Would you rather be doing backbreaking farmwork in the blazing sun all day or working in an air-conditioned factory or office, with health-care and retirement benefits? My 45-year Innovation Cycle shows that mainstream disruptive technology or innovation won't sweep through our economy again until around 2032–33 through 2055.

In other words, the hottest and strongest new technologies—like robotics, biotech, nanotechnology, and 3-D printing—won't go main-stream enough to tip the scales for another 16 years!

Many recent innovations, like Uber and Airbnb, autonomous cars and artificial intelligence, will replace some jobs, yes, but they won't create whole new industries and ways of working and living (like the suburbs) just yet! They're not like the assembly line, which made everyday workers ten times more productive. They're not dis-ruptive only because they're confined to niche markets or they make minor improvements to mature, existing industries.

Today's innovations are only enough to make a dying economy a bit more efficient. . . . They don't create a new economy that launches into a new era, as did the mushrooming of steamships, railroads, autos, and the Internet—all 45 years apart.

That said, artificial intelligence is on the road to becoming a disruptor. It's still too early to change the game altogether, but it will increasingly automate almost all left-brain, white-collar work and free up more people to do creative things, like entrepreneurial cre-ation of new and better products and more customized service for customers.

That is the modern-day equivalent of the assembly line.

That will be revolutionary.

But before we reach that point, we have a political, cultural, and social revolution right on our doorstep, and, as I'll show you in the following pages, it was preordained . . . and is playing out exactly on schedule.

You see, every 250 years, we experience a massive, life-changing revolution. The last cycle brought us the convergence of democracy and free-market capitalism. The one before that ushered in the Protestant Reformation in Europe. And so on.

Now it's bringing home the greatest political and social revolution since the emergence of democracy.

The financial crisis before us is not just about another debt and financial-asset deleveraging, like the 1930s. . . .

The political crisis spreading across the globe is not just about another regime change or a "populist revolution," like the one led by Hitler and Mussolini (which take place every 84 years).

This is about the destruction of the old ways—top-down management, establishment politics, social engineering, financial and monetary manipulation, wealthy elitism—and the rising up of a new world.

This revolution, marked by an initial backlash against globalization, will take decades to unfold. It'll break the world as we know it back down to its individual elements, focused around local and regional cultural roots. Then it will start to re-form into a more powerful, cohesive entity that will surge into the final peak of globalization (which is on predictable 100- and 500-year cycles, by the way).

One of my favorite, paradoxical principles of growth and evolution is this:

Technologies change faster than cultures, and cultures change faster than genes.

This is why any extended periods of strong growth and progress create divergences in incomes and values that eventually become unsustainable.

The typical developed country has 6 times the GDP per capita of the typical emerging country. At the extremes—Norway versus Kenya—it's 30 times.

Southern and Eastern European countries have as little as half the GDP per capita of Northern and Western Europe.

Globalization has succeeded so much that it has put incompatible cultures, religions, and income groups into the same cooking pot. This chart, from the World Values Survey, shows this best.

Figure I-1: The Global Cultural/Religious Divide: Nine Global Cultures from the World Values Survey

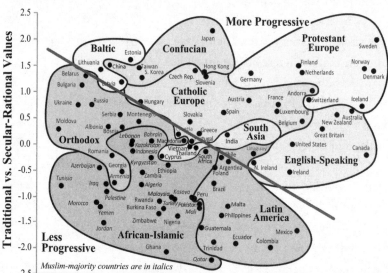

Source: Courtesy of www.worldvaluessurvey.org; annotations by Dent Research

You'll see nine distinct global cultures around two variables. On the *x* axis are survival (conformist) versus self-expression (individualistic) values. On the *y* axis are traditional (faith) versus secular-rational (scientific) values.

As you move from the bottom left to the upper right, you're going from conservative to progressive. From the bottom left to the top left, you're going from more traditional to the most secular-rational. From the bottom left to the bottom right, you're going from survival-based psychology to greater self-expression (Abraham Maslow's hierarchy of human needs).

The group that is the most rational and self-expressive is Protestant Europe. The English-speaking countries (often called the British offshoots) are equally self-expressive but a bit less rational and scientific. The Catholic or Southern European countries are a bit less affluent, less self-expressive, and more traditional.

Confucian East Asia is very high on the rational side (try to compete with them in science!), but also less self-expressive and more conformist.

The Orthodox countries of Eastern Europe and Russia are pretty high on the rational scale but much less self-expressive.

The least progressive on both values is the African-Islamic group—and that's why they often have such a hard time integrating into Western countries.

And then there is Latin America, which is more traditional but more expressive—can they dance or what?!

Looking at it this way, you can see why the more affluent Christian cultures of Europe and the English-speaking groups clash with the African-Islamic ones. They're quite literally on the extreme opposite sides of both value dimensions.

You can also see why Russia and the Eastern European Orthodox countries don't get along very well with Western Europe and North America!

Rapid globalization and population migration, especially since World War II, have thrust all of these very different cultures in one another's faces. Quite frankly, a lot of people have had enough of it . . . particularly those who find themselves on the lower rungs.

This breakdown of the current situation helps us see what things might look like in the years and decades to come as this revolution unfolds.

Think about more effective trading and political zones.

The United States seems destined to break into red and blue political zones that still share a common trade zone. The clear blue zones are the Northeast, the upper Midwest, and the West Coast. The rest of the country is mostly red.

Europe could break into a distinct North (Protestant) and South (Catholic). We could even have two euros and correct the economic imbalances in trade.

With Britain free of the European Union, why shouldn't there be a stronger alliance between Great Britain, the United States, Canada, Australia, and New Zealand? After all, they're highly compatible, sharing similar heritage, religions, lifestyles, and language.

The Asian Tiger countries—Japan, South Korea, Taiwan, Singapore, Hong Kong, and coastal China—would make a great trade zone and alliance. Most people don't realize how different the highly urban coastal cities of China are from the interior regions, which are still very third-world.

Southeast Asia could be a separate zone and possibly ally with India and the interior of China to make up a trade and political bloc that would be home to the biggest population in the world.

Vladimir Putin's desire to reunite the constituents of the Soviet Union could happen, given the weakening resolve in Europe and NATO to defend the eastern zones—and President Donald Trump is making it clear that the United States will not be there!

BUT in this revolution, which requires more compatible sovereignty first, a broader Russian and eastern zone would be likely only if the Orthodox countries remained sovereign and independent while forming a trading alliance like the EU. Putin will likely fail if he tries to conquer them.

The dominant Sunni nations of the African-Islamic group could be a major alliance, with the smaller and more concentrated Shiite-dominant countries or regions allying around Iran, parts of Iraq, Syria, Lebanon, and Yemen.

Almost all of the civil wars and bloodshed in the Middle East occur in countries where Sunnis and Shiites occupy the same political structure. Realigning the Middle East into a clear Sunni/Shiite divide would alleviate massive conflict.

And of course, Latin America makes sense as a more integrated political and trading bloc, with a common religion and language (although there are different versions of Spanish). And Latin America largely allies well with the United States, due to a common religion.

Even up-and-coming India could see a split between Hindu and Muslim regions and between a north and south that have different income and demographic trends.

This is what I mean when I say we're in the jaws of a revolution here. Literally, the face of the world will change, on a macro *and* a micro scale.

We'll see a breakdown into more coherent nations and a realignment of countries around their progressive/conservative and religious/cultural divisions.

We'll see national borders redrawn and political policies rewritten so there's more unity and commonality in each sovereign entity.

Only once all that chaos has unfolded—and the revolutionary spirit has been appeased, and corrupt or ineffective governments have been overthrown—will we build back up to greater growth and global integration again, wherein stronger parts can mold and network into a greater whole.

This is going to be the major trend in coming years. And it will lay the groundwork for another mega-global boom later in this century! Although there was much progress after the American Revolution, the greatest payoffs came decades later, when globalization first accelerated with steamships and railroads.

And ALL of this was (and is) completely predictable . . . thanks to the power of cycles.

That's what this book is all about: the greatest political, social, and cultural upheaval since the American Revolution, 250 years ago, and the Protestant Reformation, 250 years before that.

And how cycles give us advance warning.

It's why we publish the free e-letter—*Economy & Markets*—daily, and I urge you to sign up at economyandmarkets.com. While you're at it, also go to dentresources.com for a free report to help you navigate this chaos of cycles.

People don't really like to think about cycles, for the obvious reasons: a challenging phase always follows a good one. So Andy and

I do that for you, so that we can warn you when major shifts—good and challenging—are coming, and you don't have to be constantly thinking about cycles.

Only an understanding of the key cycles that drive economic growth, innovation, and progress will empower you to understand WHY major shifts like the Great Depression and major booms like the Roaring Twenties and the Roaring 2000s (1983 to 2007) happen . . . WHEN they'll happen . . . and HOW you can benefit from them.

Make no mistake: the current worldwide backlash against globalization and immigration isn't just a passing phase or a minor event.

This is bigger than Brexit or Trump, and it will end up much differently than it started.

There will be a major financial crash and a deflationary economic crisis like we last saw in the 1930s.

That changes everything about investment and business . . . everything!

It will force businesses to embrace a new network model of business and organization that top-down managers and governments have been resisting.

New bottom-up digital currencies that central banks can't manipulate could ultimately emerge on a much larger and more efficient scale.

The folly of central bank policies will become very clear when the greatest bubble in modern history finally bursts, between late 2017 and late 2022.

And it will change everything in the decades ahead, creating a very different economic landscape from what we experienced during the last boom.

One where emerging countries will flourish, while developed countries will limp along or die (RIP, Japan). Developed countries will have to force later retirement, in line with our much longer life expectancies, or the clear demographic trends will cause us to age and slow unacceptably.

One where aging industries, like healthcare and nursing homes, will prosper, while real estate crumbles and autos roll down the hill to the junkyard.

But most of all, the new world will be one where bottom-up, network-designed companies and countries will trump the old top-down hierarchies that have dominated since the Industrial Revolution.

My motto is: Every customer a market, every employee a business.

There is no way to make America great again by returning to the rote assembly-line jobs of the past.

In the not too distant future, we'll enjoy decentralized and instant access to information technologies that allow a more egalitarian, democratic, inclusive, and productive economy and culture.

Ironically, it'll be the complete opposite of how this revolution started, with its nationalistic and racist policies aimed at protecting against the extremes of globalization.

The history of economic and human progress is crystal clear: while there is a constant play of opposites between liberal and conservative values, the trend is in favor of the progressive spirit.

The end of slavery . . . the rise of women's rights . . . lesbian and gay rights . . . transgender rights . . .

Farm jobs to factory jobs . . . office jobs to entrepreneurs.

History clearly progresses toward higher affluence, greater individual freedom, more knowledge, more profound individuality, and grander self-expression. What's more self-expressive and potentially more profitable than having your own business that speaks to your greatest passion, either in your own small company or designed like a small business within a much larger one?

That's why that first chart I showed you is so telling!

More traditional and conformist values ultimately give way to more progressive ones. Cultures that go against that progression regress or fail (ahem . . . Japan).

It's constructive that conservatives challenge new liberal technologies and values. That's how we test these things and separate what's productive and acceptable from what's nonproductive and unacceptable.

It demonstrates the ultimate principle of cycles and progress: the play of opposites.

Like male and female, boom and bust, inflation and deflation, liberals and conservatives aren't right or wrong. They are yin and yang. Inseparable. Together, they create the energy and innovation necessary for real life to function and evolve, just as opposite poles create energy in a battery.

This dynamic has created the differences and comparative advantages in our global culture today . . . the very ones the world's citizens are revolting against. And as this revolution runs its course, we'll ultimately move back toward globalizing . . . to our mutual advantage and pain.

The backlash against globalization is necessary at this extreme point, and it will take decades to work out.

But it's not the ultimate result.

It's just the pause that refreshes.

The backlash against immigration isn't the ultimate result, either, but it will be very real in the coming years and decades—to our initial detriment.

Without a monumental revolution in this Economic Winter Season, we can't move forward into a new Economic Spring Season, with its promise of growth.

And only a clear understanding of the most important cycles that repeat throughout history—like the 250-year Revolution Cycle, the Centurial Cycle, the 84-year Populist Movement Cycle, and many others—will allow you to see how this financial crisis is different and how the boom to follow will be different as well.

Any investor or business could have done fairly well in the boom from 1933 to 2017. They could have done even better in the boom from 1983 to 2017, just by throwing a dart at a list of businesses or stocks, real estate or commodities.

This will NOT be the case in the global boom that follows the greatest crash and financial crisis of our lifetimes.

Nor will the next mega-boom reach the heights of this last one in most developed countries.

The four fundamental cycles that drive the developed world (and, increasingly, the emerging world) won't converge again like they did from 1988 to 2000 for decades to come! It's this convergence that adds rocket fuel to the booms or busts.

You will have to be smarter as an investor or business (or government) to succeed in the next boom.

And that starts with surviving the greatest crash and reset of our lifetimes.

This book is all about guiding you through the threatening and opportune times ahead, especially the worst cycles, which will hit between late 2017 and last through early 2020. We keep the conversation going at dentresources.com, where you'll find a free report as thanks for reading this book. I also encourage you to sign up to our free daily e-letter at economyandmarkets.com.

If you protect your financial gains now, you can soon profit from the sale of a lifetime. But the profits will come from very different sectors than those of the past. I'll share specifics with you in these pages.

Before we dive in, let me repeat myself: All of this is predictable thanks to the power of cycles.

The first book I ever published was titled *Our Power to Predict*. Its message remains as true today as it was in 1989. I just have better and more integrated cycles after 30 years immersed in this field.

Cycles are my and Andrew Pancholi's business. It's time you started listening to experts like us, who don't pretend that the economy can just grow incrementally into the future without recessions and disruptive technologies . . . and revolutions!

What did Janet Yellen say on June 27, 2017? That we will not see another financial crisis "in our lifetimes." Sounds like Irving Fisher just before the 1929 crash: "Stock prices have reached what looks like a permanently high plateau."

Andy is a dear friend and fellow cycles nut. He's the creator of *The Market Timing Report* and general partner and portfolio manager at Fidelis Capital Management. And he has some insights to share with you in the pages of this book as well.

Before we get started and get you ready for the greatest revolution since the rise of democracy, a word from Andy. . . .

Why We're Entering the Most Critical Time of Our Lives

Andrew Pancholi

The longer you can look back, the farther you can look forward.

—WINSTON CHURCHILL

AS HARRY JUST SAID, over the next several years we'll see a complete transformation in all aspects of our lives.

As you know, history repeats itself.

Most people are foolish enough to ignore this concept. They do so at their peril.

We're witnessing huge social, cultural, and financial (investing, etc.) change, and it's a result of some of the biggest cycles coming together. Basically, history repeating itself.

This is not another case of debt deleveraging and deflation. It's something far deeper.

Let's assume that we frequent a certain café.

I sip tea there every day.

Harry joins me once a week.

George comes along every two weeks.

You join us once a month.

Eventually, we'll all end up at that café on the same day. It's inevitable. And when we're all together, we'll have a party.

Cycles are exactly the same.

We have a whole range of them, from the super-macro cycles that you'll learn about in this book all the way through to the most minute ones, which can last a few days or even seconds.

The trick is to find those time windows when they all come together. That's when we get the fireworks. The more cycles that arrive at the party, the rowdier it gets!

The greatest British statesman who ever lived, Winston Churchill, said, "The longer you can look back, the farther you can look forward."

He was no fool!

This is the nature of forecasting with cycles.

The longer cycles that people either forget or have no knowledge of create the big, "unexpected" events. This is what some people refer to as "black swans."

Only there is no such thing as a black swan.

This is just a convenient tag to pin onto something that some expert just didn't see coming, because he didn't understand a cycle—or cycles altogether. It's their get-out-of-jail-free card!

They miss these things because they don't have enough retrospection to forecast what is just around the corner. Brexit was precisely one of these events. Later in this book, you'll learn how you, too, could have predicted it.

However, it's not just a case of looking back as far as you can. You also need to know *where* to look. That's what Harry and I do best!

As this revolution unfolds, we'll feel the effects of cycles that caused earth-shattering events the last time they peaked. I'll give you more details about these in this book, but for now, we're looking at events that include:

- Martin Luther nailing his 95 Theses to the church door, in the biggest religious rebellion of its time
- the *Mayflower* setting sail from England
- the 1720 South Sea and Mississippi Bubbles

- the American Revolution
- the French Revolution
- the 1848–50 revolutions of Europe
- the U.S. Civil War
- the First World War
- the 1929 crash
- the rise of Hitler
- the Second World War
- the atomic bomb
- the Arab oil crisis
- the impeachment of Richard Nixon
- the beginning of free-floating currency trading
- the 1987 crash
- the global financial crisis of 2007-08

Yes!

I quite literally mean that the cycles that led to those events are converging on us again—now and over the next several years!

We live in exciting times!

Let us help you through them (check out markettimingreport .com).

PART I

The Forces Driving the Revolution

CHAPTER 1

The Three Harbingers of Revolution

Cycles are the dark matter of our world. We can't see them, but they affect everything we do.

Harry Dent

NEIL DEGRASSE TYSON talks about how dark matter makes up 85 percent of the universe. We can't see it. We don't know what it is. We just know that our equations for explaining the universe don't work without including it. But it does have gravity, which is why we can detect it and measure its impact.

It's the same way with life, except that our "dark matter" is cycles. We can't see them, we can't touch them, and there are too many to fathom, but every single one affects us to some degree at multiple points in our lives.

They're the invisible, underlying currents that drive us.

As this decade rolls by us, we're caught up in an armada of economic, political, financial, social, and geopolitical cycles that are changing the face of our world.

We're about to move much deeper into the most intense phase of the Economic Winter Season in my 80-year Economic Cycle (more on this later). With it comes a once-in-a-lifetime great reset of debt and financial-asset bubbles and the emergence of a whole new economy, as occurred in the 1930s. Think of the advantages if you could have seen that great reset coming—the sale of a lifetime in financial assets back then!

We're also entrenched in the converging downside of the Four Fundamentals—four key cycles that are critical to the performance of stock markets, the survival of economies, and the safety of citizens all across the globe (and I'll talk more about this later as well).

All four have been on a negative trajectory together since early 2014.

This convergence happens infrequently. The most comparable to this one occurred from late 1929 into 1934, giving us the worst years of the Great Depression. The only other such event in the last century resulted in the massive inflation of the 1970s. This cycle will continue to deepen through early 2020, with aftershocks into at least 2022.

But what really sets this century apart is the addition of the Three Harbingers of Revolution!

We last saw the most turbulent of these three cycles—the 250-year Revolution Cycle—during the American and Industrial revolutions of the late 1700s.

The 84-year Populist Movement Cycle is back. The last time this cycle rolled through, we had to endure the horrors of Hitler and Mussolini.

And there's the 28-year Financial Crisis Cycle, hanging over our heads like the sword of Damocles.

(Andy brought the 84- and 28-year cycles to my attention. I've been using the 250-year cycle for decades. I also have an 80-year cycle that is very close to his 84-year cycle.)

This is going to be fun! Let's look at each of these harbingers to better appreciate how they're going to revolutionize our world.

Harbinger #1: The 250-Year Revolution Cycle

The current revolution started in mid- and late 2016, with Brexit and then Trump, and it could last a decade or two, to as late as 2033.

The last one started in the 1760s, with the thirteen colonies' rebellion against the Sugar Act of 1764 and the Stamp Act of 1765. It culminated in the Boston Tea Party, in 1773. The First Continental Congress was formed in 1775, followed by the Declaration of Independence, in 1776. The Revolutionary War lasted from 1775 to 1783.

That period, from 1765 to 1783, was the birth of democracy. That was a very big deal, and it's still spreading through the emerging world.

From 1776 through 1789 Adam Smith published five editions of his breakthrough book *The Wealth of Nations*. He's considered the founder of classical economics and the first to express the dynamics of free-market capitalism—what he famously called "the invisible hand." Sounds like dark matter, doesn't it?

This era also marked the practical beginning of the Industrial Revolution around the emerging breakthrough innovation of the steam engine.

I call this "When Harry Met Sally."

Two opposite principles converged to create the greatest advance in standard of living in perhaps all of modern history.

Capitalism rewards individual contribution and risk-taking. Democracy is inclusive, giving everyone a say via the right to vote. This aligns the troops with the generals.

The 250-year Revolution Cycle before "Harry met Sally" saw the Protestant Reformation, starting with Martin Luther's 95 Theses, posted in 1517. This created a split in the Catholic Church and played into the power of the printing press, invented in 1455.

This period also saw the emergence of one of the greatest inventors in history, Leonardo da Vinci. There was a clear intellectual revolution in this late stage of the Renaissance, from roughly 1517 to 1532.

Here's what this cycle looks like:

Figure 1-1: 250-Year Revolution Cycle

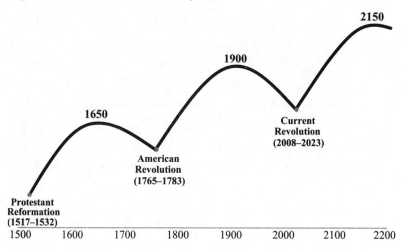

Source: Dent Research

The present 250-year Revolution Cycle corresponds with the Economic Winter Season of my 80/84-year Four Season Economic Cycle and Andy's 84-year Populist Movement Cycle. I increasingly think that these two cycles are one and the same and that the 84-year time frame is the more accurate.

Andy is a close friend and possibly the only other person in existence to be able to outcycle me at times.

We had a shootout at my Irrational Economic Summit, in Palm Beach in 2016, with many similar cycles, like 10-year, 30-year, 45-year, 60-year, 80/84-year, and 500-year. But Andy was pulling out 100-year, 144-year, and 180-year cycles that converge in this period.

He basically outgunned me on some of these longer-term cycles, and that's not easy to do.

That was when I decided we had to combine our cycle expertise, and this book was born.

Over the years, I've also increasingly turned to him for help fine-tuning my forecasts, because he excels at the shorter-term stuff. He has mastered the art of cycles analysis by developing signals that show him potential turning points and an array of other invaluable information.

Harbinger #2: The 84-Year Populist Movement Cycle

This particular cycle is easier to see in the world today, because we're witness to the countless protests and riots almost daily.

It started with the deep dissatisfaction of the everyday worker and middle-class citizens when the U.S. economy fell apart in 2008. They'd already endured falling wages since 2000, so they were ripe for revolt.

These people have been devastated by one bubble and burst after the next, all while they've watched the wealthiest 1 percent run off with 50 percent of the money. It happened the same way in the 1929 long-term stock peak and the Economic Fall Bubble Boom Season— yes, about 84 years ago.

Worse, in the United States, they've been further affected by the "Asian deflation" in middle-class wages, thanks to competition from legal and illegal immigrants coming largely from Mexico and Latin America.

In Europe, that wage pressure was magnified by the refugee crisis, in which more than a million people poured into the continent in 2015.

The Greece default and the threat to the euro in 2010–11 was another spark. Unemployment in the Southern European countries is still near record highs. Black markets thrive there.

Now we've entered the real stage, a populist revolt against globalization, immigration, and Wall Street financial trickery.

Brexit passed against the polls in the UK.

Trump emerged against the polls in the United States.

More unexpected disruptions will follow.

While the anti-EU candidate—Geert Wilders—failed in his bid
to become the next prime minister of the Netherlands, it was a close
race. . . . AND he and the far-right movements blanketing Europe
aren't going away anytime soon.

And the French election was a heated contest between the populist, anti-EU, far-right candidate, Marine Le Pen, and the more liberal Emmanuel Macron. While Le Pen also lost her bid, she and her
National Front are also here to stay.

The last time we had such a populist movement was in the early
1930s, led by Hitler and Mussolini in Europe. Hitler's whole appeal
was his promise to make Germany great again!

The emergence of Hitler as German chancellor, in January 1933,
and Trump as the U.S. president, in January 2017, occurred exactly
84 years apart. (I'm not calling Trump the next Hitler, nor am I lik-
ening the two! I'm just demonstrating this cycle and how precisely it
defines such populist movements.)

Figure 1-2: 84-Year Populist Movement Cycle

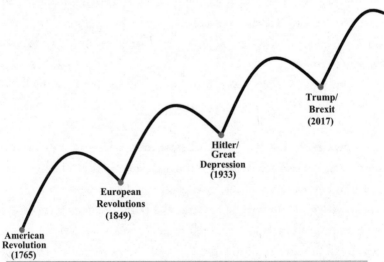

1750 1775 1800 1825 1850 1875 1900 1925 1950 1975 2000 2025 2050
Source: Dent Research

If we trace this 84-year cycle back, we get the populist movement that lasted from 1933 through World War II.

Before that, we had the European revolutions, starting around 1848.

People became fearful of losing their perceived birthright.

The masses were fed up with being oppressed by the ruling classes. But they lacked a unifying catalyst.

That is, until Karl Marx and his principles brought a torchlight of hope. The simmering discontent gathered speed, and suddenly there was unification among the masses of Europe. Communism was born!

The continent was like a house of cards. Just the slightest thing brought it crashing down.

Between 1848 and 1850, every European nation experienced uprising and revolution.

It happened quickly.

The populace had had enough.

Does this sound familiar?

No one would have expected this five years earlier.

The Industrial Revolution then; the Internet and the technology boom now. The reckless, oppressive rule of the aristocrats then; ineffective governments now.

History repeats.

The cycle returns.

Before *that,* we had the First Continental Congress in the United States, in 1774, and the Declaration of Independence, in 1776 . . . which brings me back to the 250-year Revolution Cycle.

You see, three 84-year cycles add up to 252 years!

Just look at this next chart. Look at what these cycles look like together. . . .

Andy will give you more details about this particular harbinger in chapter 2.

Seeing cycles line up like that and identifying their impact may

Figure 1-3: 250-Year Revolution and 84-Year Populist Movement Cycles Both Cycles Converge in 2017

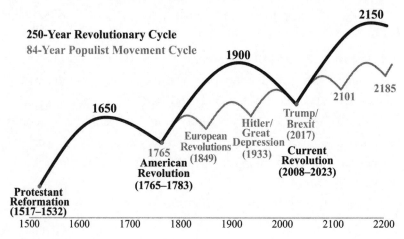

Source: Dent Research

be the most beautiful thing I've ever seen (with the exception of my lovely wife, Jean-ne).

Harbinger #3: The 28-Year Financial Crisis Cycle

Andy also has a 28-year cycle that correlates with financial crises. This is similar to my long-standing 30-year cycle in commodity prices.

In 1933, the cycle bottomed out. That was when we saw the highest unemployment in U.S. history and the worst of the world-wide Great Depression.

The next bottom hit in 1961, with twin recessions in 1960 and 1962, the Cuban Missile Crisis, and President John F. Kennedy's assassination.

Then we got the recession and savings-and-loan crisis of 1990–91 (shortly after the bottom in 1989).

The other major financial crisis, obviously, was the one in 2008–09, and that hit on my 80-year (or, more likely, 84-year) Four-Season Economic Cycle over two Generational Spending Wave booms and

Figure 1-4: 28-Year Financial Crisis Cycle

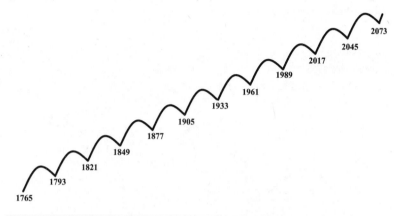

1750 1775 1800 1825 1850 1875 1900 1925 1950 1975 2000 2025 2050

Source: Dent Research

busts: the peak of the massive baby boom spending cycle and the dawn of the dreaded Economic Winter Season.

And finally, we get what Andy and I see as the next likely massive crash, from the second half of 2017 through at least late 2019 or early 2020.

That brings us back to the 84-year cycle, with a major separatist movement and backlash to globalization . . . and what a massive cycle this is shaping up to be!

Twenty-eight times three is . . . ?

Eighty-four!

Other examples of this cycle include . . .

- 1793: France stumbled through the thick of the French Revolution.
- 1821: After centuries of rule, the Ottoman Empire lost control of Greece. Panama and Peru broke away from Spanish colonization. And Faraday invented the electric motor.
- 1877: Russia declared war on the Ottoman Empire. Britain annexed the Transvaal, a province in South Africa.

Figure 1-5: 84-Year Populist Movement and 28-Year Financial Crisis Cycles
Both Cycles Converge in 2017

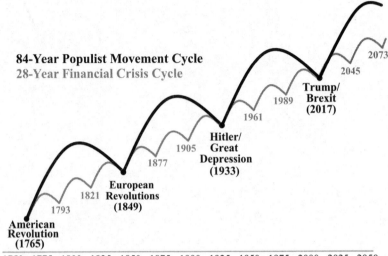

Source: Dent Research

- 1905: Russia entered a crisis. There was a huge famine and many violent uprisings. The Japanese wiped out the Russian navy.
- 1961: The Bay of Pigs invasion failed. The Berlin Wall went up. Russia won the early space race as Yuri Gagarin made history.
- 1989: The Berlin Wall came down. The Chinese army massacred students in Tiananmen Square.

Like I've said, the cycle turns.

And the next one should start later this year!

When these three Harbingers of Revolution converge, you can expect major social, political, and economic changes at local and global levels. They converge most precisely in late 2017.

Here's the beauty of it: when you're aware of these cycles, it's easy to take steps to survive and prosper as the "dark matter" rolls on over us. We share these details with readers daily in our free e-letter.

Figure 1-6: The Three Harbingers of Revolution
All Cycles Converge in 2017

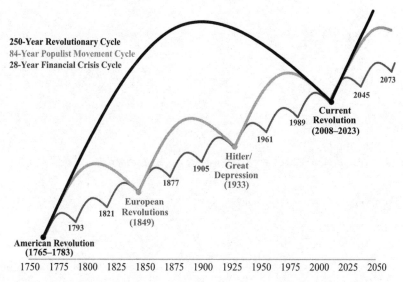

Source: Dent Research

Sign up at economyandmarkets.com. And remember to get your free report at dentresources.com, a thanks for reading this book.

The thing with cycles, though, is that the more confirmation you get, the more confidence you have about what the future holds.

While the Three Harbingers of Revolution are significant cycles individually, and while they constitute a powerful force when they converge, there's another big cycle that's joining this party.

CHAPTER 2

Which Came First? The Chicken or the Egg?

Do you see the parallels between then and now?

Andrew Pancholi

WHEN THE UK BROKE AWAY from the European Union and Donald Trump won the 2016 U.S. presidential election, it was clear: a tipping point had arrived. And 2017 would be an interesting year. (As would the rest of the decade!)

Many would say that Trump is a man of action. True to his word, he ordered construction of a wall between Mexico and the United States on Wednesday, January 25, his sixth day in office. But, as Harry would say, he's looking to build a wall for nobody. Our Mexican-born immigrant population, especially illegals, has declined since 2007 and will likely continue to do so in the even deeper downturn ahead.

But did you know that the most famous geopolitical and socio-economic wall to date, the Berlin Wall, was erected in 1961?

It was built to prevent communist East Germans from escaping to the more prosperous, capitalist West Berlin. It worked for 28 years, before it was brought down in 1989.

Add 28 years to 1989 and we arrive in 2017.

Right here, right now!

This shows the geometry of cycles.

Before we go any further, I must make one thing clear: I write this to show you how cycles unfold in geopolitical and financial arenas. Nothing more. I'm not making judgments. I'm not criticizing. I'm simply observing!

A geopolitical and socioeconomic dividing structure is in the cards once again, as an absolutely perfect repetition of cycles unfolding.

That means 2045 will be a landmark year in divisiveness and financial crisis as well, not only because it lies a further 28 years ahead but also because it will mark 100 years from the end of the Second World War.

Paradigm shifts will occur.

On Friday, January 27, President Trump signed a separate executive order imposing immigration and travel restrictions on certain groups. While this ran into legal challenges, he refused to back down.

Sure, his order placed people of certain origins under suspicion, regardless of whether they are good guys or bad guys. But previous administrations—not as innocent as they'd have you believe—pursued similarly discriminatory policies.

The 84-year Populist Movement Cycle repeats in a chilling way, and within a window of a few days.

Eighty-four years earlier, on January 30, 1933, Adolf Hitler became Germany's chancellor.

He gained power rapidly because people thought that those around him and before him had been weak. The masses had had enough. They wanted him to make Germany great again.

While I am absolutely NOT comparing Trump to Hitler, does this sound familiar?

On April 1, 1933, the German government initiated a mass boycott of all Jewish-owned shops and businesses. In other words, it placed people of certain origins under suspicion, regardless of whether they were the good guys or the bad guys.

Head back 72 years (another important cycle in my research), to January 27, 1945. This was the exact date on which the Soviets liberated Auschwitz.

Recurrent timing, to the day.

The cycle doesn't stop there. Head back another 84 years from 1933 and we arrive in 1848.

Between 1848 and 1850, the majority of Europe went through revolution. On February 21, 1848, Karl Marx, with the support of Friedrich Engels, published *The Communist Manifesto*. He called for workers to unite: "You have nothing to lose but your chains!"

In fairness, Marx was probably only a catalyst for revolution. The seeds had been sown well before 1848, and tension had been mounting.

The Industrial Revolution was also playing its part, as was the extravagant behavior of the ruling classes.

France had another revolution on its hands. King Louis Philippe I had ruled for 18 years before fleeing into exile in England. The French Second Republic was declared.

The contagion spread around Europe in a rapid domino effect.

The highly unpopular Chancellor Metternich, of the Austrian Empire, was forced to resign.

Next came Italy, with fighting in Milan and the deposing of the various rulers of the many states within that country. Pope Pius IX was forced to flee the Vatican later in the year.

The end of March 1848 saw violent disorder throughout Berlin. King Frederick William IV was forced to make massive changes and carry out huge reforms to keep order.

Meanwhile, the Kingdom of Hungary was experiencing its share of troubles. Emperor Ferdinand V approved a series of laws sweeping away the Austro-Hungarian Empire's feudal legacy.

No European power was immune.

Even Great Britain saw the Chartist uprising, but this was a relatively minor affair compared with what her neighbors were going through.

Yet, within a year or two, order had been restored. Everything just blew over.

For the most part, these revolutions were inspired by intellectuals rather than workers themselves, thus making them unsustainable.

However, 1848–50, whichever way you look at it, was a major turning point for Europe. It was also approximately when the first great surge in globalization started, as Harry will cover in the next chapter.

This disruption wasn't limited to Europe. . . .

The United States defeated Mexico in their war in February 1848.

Within America, 1848 saw social advancement. The first women's rights convention was held, and, a few months later, the first medical school for women was opened in Boston.

The links are uncanny.

But if you're still not convinced, then turn the wheel back one more 84-year cycle—straight into the beginnings of the American Revolution, in 1765, a settlers' rebellion against British lords.

And, because we can, let's take this cycle back one more time, to the 1683 Battle of Vienna. This was more than just another historic battle. Many experts point to this event as a culminating point in the wars between the Holy Roman and Ottoman empires that had been running for 300 years.

Do you see the parallels between then and now?

But let's change track for a minute. . . .

Newton's Laws

Newton was a smart man!

His third law of physics states, "For every action, there is an equal and opposite reaction."

Since President Trump won the election, there have been mass protests the world over, an opposite reaction to his policies being enacted.

We're even moving away from globalization, toward nationalization and polarization.

Then there's Newton's first law: "Every object in a state of uniform motion tends to remain in that state of motion unless an external force is applied to it." In other words, until an external force collides with it, kicks its ass, and changes its motion.

Trump wants to "make America great again." This involves a degree of isolationism. However, once in motion, we might end up with micro-isolationism.

I was contemplating this before one of my regular telephone calls with Harry. He pointed out that an activist in California was gathering signatures for a petition to hold a ballot referendum on the question of whether the Golden State should leave the United States. The petitioner had to collect a certain number of signatures by July 25, 2017. If he did, then a referendum would be held in November 2018.

While that whole situation fizzled out after the petitioner opted to make Russia his permanent home, the cycles are telling us there's still danger that the United States may not remain united for much longer.

So let's project back from November 2018. We find it's two 84-year cycles from when California joined the Union, on September 9, 1850.

That means there's a distinct possibility that the United States will no longer exist as we know it by the end of 2018 or shortly thereafter, whether it's California that leaves or another state.

Here's something else to consider. . . .

Splitting Hairs

Trump was inaugurated as the 45th president of the United States of America. In terms of number cycles, "45" represents radical change!

We're indeed 100 years on from the thick of the First World War. Most significantly, despite most Americans' wanting to remain neutral, the United States joined what was once known as the Great War on April 6, 1917.

The mathematics of this cycle is clear, but there's another key cycle sequence at play as well.

Back in December 1773, the residents of Massachusetts had had enough. On one side, they were pledging allegiance to the Crown in England. On the other, they were completely disgruntled by British oppression.

The bubble burst as crate upon crate of tea was thrown into Boston Harbor . . . not the sort of tea party the English were used to.

Obviously, this tea party was short on crumpets, jam, cream, and scones. This was a tipping point.

The half cycle (42 years) of revolution takes us straight into the peak of the War of 1812, which ended in 1815.

America was fed up with British tariffs destroying their trade, not to mention the impressment of American men into the Royal Navy. Britain was, after all, a huge shipping and trading nation at the time. It was also in the thick of the Napoleonic Wars.

To some extent, this was just a thorn in the side for the British. . . . But for America, this war was a major statement.

Move on another half cycle (45 years this time, on a 90-year cycle—another important cycle historically) and we arrive at 1857: the year of the Western world's biggest financial crisis (although for North America, the 1835–43 real estate crash in the bubbling Midwest and Chicago was worse).

The discovery of gold in the late 1840s had led America to a second boom in western migration and prosperity. Land speculation was growing again. Most important, railroads were expanding across the nation. By 1857, the boom was running out of steam.

The gun was loaded, and the trigger was about to be pulled.

In Cincinnati, the Ohio Life Insurance and Trust Company failed. Suddenly there was a run on banks. In fact, by October 1857, 62 of the 63 banks in New York had suspended payments.

A full-blown stock market crisis ensued.

Britain was also hit hard, as was Europe.

The UK was going through a currency crisis. The nation had lost its edge in global domination, due to the advancement of transportation, particularly steamships. She wasn't used to so much competition.

These two superpowers sucked the rest of the world into chaos. All on time!

Harry and I both have a chart from Robert Prechter that depicts the long-term boom back to 1787—since the last great 250-, 84-, and 28-year cycle revolution. Its first and largest set of major stock crashes and depressions occurred between 1835 and 1857—amid what Harry calls a "great reset."

Then there's 1896 (39 years later).

On December 21, 1896, the National Bank of Illinois collapsed, creating a domino effect that led to a banking panic.

By that point, America was in depression as a result of events running all the way back to 1893. There was deep disagreement about the gold standard and also the use of silver.

Some people felt that the influential families were trying to control the American economy, which led to an increase in anti-Semitism and nationalism. Harry and I will show later how 1896 marked the bottom of a 500-year cycle, after a peak in inflation in 1648. Hence, here was the coincidence of an 84-year and a larger 500-year cycle around 1896.

Now fast-forward to 1940.

By now the world was once again at war. The United States was trying to remain impartial. That is, of course, until December 7, 1941, when Japan attacked Pearl Harbor. America could no longer sit on the fence.

The cycle itself had already instigated a global crisis. The Japanese attack just escalated it. There was a second great reset between late 1929 and 1942 in stocks and the economy.

Then forward again. . . .

On Christmas Day 1979, six days before the end of the year, Soviet tanks rolled into Afghanistan, and Moscow's occupation began after a coup in Kabul. Leonid Brezhnev was expanding his empire. President Jimmy Carter declared this to be the greatest threat since World War II. Cold War tension intensified to a new level.

Meanwhile, domestically and all across Europe, the economic aftershocks of the 1970s Arab-led oil crisis had had their full impact.

High unemployment combined with persistent inflation, and stagflation had set in.

In the UK, inflation hit 20 percent in the late 1970s.

U.S. inflation reached 14.8 percent in March 1980.

So politicians got involved. Federal Reserve chairman Paul Volcker raised interest rates to nearly 20 percent.

People lost their homes.

Volcker may have solved the problem of inflation, but he also seemed to have brought the economy to its knees. (Actually, he was just bringing reality to the already out-of-control inflation and weakening demographic trends.)

And guess what?

These events all fit with cycles emanating from the Boston Tea Party.

This 84-year cycle, along with its twin 42-year cycles (averaged), is indeed life-changing. As is the next one that Harry will give you more evidence about, but it's one I have noticed in my research as well.

In fact, Harry told me he noticed the 100-year cycle I first shared with him only after he saw an important long-term chart that surprised even me.

CHAPTER 3

Witness the Climax of Globalization and the Centurial Cycle

This is a major setback for globalization . . . and it's NOT anywhere near the end, yet.

Harry Dent

A WHOPPER OF A NEW CYCLE IS EMERGING, one of great importance and potential impact.

It's the Centurial Cycle, and it sees globalization peak about every 100 years.

Lucky us! We're witness to the peak in globalization's second surge.

Andy has been tracing a 100-year cycle further back . . . but this may be its most important impact.

For cycle guys like Andy and me, seeing this next chart was a "wow" moment. . . . And we didn't even have to create it.

There are a couple of specific points I want to make about this chart.

This is great historical research, but in my view, it double-counts global trade. It takes the sum of exports AND imports as a percentage of global GDP. But they're really just the two sides of a single coin and equal out in the sum of things.

In other words, one's export is another's import.

So I halve the percentages on the left axis of the chart to consider just exports when I look at it. But I'm not going to change this great

Figure 3-1: The Second Surge in Globalization Has Peaked
Global Trade as a Percentage of Global GDP

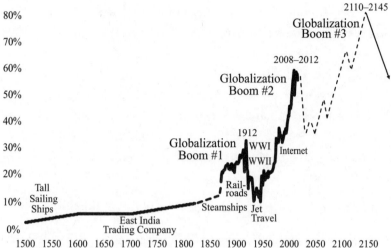

Source: Estevadeordal, Frantz, and Taylor (2003); Penn World Tables, version 8.1; Klasing and Milionis (2014); World Bank; ourworldindata.org/international-trade; Dent Research

chart. Instead, I'll just thank Estevadeordal, Frantz, and Taylor for their great research.

Doing that still gives us global trade at the recent peak of a little more than 30 percent of GDP, which is substantial compared with history, as you can see. Note that U.S. exports account for only 11 to 12 percent of its total GDP.

After we learned to navigate the world with tall sailing ships, conquer nations with gunpowder, and spread the word with the printing press in the last 500-year Mega-Innovation and Inflation Cycle, which started around 1400 (again, more on that to come), global trade grew only slowly. Those ships were slow and small, and most of the crews didn't make it back.

The first major surge in globalization came with the creation of larger and more powerful steamships. After that, it was amplified by continent-spanning railroads in Europe and, especially, America. Railroads opened and united a vast, new, resource-rich continent that generated the leading country in the world 100 years later! Did I say 100? Yes, I did!

Globalization Boom #1 was from around 1850, driven first by steamships and then railroads, into 1912. That was when World War I hit and caused a major retrenchment—and was that a major backlash against globalization or what?!

This was aggravated by protectionist tariffs in the Great Depression (we'll likely see the same effect from the proposed tariffs today) and then the most destructive conflict in modern history, World War II.

Hard to have good global trade in that environment!

Speaking the Language of Technical Analysis

I always like to describe things in Elliott Wave terms. After all, Robert Prechter has made it the language of technical analysis. And it makes the movement through cycles and trends easy to visualize and talk about, even though many Elliott Wave analysts have different interpretations of the patterns.

The first surge of globalization, from about 1850 through 1912, was "wave one up."

The 33-year retrenchment from 1913 to 1945 was the "wave two correction."

The sharpest surge was, and typically is, "wave three," up to somewhere between late 2007 and late 2016.

Now we're looking at a multi-decade retrenchment—or "fourth wave down"—ahead.

The retrenchment after the first surge was from 15 percent to 6 percent of global GDP (remember, I'm considering only exports). That's a 60 percent decline. This only made the period of the Great Depression worse.

The Great Depression would have occurred anyway on the 80/84-year Four-Season Economic Cycle, which hit again in 2008 and ends only in 2022–23.

Individual countries often think they can benefit from protecting their own industries, but when everyone does the same thing, all it does is shrink the global pie.

Again, U.S. exports are just 11 to 12 percent of its GDP.

Germany's exports are a considerably bigger portion of its GDP, at 46 percent (which is very high among Western European nations and even among East Asian ones).

Hong Kong and Singapore are off the charts.

These high-export countries will get hit the hardest by this "fourth wave down" retreat in the globalization cycle, and the United States will continue to be the best house in a bad neighborhood.

Hong Kong and Singapore are toast, and for the near term, as we move through this current globalization retrenchment, they'll be crushed by the massive drop in their exports!

Remember, the last pullback saw global export trade fall 60 percent.

Figure 3-2: The Good, the Bad, and the Ugly as Globalization Retreats
Exports as a Percentage of GDP, 2013–2015 Average

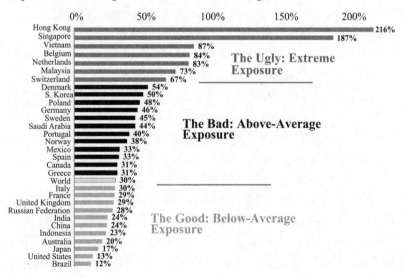

Source: World Bank

But if Bob Prechter looked at Figure 3-1, he'd say there's a fifth wave still coming. That wave should bring us up to at least 40 percent exports as a percentage of GDP (80 percent on this graph).

That would naturally occur as emerging countries, with their significantly larger populations, become more urban and middle-class.

Without Bob's input, though, I would still know there will be a fifth-wave surge in globalization over the next 100-year cycle—but this was also a cycle I first learned from him.

What makes me so certain is the 500-year Mega–Innovation and Inflation Cycle.

It Pays to Be on the Right Side of a Bigger Cycle

The 500-year Mega-Innovation and Inflation Cycle, which produces inflation during its upswing and deflation during its downswing, has pointed up since 1896 (the lowest point of deflation in modern history). It continues in its positive arc until around the 2140s.

This is a great thing.

The last such cycle was up from around 1400 into 1648, with a 100-year, stronger-than-average boom starting around 1500 that culminated in the Elizabethan Golden Age of 1558–1603.

That's why I expect one more mega-surge in globalization between the 2070s and the 2140s.

After all, we've already seen a stronger-than-average boom between 1933 and 2017. There's likely more to come up until 2055–68, when emerging-country demographics finally start to slow, just as the developed countries have since 2007 in North America and since 2011 in Europe.

The next boom will take root in the emerging world (somewhat outside of China), thanks to the strong demographic trends there.

Given the current trajectory of demographic trends, the developed world faces a wilted future unless we have a revolution in aging in the decades ahead.

People need to live and work for much longer. This still very bullish 500-year cycle strongly suggests that! Maybe we even have two sets of kids (one in our thirties and another in our sixties) and don't retire until we are 100-plus. Two sets of kids would also bolster our sagging demographic dilemma, as would much longer work spans.

Those are the two things I see reversing the current dismal demographic trends in the developed world.

There's an important point that was a big "aha" insight for me in the 1980s.

Inflation, from a longer-term perspective, is a sign of demographic progress. It's also reflected in urbanization, which fosters greater specialization of labor and a higher standard of living. We pay more for goods that others produce, and we make more money by specializing. This is possible only in urban environments, and it's been further fostered by the dynamic duo of capitalism and democracy since the last 250-year cycle.

Such specialization requires more dollars and credit to facilitate greater trade. Delegating more to other specialists raises the cost of products. That creates inflation.

But the key is that our higher wages from specialization trump that inflation. That's how we get higher inflation *and* a higher standard of living—and the long-term correlation is crystal clear.

Since 1900, our standard of living, adjusted for inflation, has increased more than eightfold . . . and all of that during one of the highest inflationary periods in history. The gold bugs always tout a chart showing that the value of a dollar has fallen by 97 percent since 1900, as if that has destroyed our wealth. . . . But clearly, the opposite happened through the facilitating of specialization and greater trade, including globalization.

Hence, if trade and specialization retreat on this 100-year Centurial and globalization cycle, then our economy is going to be worse for a time, not better.

Hey, the specialization of labor was Adam Smith's primary

thesis. He looked at it in the context of nations. It's since become more about individual workers, or labor.

So it should come as no surprise to you that there are two 250-year cycles within each 500-year one! Each revolution in innovation or politics accelerates the last one.

Cycles in cycles! It's exhilarating. . . .

(I know by now you're thinking that Andy and I need to get girlfriends. Well, we both have great ones, although it took us both a few tries!)

The Protestant Reformation, beginning in the early 1500s, accelerated a great boom in Europe, the Elizabethan Golden Age in Britain, and world circumnavigation.

This second surge in globalization was a major catalyst to growth and specialization of labor, but now it's clearly subsiding, and rapidly.

First it was jet travel after World War II, and then the Internet, that fostered this very steep and powerful second surge.

But now, too many workers feel that immigrants and foreign workers are hurting more than helping their standard of living.

There is still a massive divide in income between the peaking first world and the growing third world.

And while developed-world factory workers worry about the threat of lower-wage Asian and immigrant workers . . . the bigger threat there, to both, is robots! They don't have emotional problems, and they don't need healthcare and retirement benefits, just a little maintenance.

And then there's the EVEN greater threat of the automation of left-brain tasks in the office, including many higher professional skills.

We ultimately have to become creative, right-brain–oriented entrepreneurial workers who create more customized products and services, delivered in real time . . . to compete with computers that do as much for simple and complex left-brain tasks.

Expect anti-free-trade sentiment and trade wars to grow in the years and even decades ahead, especially in the worst economic years—likely between late 2017 and 2023.

Combined with the rapid aging of populations in most developed countries, this isn't a good trend for the global economy.

And because global leaders and their posses of experts don't understand or even see these cycles, they'll slog painfully from one blunder to the next while the world unravels despite them.

We will get a revolution, first in politics on this 250-year revolution, and then in technology on my 45-year revolution to follow, from 2032 forward. But . . .

The problem is that it's only going to get worse before such a real and deeper revolution is possible. That's why we keep the conversation going at dentresources.com.

CHAPTER 4

A World Rushing into Revolution

The only way things will get better is if they get far worse first. Everyday people become heroes only in a crisis like 9/11.

Harry Dent

THE EFFECTS OF THESE FOUR CYCLES—the 250-year Revolution Cycle, the 100-year Centurial Cycle, the 84-year Populist Movement Cycle, and the 28-year Financial Crisis Cycle—are rampaging through our world already.

In the United States, we had a historically controversial presidential election in 2016, which brought about the most substantial shifts in politics, social policies, and economic trends since the Civil War.

Abroad, the world is fracturing right before our eyes, starting with Brexit. Scotland wants to break off from the UK already, Catalonia from Spain, and there's much more to come!

This alarming trend toward civil division, unrest, and anger is fundamentally about a political and social revolution to realign around more common and cohesive cultural values. . . .

And, paradoxically, this is a good thing! People are happier in a political structure that has more commonality in values, especially in religion.

As I explained in the previous chapter, globalization has peaked. It's gone too far ONLY after succeeding so well, which is typical of any trend or cycle.

In today's world, we're so connected that everyone now hates everyone else, and we're all at one another's throats!

Shiites versus Sunnis . . .

The affluent versus the evaporating middle class . . .

Conservatives versus liberals . . .

Ethnic minorities versus majorities . . .

Young versus old . . .

You name it and you'll find a gulf dividing the two sides. It's turning into a modern-day civil war. But this time it's global, and for the most part, it's not likely to be fought by big armies on traditional battlefields . . . just by way of a lot of political, cultural, and social conflicts.

The American Civil War (fought between 1861 and 1865) emerged out of an insurmountable economic, social, and political divide between the industrial and urban North and the agricultural and rural South.

The South started it, because it was home to the disgruntled faction. As we know, the developing North won, with its new technologies, growing urbanization, and rising demographics. Recall that the trajectory of history ultimately favors the more progressive side.

In our emerging "civil war," the winners will instead come from the less affluent developing world—especially in Asia, including India and Southeast Asia. They have the momentum and demographics working in their favor (except China)—and, most important, urbanization.

In the United States and almost all other developed countries, the economic progress of the late 1960s and the late 1990s has increasingly vanished. A good indicator of this is income gains. As an economy grows, so, too, do incomes.

Figure 4-1: Why People Feel Poor
Ten-Year Change in Real U.S. GDP Per Capita Slowing Since the 1960s

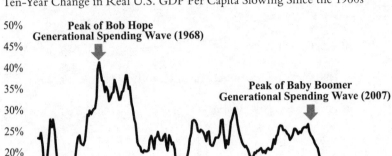

Source: St. Louis Federal Reserve

Look at the above chart of real income gains in the United States since the 1960s. And note how GDP per capita in the United States has been declining sharply for nearly ten years now!

The big picture is that such gains became less and less significant after the late 1960s. It's also now approaching the zero point of GDP gains per dollar.

Not helping the matter any is the fact that economic mobility in the United States is disappearing fast.

If you were born in 1980, you have only a 50 percent chance of making more money than your parents. If you were born in 1950, you had a 79 percent chance, according to research done by Raj Chetty and his team of economists.

That's one hell of a drop over just three decades!

Upward mobility in the United States was once one of the easiest accomplishments in the developed world. Now it's ranked as one of the hardest.

Compounding people's dissatisfaction is the economic malaise

Figure 4-2: Economic Mobility Has Vanished

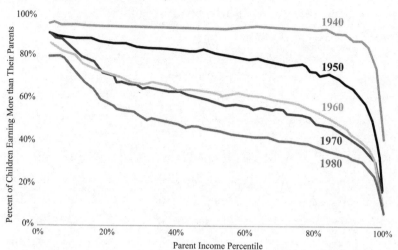

Source: Raj Chetty, *The Fading American Dream: Trends in Absolute Income Mobility Since 1940.*

that has plagued the world since 2008. And for that we have slowing demographics to thank.

I've forecast this demographic demise since the late 1980s. This trend has gathered speed since 2007, but it's been killing Japan since 1990.

The Land of the Rising Sun has had a coma economy since the last decade of the last century, when its demographic trends rolled over, along with its stock and real estate bubbles. Japan should henceforth be known as the Land of the Setting Sun.

The result of all of this is a steady uprising by the people who've just had enough!

The Weirdest Election Ever

The 2016 U.S. presidential election was the weirdest one ever.

"Mister Magoo," Bernie Sanders, almost upset "Lisa Simpson," Hillary Clinton, for the Democratic nomination. (Everyone likes Bart more; now you know why charismatic Bill Clinton was more popular.)

Meanwhile, "Mad Max," Donald Trump, upset the applecart by winning the presidency, against both the polls and his own party's wishes.

Even "Mister Rogers," third-party candidate Gary Johnson, polled as high as 7 percent, a rare accomplishment for a third-party representative.

Most of the rest of the world watched and wondered, "What the f!@#?"

Many U.S. voters said the same thing. (And they still are!)

Trump had a 61 percent unfavorable rating in polls even before his devastating sexual comments leaked across the media pages. Clinton wasn't much better, at 56 percent unfavorable.

They were the two least popular candidates ever to run against each other, surpassed only by a hypothetical matchup between Goldwater and McGovern!

The French election was also fought between two undesirables . . . as was the Dutch one.

This is a symptom of the most radical polarization of U.S. (and global) politics since the American Civil War.

Look at this chart from stellar-as-usual Pew Research, depicting how polarized the United States has become, primarily since 2004.

We went from about a 10 percent differential in ideology between the average Democrat and Republican in 1994 and 2004 to a 35 percent differential in 2016.

But it gets even worse if you look at the spread between the most politically engaged, on the far right side of the chart. There, the differential is about 55 percent, with the majority of each party on the extreme right or left.

How do you resolve such polarization, or get anything passed, regardless of who's in power?

You don't! And Trump is already finding this out.

Trump preached to the working class about why they were feeling so hard done by. He pointed a finger at globalization, bad trade

Figure 4-3: Political Polarization Is Straining the United States
Democrats and Republicans More Ideologically Divided than in the Past

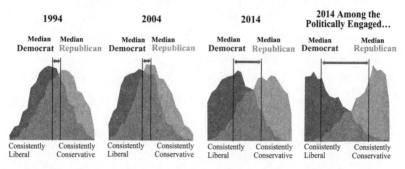

Source: Pew Research, *Political Polarization in the American Public*

agreements, and faulty immigration policies. That's why he was able to take over the Republican Party, against establishment interests.

How did he defy the polls?

By winning the rural, white, working-class vote by margins of 80 percent. These are the most dissatisfied voters, and he hit them right between the eyes, with a lot of coaching from Steve Bannon.

Just an interesting sidenote:

My father was a political strategy adviser to three presidents, most notably Richard Nixon. He always told me that it isn't the average voter who decides elections—they're largely predictable and vote according to their more conservative or liberal ideologies. It's the swing vote—about 15 to 20 percent of the electorate—that most often decides the winner.

Trump absolutely captured the hearts and minds of that sector of dissatisfied white working-class voters.

His victory is indicative of the massive chasm dividing this great country of ours.

But there's another important point to understand here.

The South started the Civil War, but it didn't end in Dixie's favor. Similarly, these most dissatisfied voters are starting this revolution and backlash against globalization. But the only solution in the end is an economic revolution that taps the right-brain, more creative and entrepreneurial capacities that aren't the strong suit of either emerging-world workers or left-brain computers.

But many of our everyday workers *do* have this capacity, and more will when they see it happening.

Jack Stack is an entrepreneur who has proven he can turn his Midwest factory workers into millionaires by turning them into entrepreneurs and owners. More on him and his company later.

Now *that's* how you make America great again!

Trump America

The United States is split by extreme political polarization, and this chasm only continues to grow under Trump's presidency.

The right-wing factions have grudgingly accepted more progressive social policies, from women's rights to black and minority rights to gay marriage. But transgender issues may have been the straw that broke the camel's back for this crowd.

Ever-rising debt with no ceiling is another major issue for the traditional conservatives. They see mounting debt as an arrow to the heart of our financial system. I agree 100 percent on that one!

In addition to the now 35 percent spread between the average Republican and the average Democrat, and the 55 percent divide among the most politically engaged, we can see this shift from other angles in the Pew study.

In 1994, 64 percent of Republicans were more conservative than the average liberal. Today, that's 92 percent.

Democrats shifted from 70 percent more liberal than the average Republican in 1994 to 94 percent now.

What's more, 36 percent of Republicans see the Democratic Party as a threat to the nation's well-being, while 26 percent of Democrats view the Republican Party as the threat.

Twenty-eight percent feel it's important to live in a place where most people share their political views, but that's a whopping 50 percent for the consistently conservative, compared with 35 percent for the consistently liberal.

This sort of thinking creates rigid ideological silos, with no middle ground for compromise.

It's also fodder for a political/social revolution.

The most surprising part is that most of this great divide has formed just since 2004.

That tells me that this revolution isn't all about the extreme growth of the top 0.1 to 1 percent in income and wealth, which exploded in the second half of the 1990s and first peaked in 2000.

Political polarization wasn't as extreme in the Roaring Twenties and the Great Depression, and back then our country was experiencing similar extremes of wealth and income inequality.

The radical political divide and voter dissatisfaction set up Trump for the win that broke the nation!

While Bernie was aiming at income inequality and the 1 percent, Trump aimed at foreign trade and illegal immigrants. And that's who the working class feels most injured by.

And, of course, Hillary represented the establishment, which even more people had become fed up with.

The medium gray states in the map on page 56 are ones that were previously borderline blue but voted red in 2016—and it was the rural areas that swung 80 percent or so to Trump.

Red (light gray) makes up the largest number of states, but look where they are concentrated. They're in the Southeast, the Southwest, the northern Rockies, and the Great Plains—all of which have more rural areas.

The blue states (dark gray) have a similar overall population, but they're concentrated in the Northeast, the Upper Midwest (not as much now), and the West Coast, with a few outliers in Colorado, New Mexico, and, marginally, the southern half of Florida. They're typically more urban.

Figure 4-4: Red States and Blue States Largely Aligned Regionally
2016 Presidential Election Results

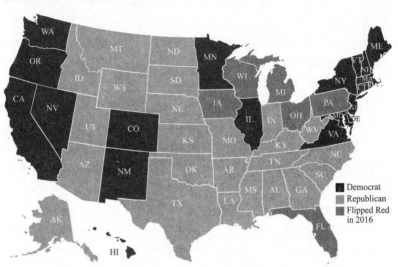

Source: Dent Research

The extreme economic decline we face over the next few years—
and my cycles tell me the worst time could be between late 2017 and
2020 (more on this later)—will only widen this split and fuel greater
civil unrest.

But if you look at the red-versus-blue divide in the United States
at the local or county level, what you see is more of a rural-versus-
urban split. The red states have more rural areas, while the blue states
have more urban areas. But even within the bluer states, you have a
lot of rural red areas. And red states like Texas have large cities like
Dallas, Austin, and Houston that still lean blue.

Those more rural regions were the swing areas that elected
Trump on ratios of 80 percent. It was political genius to target these
disgruntled people. They're the ones starting this anti-globalization
and anti-immigration trend. But they won't be the ones who end up
winning, because they're not on the progressive side of history (just
like the South wasn't on the right side during the Civil War).

These more conservative, central, rural areas have bubbled up the least in this great bubble boom and will tend to see the fewest crashes and breakdowns in the great crash ahead.

But Trump has also walked into what is likely the worst economy of our lifetimes. I predicted that whoever won in 2016 would be a one-term president at best.

Do yourself a favor: Don't just protect your capital. Consider where you can live that will be the safest place geographically. I'm talking about areas like the middle of the country, or smaller, less bubbly cities, and the exurban areas of larger cities. Maybe even the Caribbean. (This is one of the reasons I now live in Puerto Rico, even though it's bankrupt! At least it's dealing with its crisis rather than printing money to cover over the problems. Even better, there's no significant civil unrest here, even after ten years of recession.) I did not anticipate that Hurricane Maria may be a killer wound to this affluent island. But even in the early days following this unprecedented hurricane . . . no significant civil unrest!

If you're one of those growing number of households that wants to live where people have similar values, consider whether you're in the right state, region, or country.

Social and fiscal policies could change rather dramatically in the years ahead, depending on whether you're in a red or a blue zone. Make sure you're in the right place. . . . Either is okay—both will survive, as always.

Remember, the broader 100-year and 250-year cycles are about regrouping around more common and cohesive cultures and values.

A Global Protectionist and Separatist Movement

What I call "markets on crack" continue to discount and dumb down news that should be a bit terrifying. Talk about "fake news" from Trump's protectionist, America First policies? Stock markets take bad news as good, because they see that there will be more free money and stimulus.

Is that crazy or what? So are people on crack!

From screaming debt levels—especially, more recently, in China and the emerging world—to crashing bank stocks and nonperforming loans, especially in Greece and Italy . . .

From negative interest rates with little to show for them to the second China stock bubble crash . . .

From the unexpected Brexit vote to the even more unexpected election of President Donald J. Trump . . .

Based on current world affairs and knowledge of the cycles I study—particularly the 500-year Mega–Innovation and Inflation Cycle, the 250-year Revolution Cycle, the 84-year Populist Movement Cycle, the 28-year Financial Crisis Cycle, and the Four Fundamentals (details ahead)—here's what the world could look like in a few short years. . . .

With the United Kingdom leaving the EU, Scotland could well leave the UK.

Catalonia could leave Spain, and that includes the highest-growth city, Barcelona.

Italy is likely to have to leave the EU as it deals with a banking and debt crisis that won't generate the same, if any, major bailouts that Greece got.

Greece, Portugal, and, ultimately, Spain could follow.

The EU and the euro are not very popular in the larger and more competitive northern countries, either—like France. Though Emmanuel Macron won the French election, Marine Le Pen is still a disruptive force, and nearly a majority of French people aren't happy with the common currency.

The handling of the 2015 migrant crisis, along with the bailing out of banks and governments, were very unpopular in Germany—which has the worst demographic trends of them all! How is Germany going to save the euro if it demographically looks like Japan in 1989? And it does!

What if France and/or Germany leave the EU because they don't

Figure 4-5: Europe: The North/South-Versus-East Divide
Regional Income per Capita, Europe

Primary income of private households relative to population size, by NUTS 2
regions, 2013 (purchasing power consumption standard [PPCS] per inhabitant)

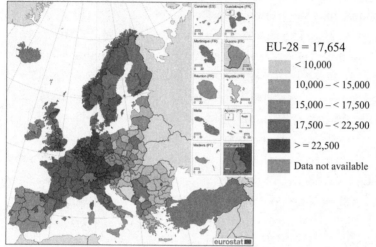

Administrative boundaries: ©EuroGeographics ©UN-FAO ©Turkstat Cartography: Eurostat - GISCO, 04/2016

NUTS: Nomenclature of Territorial Units for Statistics; source: Eurostat

want to bear the brunt of more failing bank and loan defaults in
Southern Europe? Germany has the most exposure to loans to the
central bank in Italy. France has the most exposure to real bank loans
to failing businesses.

The eurozone and the euro are likely to see a major restructuring
in the years ahead.

The great polarizing spirit in Europe is more about the income,
wealth, and productivity divide between the northern and southern countries. Just take a look at the GDP per capita differences in
Europe.

Scandinavia, the UK, France, the Netherlands, Belgium, Germany, Switzerland, Austria, and northern Italy make up a higher-
income, higher-productivity, export-strong bloc to the north.

Southern Europe is the complete opposite: it's made up of lower-income countries with lower productivity, and largely net debtors and importers.

The best example of this north/south divide is found in Italy.

The creation of the euro only exaggerated this split of trade and borrowing capacities. It reduced the currency values of the northern countries leading to greater exports and trade surpluses and lower debt compared with the southern countries with their lower borrowing costs and more debt so they could afford imports from the north.

Northern Italy has an average GDP per capita of $34,147, compared with southern Italy's $20,850. That's a 1.64-times difference.

But it's more extreme than that. A region in the very southern part of Italy has just $18,115 GDP per capita, while the most northern part of the country is as high as $41,471—a 2.29-times difference.

Talk about an extreme divide within the same medium-size country!

Figure 4-6: The Extreme North/South Income Divide in Italy
Regional GDP per Capita

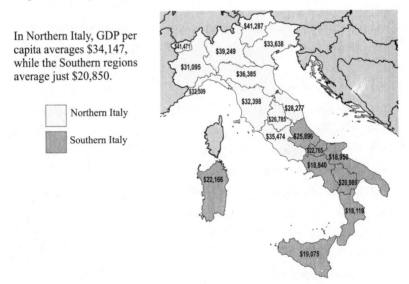

In Northern Italy, GDP per capita averages $34,147, while the Southern regions average just $20,850.

Northern Italy

Southern Italy

Source: Istat, Dent Research

Naturally, the more urban and higher-income northern part of Italy is going to be more liberal, and the southern part more conservative.

A quick visit to Italy will show you the bustling and world-leading fashion and textile industries, auto plants, high-end vineyards, and more urban/hip culture in the north. But in the south . . . there are more fishermen, farmers, goatherds, and the like. They're the more conservative and traditional, salt-of-the-earth kinds of people.

They're two very different worlds, united only by a common language.

Even the pizzas are different!

Back on the broader European map, Eastern Europe is similar to Southern Europe, with much lower incomes and lower skill sets.

Northern Italians constantly complain about the "inferiority" of the Eastern European immigrants and how they have to support the higher debts of the "laid-back" southern Italians!

I'm not being a bigot here, just reporting the truth!

Europe ultimately needs to restructure into two zones: the strong euro and the weak euro, with, hopefully, a still larger eurozone of trade.

The stronger, northern eurozone would naturally revalue and continue to have greater competitiveness. The weaker Southern and possibly Eastern European zone would devalue to help shore up their lagging competitiveness and productivity with rising exports and growth again. They'll struggle, especially because of their very weak demographic and productivity trends.

The cost to the northern zone would be slower export growth and lower trade surpluses, which would mean slower economic growth. Also, it would have to deal with rising debt defaults from the weaker southern and eastern zones. Italy alone owes the central bank in Germany about $360 billion!

So that would be especially painful for Germany!

French banks have the largest share of Italian-owned bad bank loans. And Italy has half of the bad bank loans in all of the eurozone!

The cost to the southern zone would be inflation from higher import prices (ask Iceland about when it devalued in the global financial crisis), but ultimately this would lead to rising exports and stronger economic growth, and debt relief from defaults on foreign loans. (Put Iceland on speed dial.)

Iceland was one of the few European countries that was not on the euro and was forced to let its currency fall while it defaulted on foreign debts. It suffered high short-term inflation from rising import costs. Iceland imports a lot because most of what it has is ice and fish!

Yet it came out of that crisis stronger than most other European nations.

Deleveraging and detoxing of financial excesses works better than not dealing with the imbalances and just printing more money to kick the can further down the road.

Only painful restructuring helps cure the extreme disparities in trade, debt, and demographics in Europe (and everywhere else, for that matter, at any time in history).

In short, I anticipate a major restructuring in the eurozone, along with weakness in the euro and strength in the dollar for a while yet. After that, it's likely a more neutral currency game, with a bias toward the stronger countries. This means they'll be able to attract more foreign investment and lower-cost imports, but their exports will decline as a result.

The Islamic Hotbed— Especially the Sunni/Shiite Split

The lines drawn by victorious countries after World War II were arbitrary. This has led to a hotbed of civil unrest and civil wars in the Middle East.

Figure 4-7: Sunni Dominates the Islamic World, Except Iran and the Eastern Middle East

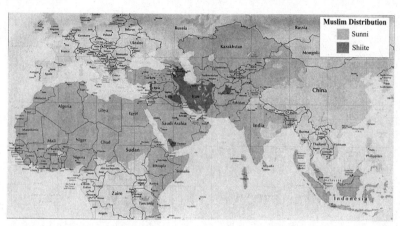

Source: University of Texas Library

The Islamic world is overwhelmingly Sunni, not Shiite, as you can see in this map showing the Sunni-dominant areas in light gray.

North Africa is Sunni and enjoys higher income, while sub-Saharan Africa is mixed among mostly Christian and Sunni Muslims, with lower income, except for South Africa and Botswana.

I don't see a reason why these two regions couldn't split into northern and southern African districts.

Shiites are a minority globally, concentrated in Iran, western Iraq, central Afghanistan, Lebanon, and Yemen.

That's why there's no way to unite Iraq. Not with its current mixture of Shiites, Sunnis, and Kurds.

That's why the war there never ends.

This region needs to realign. Western Iraq should merge with Syria as a Sunni region, while the larger eastern part of Iraq could merge or align with Iran as a Shiite region. The Shiite section of Afghanistan could also align with Iran. The northeastern part could merge with the southeastern Kurdish part of Turkey (and perhaps split off as a separate country or area within Turkey).

In this way, these distinct religious areas could be more unified

Figure 4-8: Iraq's Unstable Sunni-Shiite-Kurd Divide
Ethno-Religious Groups in Iraq

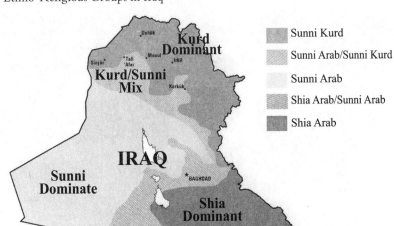

Source: University of Texas Library

and culturally stronger. Only then could we finally see peace in the Middle East. But currently, Saudi Arabia and other Sunni countries are increasingly aligning against Iran, the leading Shiite country. Will there be a war there?

This could start to manifest more positively as soon as 2020, when my 34-year Geopolitical Cycle bottoms out and starts to turn up again (more on that ahead).

When I look at the issues of growing terrorism and civil wars in the Muslim world, there are some clear distinctions that many people don't understand. First, the great majority of the Muslim population lives outside of Northern Africa and the Middle East. South Asia by itself has nearly twice as many Muslims as those two regions combined.

Figure 4-9: Insurgency Countries
Poor and Highly Muslim

Country	GDP per Capita (PPP)	Muslim Population, Percent
Somalia	$600	99%
Niger	$800	99%
Afghanistan	$1,100	99%
Yemen	$2,500	99%
Nigeria	$2,800	50%
Pakistan	$3,100	97%
Syria	$5,100	90%

Source: *CIA World Factbook*, Wikipedia

But that's exactly where we get most of the terrorism and civil wars, because the region is largely desert, with scarce resources and a tribal mentality of mistrust and warfare.

The chart above shows a second dimension. It's the poorer countries that tend to have strong insurgencies: Somalia, Niger, Afghanistan, Yemen, Nigeria, Pakistan, and Syria.

The countries seeing the highest levels of civil war are those that have Sunnis and Shiites mixed together but are also more affluent, like Iran, Libya, Tunisia, Iraq, and Egypt. Perhaps poor people can't afford to revolt against their government but they can afford to become terrorists.

I add these comments to reinforce that terrorism and civil war are not, broadly, a Muslim problem. More than 70 percent of Muslims live in countries and regions that are NOT significantly plagued by insurgencies or civil wars.

India is divided into north and south on ethnic and language lines. It also has dominant Hindu but strong Muslim lines to the west.

Northern India leans more toward the progressive party of Prime Minister Narendra Modi and his allies, while the south leans toward the more conservative Congress party and its allies.

The southern region also has lower fertility rates and higher literacy and is a bit more Muslim-leaning, meaning that the second divide is between the clearly dominant Hindu religion and the minority Muslim group.

There are also small concentrations of Muslim areas in the northeast region around Rajasthan, closer to the eastern Pakistani border, and, to a lesser degree, along India's northern borders.

I got to see the daily closing-of-the-gate ritual at the Wagah border, separating the two countries, and it's obvious from the military rituals that the Pakistani Muslims and the Indian Hindus do NOT like one another.

The greatest incidence of civil war has been in the northeastern Kashmir region, which is actually the only major Muslim-dominant area. That is the most likely region to realign with Pakistan.

And why not have countries and regions that are more aligned internally? It makes for stronger global innovators and traders.

What about Russia?

The country is suffering from three things I've predicted: crashing commodity prices, especially for oil and natural gas; rapidly falling demographic trends; and a corrupt, centrally planned, top-down communist/authoritarian government with an expensive and unaffordable military.

In this time of revolution, why wouldn't Putin take over or annex former Soviet satellite countries, especially the ones that have a higher Russian ethnic and/or Russian-speaking population—like Crimea, eastern Ukraine, and Georgia?

But there are many other countries, from Belarus to Kazakhstan, that could be vulnerable and might even benefit from again becoming a part of Russia in a declining world.

The weaker the European economy gets—and it will get much weaker for years and decades ahead—the easier it is for Russia to keep pushing into more areas.

Europe and NATO won't have the finances or strength to fight it, particularly now that it looks to receive less support from Trump and America.

But it's like everywhere else: Consolidating—or, in this case, expanding, like Iran—sovereign nations around more homogenous religious, political, and ethnic populations will enable the growth of internal strength, which can be a foundation to expand and trade globally again in the future.

Putin will be more likely to succeed if he keeps the eastern zones independent but still aligned with a broader trading zone like the EU. Why? Because this revolutionary cycle strongly suggests that everyone is going to revolt against top-down control and bureaucratic power.

And then there's China. . . .

The Red Dragon has great divisions on all three lines: religion, ethnicity/language, and income/wealth.

The most obvious division is between the eastern/coastal areas and the central/western regions in income and wealth.

Tibet and Mongolia are so different from the rest of rapidly urbanizing and modernizing China that they're more like centuries apart in culture and incomes, rather than decades.

This next chart shows the dominant religions in the north/south and east/west regions. But still, religion doesn't feel like the greatest divide in China, except in Tibet, since China is used to diversity there. The real divide is between the massive new affluence and wealth on the coastal region and the rest of the interior. These are two very different countries now.

The greatest divides I see on the income and wealth scale, due to the extreme bubble economy in the Middle Kingdom, are:

Figure 4-10: China Is the Most Ethnically Diverse
Ethno-linguistic Groups in China

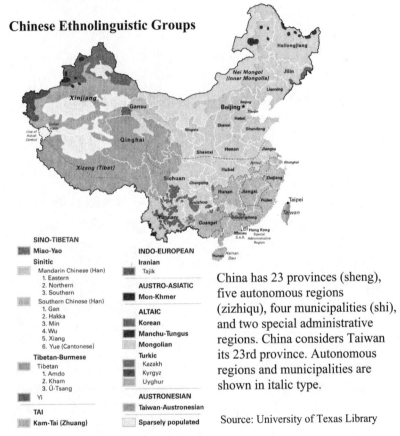

Chinese Ethnolinguistic Groups

China has 23 provinces (sheng), five autonomous regions (zizhiqu), four municipalities (shi), and two special administrative regions. China considers Taiwan its 23rd province. Autonomous regions and municipalities are shown in italic type.

Source: University of Texas Library

1. The east and northeast, including Hong Kong, Shenzhen, Guangzhou, Shanghai, and Beijing.

2. The middle region, including Chengdu and Ordos and 20 others, largely in central areas that are more commodity-based and propped up by overbuilding projects and debt.

3. The west and northwest, including Tibet and the Mongolian-oriented regions, with their completely different cultures.

The religious divides are also largely concentrated and clear: northeastern China leans more toward Christianity, southern China and Tibet more toward Buddhism, and northwestern China more toward Islam.

There's also a growing north/south divide for water and natural resources. The north consumes more and the south has more, especially rivers and water.

China is the hardest to forecast, but the punishing hard landing it'll experience after the most extreme bubble in top-down planning and real estate in all of modern history suggests it'll have the highest civil unrest of any major global power (the United States likely being second). Only an aging population will temper that somewhat, but aging is not a good thing economically, as my research has proven.

Don't forget, there are 250 million unregistered rural migrant workers who are now trapped in urban areas, building stuff for no one.

The one benefit will be squatting in such empty condos, especially in urban areas with high vacancy rates. If the Chinese government tried to kick them out, after creating this urban crisis with its top-down, unaccountable overbuilding and super-rapid urbanization policies, it would be the spark that lit the bonfire.

I know that younger populations are more likely to revolt than older ones. But the extreme imbalances in overbuilding, debt, and excessive urban migration would get even a 50-year-old's blood boiling in China. And most of these 250 million trapped and degraded rural migrant workers are younger—I'm talking in their twenties or thirties!

Before we move on to the next chapter, take a look at the map on the next page.

My research specialist, Dave Okenquist, found this map of terrorist events around the world.

Guess what?

They're almost all in the Eastern Hemisphere—east of Western

Figure 4-11: Terrorism Almost Exclusively in Eastern Hemisphere
Terrorist Attacks, 2015: Concentration and Intensity

Source: National Consortium for the Study of Terrorism and Responses to Terrorism (START),
2016; "Terrorist Attacks, 2015," Global Terrorism Database, www.start.umd.edu/gtd

Europe, with the exception of the northern part of Nigeria and Niger,
where Boko Haram operates.

This is historic, because most geopolitical conflicts in recent centuries have occurred more in the Western Hemisphere, including, of
course, World War I and World War II. (Historically, Europe has been
aligned more with North America and the Western Hemisphere culturally and in religious terms.)

But that also indicates that the greatest expansion in the future
will come in Asia, the Middle East, and Africa, with the greatest
population concentration in Asia.

I have a 165-year cycle (take that, Andy) that says the East will
continue to dominate global growth into the next century. The rising Eastern Hemisphere trends started in the early 1980s and will
continue until around 2065.

Growing conflict, like emerging innovation and technological
disruption, foreshadows higher growth and change in the future.

After the 2016 peace accord was signed in Colombia, an international agency claimed that the entire Western Hemisphere was now
free from major armed conflicts.

Wow!

Except it's actually a bit of a contrary indicator, longer-term.

Greater peace is a sign of maturity and slower growth, which perfectly describes the Western Hemisphere. Older and aging countries will tend to be less violent and rebellious. But they'll also grow slower or decline.

Bigger than Brexit or Trump

All of this is to say that Brexit and President Trump are just the beginning of this revolution.

The effects of zero and negative interest rates are now finally showing signs of hurting more than helping.

This is the peak of the massive demographic and technological trends that created the second phase of globalization on a large scale starting after World War II.

Globalization is peaking, with a sharp backlash toward greater sovereignty and protectionism, exactly like the 1930s.

But every cycle has its expansionary phase and then its consolidation and deleveraging phases. This is the peak of the dramatic growth of Western and developed countries and will lead to the continued rise of emerging and Asian countries.

That's why we see more volatility and civil unrest in those areas.

We need to buckle our seat belts now to prepare for not only a great debt and financial-bubble deleveraging and deflationary period in the next several years, but also a time of true revolution in everything. I'm talking everything from political and social structures to business organizations reshaping and re-forming for many years, and even decades to come, just like after the Civil War. I'm talking the bottom-up network revolution in everything!

It's time to hunker down in your business and household finances.

Cash out of the bubble in all risk assets for just a few years, even if you get out a bit too early. Crashes happen much faster than the bubbles build, so don't wait for the horse to bolt before closing the barn door.

Consider where you should be living and target less bubbly areas that are safer and more aligned with your political and social values.

And if you get ready now, you'll have plenty of opportunity to profit when the time comes. I'll give you the details in part III. Also, check in at dentresources.com regularly.

CHAPTER 5

An Even Bigger Cycle

Inflation is a sign of progress in the longer term, not the monster that economists make it out to be.

Harry Dent

AS I EXPLAINED IN CHAPTER 1, we're seeing world-changing shifts in politics, economies, and societies, thanks to the 250-year Revolution Cycle rolling over us, on top of the 84-year Populist Movement Cycle and the 28-year Financial Crisis Cycle.

Besides that (and I'll tell you more about this in later chapters), we have a continuing adverse 34-year Geopolitical Cycle that turned down in 2001 (on the day of 9/11, to be precise) and will remain negative into early 2020, with terrorism, ethnic tensions, civil wars, and so on.

We've been in a downward-trending Boom/Bust Cycle (see chapter 6) since early 2014 and will continue on this path into late 2019 or early 2020. Governments can fight such a declining trend with free money for only so long.

And aftershocks in demographic trends will be felt into late 2022.

But there's also an even bigger cycle at play that I briefly referred to earlier: the 500-year Mega–Innovation and Inflation Cycle.

Economists generally see inflation as a bad thing, whereas it may be the ultimate dark matter for the economy.

Figure 5-1: 500-Year Mega–Innovation and Inflation Cycle
Consumer Prices in Britain, 950–1985

Source: E. H. Phelps Brown and Sheila V. Hawkins

What's wrong with these pinheaded pencil pushers?

They know nothing about the most important principles of our economy and the naturally oscillating dynamics of innovation and change.

They think that we can incrementally grow with few and only minor setbacks and then settle into a nirvana-like state forever, with no more recessions—and no more substantial inflation or deflation. . . . Do they think they can design a greater system than God or "the invisible hand"?

They think they can turn our dynamic economy into a machine. It's not a machine. It's biological, diverse, complex, and organic.

What's wrong with them is that too many of them live in academic ivory towers and don't have to run real businesses or deal with real life in any significant way.

Yes, short-term inflation can be a bad thing.

Like the falling productivity and rising prices in the 1970s and the oil embargo that made it worse.

Or when we have great wars at short-term costs, and inflation that we can't pay for at first . . . but that can bring great innovation and changes in global markets and powers.

Or when a short-term natural disaster makes certain things radically more scarce and expensive, like a bad freeze in Florida that raises orange juice prices.

But even those short-term challenges bring innovations that offset the setback and allow for growth again.

In the long-term, inflation is *clearly* a sign of progress, and of a rising standard of living. There is no question about that, historically speaking.

When did we have the greatest decline in living standards in modern history? The Dark Ages—a 500-year bear market between 450 and 950. When was the last terrible downturn? The deflation of the 1930s. But both periods were followed by major growth accelerations!

New technologies, which develop out of adverse periods of inflation or deflation, allow us to move to higher-density urban areas and specialize in labor. We earn more and contribute more. But, again, delegating to specialists and the costs of managing more complex urban areas combine to raise the costs of goods and of government.

Investments in new technologies, infrastructures, and more integrative government services and regulatory agencies create greater growth and a higher standard of living compared with what you'd find in more rural and lower-cost areas of living.

This is the paradox.

Who's richer: urban or rural households?

And which countries are richer? Urban ones!

In emerging countries, urban households tend to have three times the GDP per capita of rural ones.

Developed countries, with higher urbanization and technology, tend to have six to eight times as much income per capita as more rural emerging countries.

Urbanization and new technologies allow better and more specialized work and trade, just as Adam Smith understood in the late 1700s.

We have to pay specialized workers to do what they do best, so *we* can do what *we* do best.

But that comes with a price.

Specialization raises the costs of almost everything, except the emerging high-tech goods that become radically cheaper and drive change—from autos to computers.

At the same time, we earn much more than the added costs of our specialization, and we see greater value and greater job prospects in more urban and high-trade areas. So . . .

We get inflation and the need for more dollars and credit to facilitate such trade and specialization.

And we get long-term inflation, like you can see in the 500-year chart (Figure 5-1) that I shared earlier.

Long-term inflation is actually a sign of progress in people's standard of living. It's largely a result of increasing innovation, urbanization, and expanding demographics.

Gold bugs will argue that the value of a dollar has gone down 97 percent since 1900 due to the fact that so many more dollars are in circulation through cash and credit. **But that is such a wrong view.**

If the dollar was so devalued, how did our standard of living, adjusted for inflation, increase by more than eight times since 1900?

And how did our prosperity rise while government expenditures became a higher percentage of our economy, instead of lower?

If gold bugs want to go back to the times of Mayberry in *The Andy Griffith Show* or *Little House on the Prairie,* they can be my guest. Break your back 100 hours a week to barely survive, and then be attacked regularly by bandits or hostile American Indians?

NO, I think I will take watching Homer Simpson on TV while someone else does everything for me and takes care of my kids as well, and I at least have some healthcare and retirement benefits.

When inflation rises over the long-term, it's a sign that this broader process of the specialization of labor is manifesting successfully.

It also reminds me of my favorite classical economist today, Lacy

Hunt. He explains the same phenomenon on shorter-term "money velocity" trends. He shows that when money velocity (or turnover of money) is growing, it's a sign that money is being productively invested. That means it can be reinvested and create even more growth in the future—more jobs, more income, and more wealth.

When money velocity first starts to fall, even from higher rates, it means that money is being invested in more speculative pursuits that don't create real growth, just short-term gains and "bubbles"! Then it finally falls below average, and that means we're into the deleveraging of debt and financial-asset bubbles . . . and a depression wherein the excesses get wrung out of our economy.

Look at this chart from Lacy.

What I'm talking about happens in longer- and shorter-term cycles.

Longer-term, rising inflation means rising investments and returns. Slowing inflation means less! This occurs in 500-year and in 60-to-80-year cycles as well.

Urbanization is the greatest single driver of that, and that's pro-

Figure 5-2: Money Velocity—and Intermediate-Term View of Inflation/ Deflation

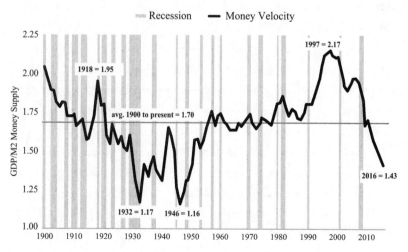

Source: St. Louis Federal Reserve, Hoisington Investment Management

pelled by innovation in new technologies when they finally move into the mainstream.

Periods of falling inflation or deflation are signs that the process is deleveraging or resetting to foster renewed innovation again . . . and that seems to be unproductive in the near term but is actually very stimulating to innovation and productivity over the longer term.

The Most Powerful Factor in Human Progress

The greatest period of deflation in modern history didn't come during the Great Depression but during a period that occurred in the Dark Ages. This was after the breakdown of the Roman Empire and the great 1,000-year boom, sparked by Greek innovations starting around 500 BC and Roman expansion to follow that created a monumental bubble.

Marcus Lemonis, on his hit TV show *The Profit,* has three key principles for growing businesses: "People, Process, and Product."

For the long-term economy, technological innovations are the products, urbanization is the process, and demographics are the people.

Globalization, with increasing urbanization and demographic growth since the latter 1800s, has been a major part of the rise in inflation and standard of living.

And, again, our income adjusted for inflation has expanded more than eight times—just since 1900, just after this 500-year cycle turned up in 1896 (but only after a longer-term deflationary trend finally bottomed out in the wake of five depressions between 1820 and 1896).

My view now, with this new chart, is that the globalization trend accelerated on a larger scale around 1945, with the meteoric rise of Japan following post–World War II reconstruction.

But that phase of globalization has peaked and is fading fast, as I've explained. Its very success has put radically different political,

Figure 5-3: Global Urbanization Has Accelerated Since 1920
Percentage of Global Population Residing in Urban Areas

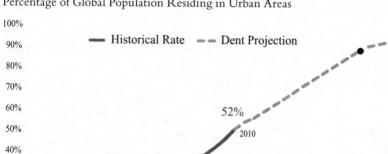

Source: United Nations, Dent Research

religious, ethnic, and income factions in each other's faces, increasing discontent and hate.

Look at the increasing accelerating urbanization rate globally since 1920.

It—urbanization—is the most powerful factor in human and economic progress.

And what was the first major country to urbanize in response to industrialization?

Great Britain!

The power it gained from urbanizing allowed a small island nation to largely rule the seas and the world for more than a century.

In China, the rate of urbanization will slow for a decade as the country works off its massive overinvestment in infrastructure and its rural migration continues to abate and even move backward.

But the longer-term trend in urbanization, in emerging countries, will continue to the point of 90 percent full global urbanization

Figure 5-4: Two Globalization Surges: After 1852 and After 1945
Global Trade as a Percentage of Global GDP

Source: Estevadeordal, Frantz, and Taylor (2003), Penn World Tables, version 8.1; Klasing and
Milionis (2014); World Bank; ourworldindata.org/international-trade; Dent Research

near 2145, precisely when the 500-year Mega–Innovation and Inflation Cycle is due to peak.

Look at the growth in global trade as a percentage of GDP, going
all the way back to 1500.

**This is globalization, urbanization, technology, and the spe-
cialization of labor at work.**

Like any long-term trend, it's exponential and driven by new
technologies that allow for it.

Economies were isolated before tall ships sailed in the late 1400s.
They were still insolated before faster and larger steamships barged
through the waters in the mid-1800s. It wasn't until railroads that
crossed national and regional borders, largely built in the latter 1800s,
that we slowly moved toward becoming a global community. Jet
travel began accelerating that trend in the 1950s, and then the Internet became the largest global catalyst.

As a percentage of global GDP, trade grew from 2 percent in

1500, after the advent of tall sailing ships in the late 1400s, to 5 percent by 1700.

Then trade grew from 5 percent to 10 percent by the early 1800s, following the first stock-financed global trading companies. The East India Company in 1706 was the first.

Then there was the first rapid globalization surge on the Centurial Cycle, from around 1850 into 1912.

The first large-scale steamships fueled that, with a 45-year Innovation Cycle rising from 1852 through 1875.

Railroads came along with the next rising cycle, from 1897 to 1920.

(This 45-year cycle is critical. I'll talk about it more in chapter 6.)

But World War I, the Great Depression, and World War II interrupted Globalization Boom #1.

An approximate 67-year trade boom started around the mid-1840s (after a major depression) and peaked in 1912. A 33-year bust followed, from 1913 to 1945. That was a "wave one" uptrend in Elliott Wave terms, followed by a "wave two" correction. It also demonstrated the 100-year Centurial Cycle I discussed in chapter 3.

Globalization Boom #2 started in 1946 and peaked somewhere between 2008, when the Great Recession hit, and 2012, when the euro hit its first major crisis, a 63-to-67-year expansion. That was "wave three." That was approximately 100 years after Globalization Boom #1 peaked.

And if this 100-year cycle holds, it will take until 2041–45 for this backlash against globalization to bottom out. Then we could start to see the beginnings of the next great surge, but likely not the strongest part until after the next global depression has run its course, by the mid- to late 2070s.

Here's why . . .

When I adjust my Generational Spending Wave in the United States for falling immigration and births in this Economic Winter Season, our economy is projected to go sideways for decades. Then it'll hit its lows in the early to mid-2070s, before potentially turning up longer-term.

This is based on rising births from 2024 onward, during the next global boom and positive Geopolitical Cycle.

The combined demographic trends in the emerging world will also peak around 2065, and a marked economic slowdown will ensue. That's when I see the next great depression and Economic Winter Season: between 2066 or so and 2074–77.

This suggests weaker global growth as developed countries decline modestly, offsetting much of the stronger emerging-world gains. But emerging countries are not and will not be nearly as high in income/GDP per capita, and typically only about 20 to 25 percent as affluent, even when they fully urbanize.

Slowing developed-country growth is the reason why investors and businesses have to get very serious about focusing on emerging countries, where the demographic growth and urbanization will take place. More on that ahead.

Two Sets of Kids?

By the top of the next 45-year Innovation Cycle, around 2055, when the peak of the second wave of the millennial generation's Spending Wave is due, we will almost certainly see breakthroughs in technologies that create much longer life spans and higher fertility into later age ranges.

That, coupled with suburban sprawl in emerging countries, could lead to a second global baby boom, with globalization returning stronger than ever.

Then we could see a stronger and final phase of demographic growth and urbanization that doesn't peak until the mid-2140s, on this 500-year cycle.

Humans could start living to celebrate their 120th birthdays, and that would greatly expand and enhance our earning-and-spending cycle . . . and maybe make it possible for parents to have two rounds of kids.

You could make all your mistakes on the first set but then have perfect kids the second time around . . . and more finances to support them (and for psychological counseling for your first set).

This would finally reverse slowing demographic trends, especially in developed countries, and create a whole new and more expansive dynamic.

We won't be around to see any of that, of course, but the point is that we're only partway through the long-term 500-year cycle in progress and inflation. It started in the mid-1890s and runs through to the mid-2140s.

The next global trade regression could last many decades before the 60-year-plus Globalization Boom #3—a fifth-wave advance that suggests globalization and inflation would peak for a long time ahead.

But the most important insight here is that the next global economic boom will see slower growth and will be much more mixed and selective, favoring emerging countries that will continue to urbanize with still-rising demographic trends and the commodities that they both export and consume.

You, as an investor or business owner, need to focus in these areas after the crisis ahead. As I said in my last book, *The Sale of a Lifetime,* this will not be a time to invest in just anything, as was the case from the early 1930s onward.

As a very long-term overview, I see a four-stage globalization cycle.

The worst crisis would be over the next several years, and it would then take decades to really pay off in a rising economic-productivity cycle again.

Here's what that four-stage trend looks like:

Stage #1: From the late 1800s to 1945, the *innovation* stage of globalization saw Globalization Boom #1 peak in 1912. Two world wars and the Great Depression sorted out political imbalances before globalization could fully blossom again . . . and blossom it did.

Stage #2: From 1946 to 2012 or so, we got the *growth* phase, or Globalization Boom #2.

Stage #3: From 2012 into as late as 2078, we'll get a *shakeout* period in globalization. Geopolitical imbalances must first be corrected before the next global boom can occur . . . and this will be a great challenge and take decades, not years.

Stage #4: From around 2078 to around 2145, we'll get the *maturity* boom phase with Globalization Boom #3.

So, by 2140–45, the world should be nearly 90 percent urban, with peaking long-term demographic trends and middle-class living standards higher almost everywhere. This is likely to be the best the world economy will look for a long time to follow, and the next dynamic longer-term global boom from around 2078 into 2145 will rival 1945–2007.

But between now and the 2070s, the global boom will be a much more mixed picture than the blockbuster period of globalization that ran from World War II to 2016.

CHAPTER 6

The Four Fundamentals That Shape Our World

When two of these cycles converge, it's distinctly noticeable. When three of them converge, it's exhilarating. When all four converge, it's a life-changing bubble.

Harry Dent

AS IF THE 500-YEAR MEGA-INNOVATION AND INFLA-TION CYCLE, the 250-year Revolution Cycle, the 100-year Centurial Cycle, the 84-year Populist Movement Cycle, and the 28-year Financial Crisis Cycle weren't enough for this revolution, we also have the downward convergence of the Four Fundamentals—four cycles that are inseparable from our booms and busts and our successes and failures economically.

Out of the infinite array of cycles that impact our economy and our lives, I have distilled it down to these four fundamental cycles that have really mattered over the last 30 years—starting with my first great discovery, the demographic-driven generational cycles.

Here they are in Figure 6-1.

Let's look at each one in detail. . . .

Figure 6-1: The Four Fundamentals
Developed Countries

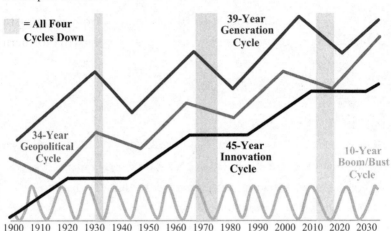

Source: Dent Research

Fundamental #1: The Generational Spending Wave

The Generational Spending Wave tracks the movement of a new generation as its spending predictably increases, peaks, and then decreases as it ages. This is totally predictable with modern demographic statistics.

Because the baby boomers were (and remain) such a powerful force in the economy, to know in advance what their impact would be on stocks, markets, real estate, and anything else, I simply moved the birth index forward by 46 years (in the United States). And, of course, I adjusted for immigration.

At 46 years old, most baby boomers were peaking in their spending, having bought the largest house they'll own when they were about 41 and helping their kids through high school, maybe college, and then into the big, wide world.

For the Bob Hope generation, I moved that birth index forward just 44 years to match up with their peak in spending. They got married earlier, went to school for a shorter time, and had kids earlier, on average.

For the millennial generation, I move the birth index forward by 48 for the first wave, and 50 for the second wave.

(The peak spending age also differs slightly from country to country; for example, it's 47 in Japan and likely the same in Northern Europe.)

It was thanks to this cycle that I was able to forecast the unprecedented boom and bubble into late 2007 in the United States, and the collapse of Japan in 1989.

And when I back-tested it, it also called the 1950s and '60s boom *and* the '70s extended recession and inflation crisis.

That's because demographics really drive the economy. They're that unseen dark matter again. New generations of consumers do predictable things at predictable times.

The average person in the baby boom generation entered the workforce at age 20.

They got married at age 26.

Apartment rentals peak shortly after, and typically the first baby arrives when his or her parents are 28 or 29 years old.

That stimulates the first home purchase at about age 31.

As the kids become teenagers, parents buy their largest house. That's between the ages of 37 and 41.

Boomers continued to furnish their homes into their forties, and thus spending on furniture peaked around age 46. This is also the peak in spending overall for the average household.

In the downward phase of spending, some sectors continue to grow. . . .

College tuition peaks at around age 51.

And cars are the last major durable-goods item to peak, at around the age of 54. That's when parents finally trade in the minivan for carting around kids and splurge on a luxury car.

Savings start to rise from 46 forward but surge the most from age 55 to 63, toward a net worth that peaks at age 64 (a year after the average person retires, at age 63).

Figure 6-2: Predictable from Cradle to Grave

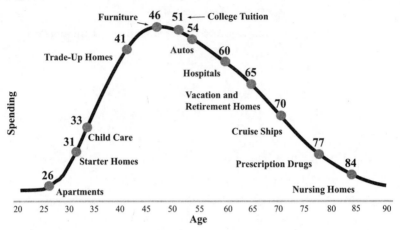

Source: U.S. Census Bureau, Dent Research

Spending on hospitals and doctors peaks between the ages of 58 and 60, when people are still paying more out of their pockets instead of using Medicare and Medicaid.

Vacation and retirement home spending peaks around age 65.

Cruise ship travel peaks at age 70.

Then there are the peak years for prescription drugs (age 77) and nursing homes (age 84, mostly women).

I've highlighted only the key areas here. The data can tell you much more, such as when consumers spend the most on camping equipment, babysitting, or life insurance.

If you want to see more, get a copy of my in-depth research report, *Spending Waves: The Scientific Key to Predicting Market Behavior for the Next 20 Years*. It delves into hundreds of categories of consumer spending, with charts that show you the trend for each. This research could cost a large corporation $20,000, if not more. You can get it at less than $200. Find more information on that at dentresources.com.

All of this is critical to understanding and forecasting the markets and economy because, as a generation moves through its predictable spending pattern, we see this . . .

Figure 6-3: The Spending Wave
Births Lagged for Peak Spending Versus the Real Dow

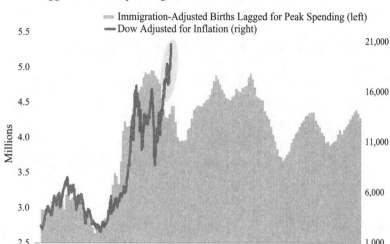

Source: Dent Research, U.S. Census Bureau, Bloomberg

That's an undeniable correlation.

The only exception came from late 2008 onward, when central banks started printing money to mitigate the impact of the Great Recession and its brief deflationary trends. . . . And I have been saying for years that it won't end well, as the massive divergence in this chart would clearly suggest.

This unprecedented overvaluation represents the greatest divergence from my most fundamental trend and strongly suggests that the greatest stock market crash in our lifetimes is just ahead.

To summarize: The Generational Spending Wave peaked in the United States in late 2007, as forecast two decades ago, and continues to point down into around late 2022. It peaked in Japan in late 1996, and the Land of the Rising Sun's economy has suffered bubble crashes and been on massive QE (quantitative easing) life support ever since. The baby boom in Europe peaked in 2011.

This is the biggest reason that the Great Recession hit in 2008 and why economic growth has been so slow ever since, despite unprecedented monetary stimulus and the biggest something-for-nothing "free lunch" in history.

Fundamental #2: The Geopolitical Cycle

The Geopolitical Cycle is roughly 34 years long (32 to 36 years, going back 200 years) and oscillates from favorable to unfavorable about every 17 years.

The last positive arm of this cycle was between 1983 and 2000, during which time nothing significant went wrong in the world and the Cold War quickly faded. The first Iraq war lasted only 100 hours and didn't occupy and seek regime change.

Since the cycle turned negative in 2001, however, we've seen an endless series of destructive geopolitical events: 9/11, two failed wars, endless civil wars including Syria, the Arab Spring, Russia's invasions of Crimea and Ukraine, the rise of ISIS (worse and more brutal than Al Qaeda), the twin Paris attacks followed by incidents in Brussels, Nice, and England, extreme racial tensions in the United States over police brutality—you name it!

Here's what it looks like (see Figure 6-4).

This cycle has an impact not so much on GDP growth or corporate earnings, but on the risk perceptions of investors, because markets and economies are highly charged during the negative period of this cycle.

Volatility is high.

Fear simmers just under the surface.

As a result, stock valuations during negative turns tend to be half of what they are during the positive swing. That's a big deal, as the following chart shows (see Figure 6-5).

It's the valuations of stocks, or the price/earnings ratios (P/E), that are most impacted. Robert Shiller has come up with the best measure of that by averaging earnings over ten years to take out the distortions of shorter-term earnings swings.

Figure 6-4: The 34-Year Geopolitical Cycle

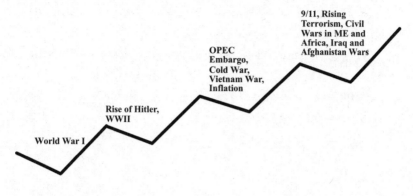

Source: Dent Research

The Geopolitical Cycle nails these swings in higher or lower stock valuations . . . more so than any other cycle I have.

Figure 6-5: Geopolitical Cycle Versus P/E Ratios
Shiller's 10-Year Cyclically Adjusted Price-to-Earnings Ratio

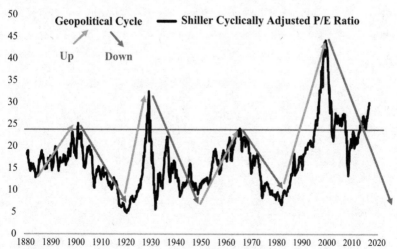

Source: Robert Shiller's 10-Year Cyclically Adjusted Price-to-Earnings Ratio, Dent Research

I used to rely more on the Generational Spending Wave for that, but the much lower stock valuations since 9/11 caused me to seek out and find this powerful cycle.

This cycle continues to point down into around late 2019 or early 2020. And it's another reason why the huge divergence from quantitative easing and money printing shown in the Spending Wave chart is due to crash and burn.

Valuations on stocks are likely to fall from as high as 32 in late 2017 to as low as 5 to 8 by early 2020. . . .

That's a big deal.

In November 2015, I recorded a monthly *Ahead of the Curve* webinar for my Boom & Bust Elite members, in which I broke down the events that have taken place since this Geopolitical Cycle turned down in 2001.

In *The Sale of a Lifetime,* I broke that chart into a series that high-lighted events per year. It was shocking to see the timeline of events, but it reinforced the power this cycle has on every aspect of our lives.

I'll share a compilation with you here:

Figure 6-6: The Geopolitical Timeline Since 2001

And this timeline doesn't even cover every single event!

Fundamental #3: The 45-Year Innovation Cycle

The peaking of major mainstream technology surges every 45 years.

In 1875, steamships peaked and then dropped off rapidly.

Up until 1920, railroads laced the dirt across continents before cascading downward.

By 1965, cars had raced into the hearts and homes of middle-class citizens, and almost everyone finally owned one.

By 2010, the Internet and mobile computing were ubiquitous and had changed how we work and interact with one another. . . .

Right about every 45 years!

And that's the key here. This cycle turns positive when clusters of technology go mainstream for about 22.5 years. This is what happened with portable computing and the Internet from 1988 to 2010; with cars from 1942 to 1965; with railroads from 1897 to 1920; and with steamships from 1852 to 1875.

And recall that the grand globalization cycle surged twice with these past four cycles.

This creates high-growth, high-productivity periods, due to the advance of such major driving industries. Higher productivity means better wages for workers and bigger profits for businesses.

Although I'm highlighting the most dominant technology in each cycle, they always come in clusters:

- steamships, canals, and the McCormick reaper
- railroads, telegraphs, penicillin, and elevators
- autos, electricity, phones, radios, and TVs
- personal computers, wireless phones, the Internet, and broadband

For example, a cluster of key technologies enabled mass production and the assembly-line revolution, which was followed by the massive shift from city living to the suburbs from the 1940s into the 1960s. That was a big deal! Suburbs were cheaper and safer. It wouldn't have been possible without the convergence of autos, electricity, phones, radios, and TVs.

Suddenly, everyday people could have more land and space, enjoy safer living conditions, and commute to and from work with ease. They didn't have to be within walking distance of their job, or the nearest bus terminal or train station . . . and they were still connected to the growing and globalizing world.

The other side of this cycle is more neutral. It's not as much like the other cycles that turn negative. After all, there is *always* innovation. Only, it's during those neutral periods that the next new technologies are emerging into niche markets, while the older wave is maturing and declining.

A perfect example of this is biotechnology.

Innovation continues exponentially in this arena, but many of the breakthroughs are not yet accessible to the masses. Watch out for this to burst into the mainstream when this technology cycle turns upward again, around 2032, along with nanotechnology, robotics, 3-D printing, and alternative energy.

And biotechnology is likely to break out earlier, as electricity did in the early 1900s.

This cycle causes me to argue with some of the gee-whiz technologists. Yes, I agree that technological innovation is exponential, not linear. But it still comes in cycles.

I don't expect to see as much progress in standard of living or longevity in the next decade, except in emerging countries that continue to urbanize and adopt the technologies that are already ubiquitous in developed countries.

I know to look for the next mainstream technology revolution in developed countries between 2032 and 2055. That's when we're likely to see our real wages and life spans expand more assertively, as occurred from the 1940s forward—two such cycles back.

And such longer life spans are the only way out of the demographic rut that aging developed countries are in and emerging countries will ultimately find themselves in as well.

And finally . . .

Fundamental #4: The Boom/Bust Cycle

The fourth fundamental cycle I watch closely is driven by sunspot cycles that vary between 8 and 13 years—not as clockwork-like as many cycles I study, but the most invaluable in calling crashes and recessions. Have we not had significant recessions about every ten years?

Now, hear me out on this one. . . .

When I mentioned this cycle to my colleagues and loyal subscribers, they were skeptical at first. Then some begged me not to talk about it in public or even to subscribers, because it could make me look like a crackpot.

I didn't need to lend any more credence to the popular view that I'm just plain crazy.

But my live-and-die-by-the-sword personality wouldn't let me follow their advice. In fact, their warnings just drove me deeper into the research to prove the value of this cycle.

And the more I researched, the more evidence I found that this cycle is very real, very powerful . . . and has impacted markets and the economy for as long as we have economic data to review (back to the mid-1800s, and we have sunspot cycle data back to the 1600s)!

And by the way, I'm not the only economist or financial researcher who believes in the power of this cycle. In fact, I first came across it when reading an article in *Barron's*.

One of the largest fund managers, formerly at PIMCO, said it was the sunspot cycle that saved him from the 2000–02 tech-wreck crash.

As I've since discovered, sunspot activity affects many things, from satellites to electronic infrastructures to sunshine to rainfall to human psychology . . . all from higher solar energy at its peaks and lower solar energy at its bottoms.

Do you know that both sunshine and rainfall are 20 percent higher at the peak of the sunspot cycle?!

In the recent cycle, the best scientists called for a peak in late 2013. They were early by a couple of months—it finally peaked in February 2014. But in the world of cycles, that's close enough to count as spot-on.

Now the scientists are calling for the next bottom to occur around late 2019 or early 2020, which just happens to be when the Geopolitical Cycle is due to bottom and turn more favorable again . . . and when the worst of the United States' demographic downturn should be over.

The good thing about this cycle is that it's more intermediate and better focuses on booms and busts within the larger cycles that the other three Fundamentals are good at forecasting. It can tell you when there'll be recessions or stock crashes, even in longer-term boom periods. It also targets when the biggest crashes are likely to happen in longer-term down periods.

This makes it the best cycle I have discovered since the Generational Spending Wave!

And if you don't see a rough ten-year cycle over your lifetime, you're blind: early 1960s, early to mid-1970s, early 1980s, early 1990s, early 2000s, 2008–09 . . . and now late 2017 into early 2020?

All of our major recessions are close to ten years apart.

Again, it's not as clockwork-like as many other cycles Andy and I have, but scientists are good at predicting the up and down swings that we don't have the specific skills to calculate.

This cycle is best at pinpointing when we'll see major crashes, financial crises, or recessions/depressions within the three larger fundamentals.

Going back further to prove the value of this cycle without the shadow of a doubt: 88 percent of the recessions (and stock crashes) since the mid-1800s (where we have good economic data) have come in the downward phase of the Boom/Bust Cycle. And the other 12 percent have come close to the down cycle and perhaps just got triggered by geopolitical events a bit early or late.

Figure 6-7: 88 Percent of Recessions Happen in the Downturn of Sunspots

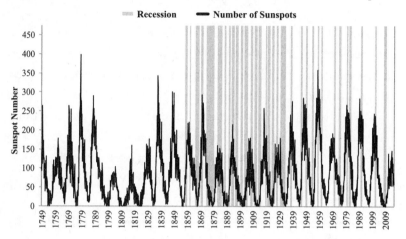

Source: nasa.gov

There is no chance this is a coincidence!

The last sunspot cycle peaked in March 2000, and the dot-com crash followed.

It bottomed between 2008 and mid-2009, right when the Great Recession was at its worst.

These last two cycles were the longest from top to top, at almost 14 years—from March 2000 to February 2014. That threw off Ned Davis's classic ten-year cycle, which predicts that the worst recessions and stock crashes come in the first two to three years of every decade . . . but not in 2010–12, when I most expected it.

Ned Davis's cycle is right, but it's not as clockwork-like.

The Boom/Bust Cycle is my new secret weapon, because scientists can predict the sunspot cycles that drive it pretty darn accurately, and very few people know about this cycle and what actually drives it.

When I had to dig deeper to figure out why Ned's cycle didn't work as well as it should have, after my other cycles suggested a major crash between 2010 and 2012, I found the sunspot cycle.

I knew this would be controversial for my readers and subscribers, so I made sure that it worked in history, and I found that it did—in spades.

When I revealed it to a broader audience at our annual Irrational Economic Summit, there was still skepticism, until a lady stood up and proclaimed, "I'm a nurse in an emergency room, and my husband is a police officer. We can testify that when there's a full moon, with slightly higher reflection of light and energy, there are more extreme events. More accidents. More murders."

So how could 20 percent higher solar energy not make people feel more optimistic or act more extreme? Why would such higher solar energy not create greater bubbles?

That was when my audience got this cycle beyond my long-term documentation.

So be skeptical about this cycle at your expense!

Like I said earlier, the current sunspot cycle peaked in February 2014 and points down until around late 2019 or early 2020, after being one of the most extreme in history.

With this more precise cycle pointing down, along with my three other fundamental cycles, I say: If we don't see a major financial crisis hit by early 2020, I'll quit my profession and become a limo driver on the Gold Coast of Australia.

And I'm not only betting on the Boom/Bust Cycle. When these Four Fundamentals converge, as they have done only twice in the past century (in the early 1930s and the early to mid-1970s), a major financial crisis and deeper downturn are almost certain.

When they converge with the Three Harbingers of Revolution and the Centurial Cycle . . .

That's world-changing!

That's revolutionary.

The only major cycle pointing up is the 500-year cycle, and that's why I don't see the deep economic and financial crisis ahead as the end of the world as we know it, as some of my bearish colleagues would have us believe.

It's criminal that the president and his men and women (and, in fact, all world leaders and their "support staff" and their economists) can't see what's right in front of their faces!

The worst years for these Four Fundamentals will be between late 2017 and early 2020. Period! There will be aftershocks into at least late 2022, before three of my four cycles turn back up again together.

The demographic cycle turns up around 2023.

The Geopolitical Cycle and the Boom/Bust Cycle turn up again after early 2020.

Only the Innovation Cycle continues to move sideways until 2032–33.

If we don't see that happen, it'll mean that central banks have conquered the business cycle. But I don't think that's even a remote possibility. I just don't see how it can happen, based on my three-decades-long study of history and cycles, especially the rare bubbles that come only once in a human lifetime.

Central banks have only created a greater bubble since the "real" bubbles, based on strong and predictable fundamentals, peaked between early 2000 and late 2007, just as my longer-term indicators predicted. This last bubble is all about artificial stimulus and the higher energy from a rising sunspot cycle.

The Economic Winter Season started in 2008 is getting ready to come back with a vengeance!

CHAPTER 7

Deep in the Heart of Winter

There's just no denying that major winter cycles come once in a lifetime.

Harry Dent

I'VE TALKED ABOUT THE PERVASIVE IMPACT of demographic and generational cycles on spending and our economy, especially since the first middle-class, broadly affluent generation emerged out of World War I—the Bob Hope generation.

But many economists are surprised to learn that the greatest driver of inflation is workforce growth. It costs a lot to raise young people until they enter the workforce. In fact, they cost everything and produce nothing until then.

The simple truth is that younger people are inflationary.

People in their rising family cycle are disinflationary, due to their rising productivity.

Older people are deflationary as they downsize, retire, and then die.

Shortly after I developed the Generational Spending Wave, in 1988, I found an incredibly close correlation with inflation and a two-and-a-half-year lag on workforce growth. And that indicator told me that inflation would fall into the peak of the baby boom spending cycle in 2007, and then, ultimately, we'd get deflation.

Here's that chart (Figure 7-1).

The combination of the generational Boom/Bust Cycle and the

Figure 7-1: Inflation Indicator and Forecast
Consumer Price Index Versus Workforce Growth on a 2.5-Year Lag

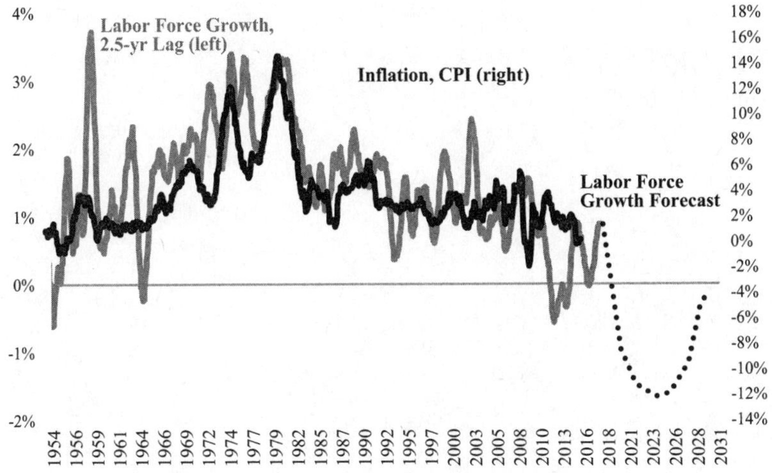

Source: Bureau of Labor Statistics, Dent Research

inflation/deflation cycle led me to an 80-year Four-Season Economic Model, which you can see in the next chart.

(As I mentioned earlier, this 80-year cycle correlates closely with Andy's 84-year cycle, and I now believe they're one and the same, with 84 years being the more accurate duration.)

The great part is that I could forecast both of these dimensions with simple demographic indicators.

The last full cycle materialized over two Generational Spending Waves: the Bob Hope boom, from 1942 to 1968, on a 44-year lag on births, and then the baby boom bull market, from 1983 to 2007, on a 46-year lag.

Strauss and Howe's work in generational cycles (which focused more on the political and social realm) also suggests that major cycles occur every 80-plus years, over two generational surges and in four stages.

In between, there were long recessions.

But it's the inflation cycle that gives this model its seasonal flavors.

Figure 7-2: 80/84-Year Four-Season Economic Cycle
The Worst of Winter Is Still Ahead

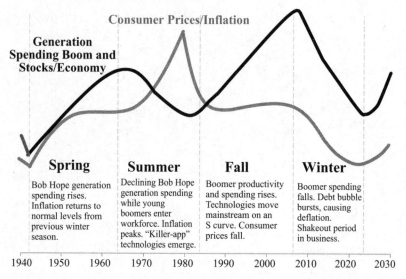

Source: Dent Research

Think of inflation like annual temperatures: the spring season comes out of the last winter or depression season—the last was the Great Depression.

In the Economic Spring boom, inflation rises mildly, as it did from 1942 into 1968.

In the Economic Summer Season, when the larger generation is entering the workforce at peak costs and low productivity, you get the maximum inflation rates, as in 1969–80.

Then inflation fell with the baby boom expansion as members of the cohort became more productive after entering the workforce en masse. This is the Economic Fall Season, with the highest growth, as well as falling inflation and declining interest rates to boot.

This is the season when you always see debt and financial-asset bubbles inflate due to high growth and ever-falling interest rates. That was the 1983–2007 period.

Then we hit the inevitable and most challenging Economic Winter Season, which sees deflation in prices and the painful deleveraging of the debt and asset bubbles, as was the case from 1930 to 1942 and as is the case right now (2008–23).

This is why central banks have feverishly created free money and stimulus: to stave off deflation and that painful deleveraging. No president or central banker wants to have the next great depression on their watch.

But, as Japan has proven, you don't get back to the spring boom if you don't go through the winter cleansing of debt and asset bubbles. That hasn't happened yet . . . but it must. And it will.

This is where the rubber meets the road.

Let's compare the Great Depression and the Economic Winter Season of 1929–42 and the one we're living through now, so you can see the impact of all these cycles you've just read about. . . .

The Great Depression of 1929–42

The 100-year Centurial Cycle of globalization peaked in 1912 and fell through 1945. There was a first great crash and mini-depression between 1920 and 1922.

The 45-year Innovation Cycle peaked in 1920 and was down into 1942, another factor in the crash of 1920–22.

The Generational Spending Wave peaked in 1929 and pointed down into 1942, then it turned into the Great Depression.

The 34-year Geopolitical Cycle peaked in 1929 and pointed down, through World War II, into 1947 . . . adding insult to injury!

Hitler became chancellor of Germany on that 84-year Populist Movement Cycle, in 1933.

The worst of the stock market crash and economic decline came between mid-1932 and early 1933, on the 28-year Financial Crisis Cycle.

The sunspot cycle pointed down from December 1929 through August 1934, the worst of the Depression, then again from July 1938 to April 1944, during which time we saw the second, less extreme phase of the downturn and the worst of World War II.

Yet the 500-year Mega-Innovation and Inflation Cycle continued to point upward from a low in 1896, telling us that there was more expansion and boom to come. This was not the end of the world or of America!

The greatest convergence of all of these down cycles came between late 1929 and 1941, especially late 1929 through 1933. That period saw the worst depression in U.S. and modern history . . . and the worst stock market in centuries.

Again, we know people don't like to think in cycles. So, as they did in the *Men in Black* movie, we'll flash the light in front of your eyes so you can forget this—after we've convinced you to make some very profitable decisions.

The Economic Winter Season of 2008–23

Fast-forward to our current financial crisis. The Boom/Bust Cycle peaked in March 2000, right at the top of the first tech bubble. That first dramatic crash bottomed in October 2002.

The next stock bubble peaked in late 2007, right in line with the Generational Spending Wave.

The Great Recession bottomed in August 2009, right at the bottom of the Boom/Bust Cycle, and it was the most extreme cycle, at 14 years from top to top. We got a two-for-one financial crisis on that extra-long down cycle.

The Geopolitical Cycle peaked right after the previous Boom/Bust Cycle, in late 2001, with the dramatic events of 9/11 and a mess of failed wars, civil wars, and terrorist attacks since then. This is why the second stock market bubble was not as strong as the first, even though earnings were as robust, as I predicted.

This geopolitical down cycle bottoms in late 2019 or early 2020. Then the terror trends should finally start to improve, slowly at first. This is also precisely when the current sunspot down cycle is expected to bottom.

The Generational Spending Wave peaked next, in late 2007, right on cue according to my forecasts dating back to 1988. It doesn't turn up again until around early 2023, although the worst of it hits by 2020.

The Centurial Cycle of globalization peaked by late 2016 and should point down for decades.

The Innovation Cycle peaked around 2010 and is neutral to down into 2032. So don't believe the extreme bullish forecasts for technology's impact until biotech, robotics, alternative energies, 3-D printing, and nanotech (potentially the largest) become mainstream.

And, again, the last Boom/Bust Cycle peaked in February 2014, after which markets went sideways for two years.

In late 2016, we got Brexit and Trump, rising together with a new populist movement on the 84-year cycle, with Trump taking office in 2017, 84 years after Hitler became Germany's chancellor, in 1933.

Andy and I both expect the worst crash to hit between late 2017 and early 2020, on that 28-year cycle, and the continued convergence downward in all four of my key indicators (the Four Fundamentals).

The negative sunspot cycle doesn't bottom until around early 2020. We should see the worst by then, with continued aftershocks into late 2022 or early 2023, before the Generational Spending Wave brings growth back again.

However, as with the Great Depression and World War II, the 500-year cycle continues to point up.

That means that this is NOT the end of the world or America.

That said, we're very unlikely to see another boom like the last one. The next boom will occur mostly in the still urbanizing and demographically growing emerging world, reflected in demand for the commodities that they most produce and consume.

The biggest difference between the Great Depression, the Great Recession, and the second great depression ahead is the 250-year Revolution Cycle.

Thanks to this, we face deeper changes in political, social, and financial institutions than those experienced in the 1930s, including:

1. Major entitlement reforms, including later retirement.
2. Reforms to global institutions like the UN, giving them more enforcement power (and teeth) against unfair trade and pollution strategies.
3. A lesser role for the United States as the global military police.
4. Stronger measures to fight global warming, not weaker.
5. Higher taxes on the top 0.1 percent to 10 percent, not lower.
6. The restructuring of massive private debt in a national "Chapter 11" process.
7. New Glass-Steagall-like financial reforms to keep traditional banking functions separate from brokerage and investment activities, to avoid collusion and conflicts of interest.
8. Greater restrictions on—if not outright bans against—corporate and special interests' lobbying of Congress.
9. Simpler, but still strong and effective, regulations for business and pollution.

More on this in chapter 8.

Taking a closer look at the impact of each of the Four Fundamentals is also enlightening. . . .

The Showstopper

My Generational Spending Wave has the broadest and most pervasive impact on stocks and the economy . . . and it's clear to see (look back at Figure 6-3).

However, the rise of a new generation into its peak family and spending cycle affects not just stocks but spending, productivity, and corporate earnings as well.

After all, as I've already said, people are the *real driver* of our economy, not government policies, as most economists would have you believe.

Governments tend to react to trends, not create them. People and business innovation create the real trends, and that is what we monitor for you.

Figure 7-3 shows you the impact of this cycle. . . .

(Note that I measure all of these indicators in real terms, adjusted for inflation.)

As you can see, stocks feel this cycle the most.

Figure 7-3: Impact of the Generational Spending Wave Cycle, 1930–2015

Years	Cycle Direction	Average Annual Growth				
		Real S&P Total Return, with Dividends	Real Corporate Earnings	Real Retail Sales	Real Personal Consumption Expenditures	Real GDP
1930–41	Down	-1.1%	1.6%	N/A	1.98%	3.32%
1942–68	Up	11.2%	3.0%	2.9%	3.96%	4.39%
1969–82	Down	-0.8%	-0.1%	1.3%	2.98%	2.57%
1983–2007	Up	9.2%	4.0%	2.6%	3.65%	3.38%
2008–Present	Down	6.5%	17.2%	0.8%	1.29%	1.14%

Source: Dent Research

That's because, historically, they rise faster than earnings. And, of course, earnings rise faster than the economy.

Stocks, including reinvested dividends, were up 11.2 percent in the longer up cycle from 1942 to 1968.

Then they were *down* 0.8 percent in the down cycle from 1969 to 1982. That's a swing of 12.0 percent!

The next bust-and-boom cycle saw 9.2 percent up and 6.5 percent down, but QE provided unprecedented support for this down cycle, which is set to continue until 2020–22 by my projections!

Corporate earnings also have very clear shifts through this cycle. The first up wave saw 3.0 percent. The down wave averaged minus 0.1 percent real growth annually.

The recent up cycle from 1983 into 2007 saw a whopping 3.96 percent increase.

Again, the current down cycle is anomalous, with the Fed's monetary policies encouraging unusually high levels of stock buybacks and fruitless mergers. Corporate earnings have been up 17.2 percent in a period of slow growth, all due to financial engineering and zero-interest-rate policies.

It hasn't come from the most anemic growth in the last century—of just 1.14 percent—and we haven't seen the worst of it yet!

And all the unprecedented monetary stimulus has just contributed to the already strong trends in income inequality that naturally occur in periods like this.

For retail sales, during the upturn from 1942 to 1968, we again see the trend for numbers to more than double during the cycle's upward wave: 2.9 percent versus 1.3 percent growth and 2.6 percent versus 0.8 percent growth in the current up and down cycle.

We can see similar trends in personal consumption, which we can measure back further.

The 1942–68 boom cycle saw real growth at 33 percent higher than the down cycle that followed.

The 1983–2007 up cycle was 3.65 percent, while the current down cycle is already at a paltry 1.29 percent.

Here again, the numbers we're seeing in this down cycle are much lower than past ones, which proves to me that the Fed's monetary policies are not benefiting the broad economy or everyday households.

Finally, real GDP also clearly correlates, but it isn't as strongly divergent in up and down cycles. That's because governments tend to counter the private economy and run deficits and stimulus programs to help offset the slowdowns.

On average, from 1930 to 2007, real GDP grew 0.94 percent faster in the up cycles. That's significant when you compound it over 26-year average boom periods.

When all is said and done, my Generational Spending Wave clearly shows how quantitative easing has boosted stocks and corporate earnings but done little for the broader economy or consumers.

It's All About Perceptions

While the Generational Spending Wave largely affects earnings, the Geopolitical Cycle largely affects what investors are willing to pay for those earnings based on their perceptions.

When a boom starts to turn into a bust as a result of a negative shift in demographic trends, investors will perceive greater risk. But they also perceive such risk when the world looks dangerous because of things like international wars, civil wars, terrorism, oil embargoes, or even droughts and plagues.

We've endured most of those things nonstop since 2001.

Prior to that—from 1983 to 2000—almost nothing of significance went wrong in the world.

And we can see the effects of this on P/E ratios.

In fact, that's what convinced me that this cycle mattered: The ratios changed so dramatically after 2000. We've never come close to the high valuations of the tech-bubble peak, despite even stronger earnings from the free-money bonanza during the QE years.

I think this cycle is one of the reasons many long-term analysts will miss this market top. They're waiting for overvaluation territory that looks like the levels we reached in 2000.

And we're simply not going to get there.

Stocks are already stretched beyond most past valuation extremes, with the exception of the once-in-a-lifetime cycles' convergence in 1929 and 2000. (I'll talk about this more in chapter 9.)

You'll find proof of the Geopolitical Cycle's impact on P/E ratios in this next figure. (We can go back much further on this cycle, but you'll get the picture just fine with the years we analyzed.)

When crunching the numbers for this table, I measured the P/E ratios at the peak of the projected Geopolitical Cycle, not when the ratios actually peaked. I did that because investors would be following the model and would not be able to guess the exact peaks.

As you can see, we saw P/E ratios ranging from 21.40 to 37.28 at the peaks of the last four Geopolitical Cycles.

Figure 7-4: The Geopolitical Cycle Versus P/E Ratios, 1883–2019

Years	Direction	CAPE* P/E at Peaks	CAPE P/E at Troughs	Trough Percentage of Peak
1883–1898	Up	21.40		
1899–1914	Down		10.17	47.5%
1915–1929	Up	22.01		
1930–1947	Down		10.68	48.5%
1948–1965	Up	23.69		
1966–1982	Down		8.47	35.7%
1983–2000	Up	37.28		
2001–2019	Down		7.0 Estimate	18.7%
Average 1883–2019	N/A	26.1	9.1	34.8%

*CAPE: Robert Shiller's Cyclically Adjusted Price-to-Earnings Ratio

Ratios were their strongest ever between 1999 and 2000, precisely when the massive baby boomer generation was growing fastest, spending, the Internet was moving mainstream at its fastest rate on the S curve, and the Geopolitical Cycle was at the peak of favorable territory.

But at the troughs of the cycle, those ratios range from 8.47 to 10.68.

I estimate conservatively that the next trough will see P/E ratios around 7.0, because the next crash will come during the worst of the Economic Winter Season . . . and crashes and ratios are always horrible during such times.

During the troughs, P/E ratios average anywhere from 19.7 to 48.5 percent of the peaks. That's a huge difference in how much investors will pay for stocks.

For the past four complete cycles (including the estimate for the next trough), the low cycles see P/E ratios average 34.8 percent of the peaks, but this should see the worst!

Given that stocks have now seen the second-highest P/E ratios in this cycle and the Generational Spending Wave peaked back in late 2007, you don't want to be sitting passively in stocks until at least late 2019 or early 2020!

The highest P/E ratios are likely to be followed by the lowest ones in centuries.

Important for Investors and Business Owners to Know

The impact of the 45-year Innovation Cycle is that it adds to economic trends by increasing things like productivity by 1 percent a year in the up cycles. That makes a big difference when compounded over its 22.5-year uptrend. That alone means the next up cycle won't be as strong. With the weaker demographic trends in most of the developed world, including the United States, the next cycle will be further limited.

Most important for investors and businesses, though, when this cycle moves into its plateau, the maturing companies of the past will fade and new sectors will emerge . . . even in a downturn. That's how you spot massive new opportunities.

This cycle entered into its sideways movement in late 2010 and will continue in this direction until mid-2033. (It doesn't turn up by 2020–23 like my other long-term cycles.)

That tells me that while there will be another global boom from 2020–23 forward, when the Generational Spending Wave and Geopolitical Cycles both turn up again, the effect won't be as strong as in past ones for the developed countries. The demographic trends say that even more so.

Here's how this cycle makes itself felt in real life (see Figure 7-5). . . .

The two strongest correlations for this cycle are:

1. Patent activity (patents per capita), which is far stronger in the up cycles.

Figure 7-5: The Innovation Cycle in Action

Years	Cycle Direction	Average Annual Growth	
		Patents per Capita	Productivity
1876–mid-1897	Down	0.6%	
Mid-1897–1920	Up	0.8%	
1921–mid-1943	Down	-1.5%	
Mid-1943–1965	Up	2.2%	2.0%
1966–mid-1988	Down	0.6%	0.8%
Mid-1988–2010	Up	3.8%	1.0%

Source: The U.S. Patent and Trademark Office; BLS; Dent Research

In the most recent upward trend, from mid–1988 through 2010, patents were up 3.8 percent a year, on average, compared with only 0.6 percent during the prior plateau, from 1966 through mid–1988.

2. Productivity, which increases as the cycle moves upward.

We don't have consistent data on labor productivity before 1947, but the first full cycle saw average gains of 2.0 percent from mid–1943 through 1965 in the uptrend, compared with 0.8 percent in the downtrend.

The last move up, from mid–1988 through 2010, was lower than in the previous cycle, at 1.0 percent, but I think that's a result of our rapidly aging society. I wouldn't be surprised if the current down cycle comes in at closer to zero.

The next upward leg of this cycle will be from mid–2033 through 2055. That's when all the great new gee-whiz technologies will have the greatest impact and finally move mainstream. Biotech will most likely be the first to break out, followed closely by robotics, clean energy, and, lastly, nanotechnology.

A 100 Percent Batting Average

Finally, besides forecasting 88 percent of recessions back to the mid-1800s, the sunspot cycle has so far forecast 11 out of 11 major financial crises correctly—a 100 percent batting average! If I didn't convince you of this cycle's power earlier, believe in it now.

A Grand Supercycle Top

After Trump's election in November 2016, stock markets launched into an irrational rally, suddenly switching from believing he was a wrecking ball to "Jesus walking on water." This looks to me to be the

Figure 7-6: Major Stock Crashes and Crises in Cycle Downturns

Depression, Major Recession, and/or Major Crash	Downturn Periods (NBER) Recession/ Depression	Down Business Cycle Period
Depression	1837–1843	Dec. 1836–Feb. 1843
Depression	Oct. 1873–Apr. 1879	May 1870–Mar. 1880
Depression	Mar. 1882–May 1885	Apr. 1882–Feb. 1890
Depression	Jan. 1893–Jun. 1897	Aug. 1893–Apr. 1902
Recession	May 1907–Jun. 1908	Feb. 1907–Jun. 1913
Depression	Jan. 1920–Jul. 1921	Aug. 1917–Aug. 1923
Depression	Aug. 1929–Mar.1933	Dec. 1929–Aug. 1933
Recession	Nov. 1973–Mar. 1975	Mar. 1969–Jul. 1976
Recession	Jan. 1980–Nov. 1982	Sep. 1979–Jun. 1986
Major Crash	Mar. 2001–Nov. 2001	Jul. 2000–Aug. 2009
Recession	Dec. 2007–Jun. 2009	

Source: Dent Research, nber.org, nasa.gov

final blow-off top in the greatest boom in modern history, as you can see in this next chart.

It isn't Trump's fault. . . . It's just not possible to create 4 percent growth again, no matter what you do with taxes and regulations. Just ask Japan!

This chart is courtesy of Robert Prechter, who used British stock prices up until 1789 and U.S. stock prices thereafter.

It's a logarithmic chart, which means it's already adjusted for exponential growth . . . yet it's *still* increasing exponentially since the last 250-year Revolution Cycle of the late 1700s. (I've updated this chart since it was originally published.)

That's how powerful this 230-year boom has been, with the next great reset to follow on the 250-year cycle we're highlighting in this book!

I also created a table to walk you through the Elliott Wave counts on this Grand Supercycle and each successive smaller wave. It says it all.

Figure 7-7: The Grand Supercycle
Stock Prices Since 1700

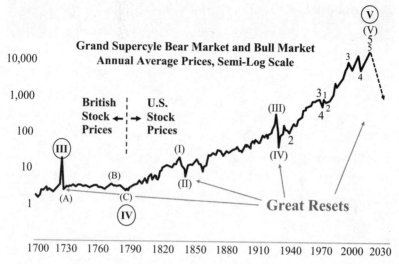

Source: Robert Prechter, *Conquer the Crash;* Dent Research

Figure 7-8: Elliott Wave Counts: Final Fifth Wave of a Fifth of a Fifth of a Fifth
The Trump Rally Looks Like the Last Orgasmic Blow-Off Rally Since,
Yes . . . 1787

Supercycle: 1787–2017

➤ 1 Wave Up: 1787–1835
➤ 2 Wave Down: 1835–1843
➤ 3 Wave Up: 1843–1929
➤ 4 Wave Down: 1929–1932
➤ 5 Wave Up: 1932–2017

➡ Mega Cycle: 1932–2017

➤ 1 Wave: 1932–1937
➤ 2 Wave: 1937–1942
➤ 3 Wave: 1942–1968
➤ 4 Wave: 1968–1974
➤ 5 Wave: 1974–2017

Generational Cycle: 1974–2017

➤ 1 Wave: 1974–1980
➤ 2 Wave: 1980–1982
➤ 3 Wave: 1982–2000
➤ 4 Wave: 2000–2009
➤ 5 Wave: 2009–2017

➡ Final Bubble Cycle: 2009–2017

➤ 1 Wave: Early 2009–Mid-2011
➤ 2 Wave: Mid-2011–Late 2011
➤ 3 Wave: Late 2011–Mid-2015
➤ 4 Wave: Mid-2015–Early 2016
➤ 5 Orgasm: Early 2016–Late 2017

Source: Dent Research

Elliott Wave counts can keep subdividing into smaller sub-waves, and this has already occurred in the past decade or so.

Quantitative easing sent many stock markets to new highs in 2017, despite the fundamental trends having peaked back in late 2007.

But you simply can't run an economy on artificial stimulus for too long without major side effects. Something will eventually go wrong.

So what could go wrong? Besides all of these cycles converging on us like an avalanche, that is?

I'll answer that question in chapter 13.

Before we get there, though, there's still a handful of other cycles you (and the president and his men and women) need to be aware of. . . .

Yes! There are more!

CHAPTER 8

What Needs to Happen to Get to Spring Again

Hey, politicians, managers, and central banks: Get the hell out of the way of the real network revolution!

Harry Dent

SO NOW YOU KNOW ABOUT the most important cycles converging on us now and in the years ahead.

The 500-year Mega–Innovation and Inflation Cycle

The 250-year Revolution Cycle

The 100-year Centurial Cycle

The 84-year Populist Movement Cycle

The 60-year Inflation Cycle

The 45-year Innovation Cycle

The 39-year Generational Spending Wave Cycle

The 34-year Geopolitical Cycle

The 30-year Commodity Cycle

The 28-year Financial Crisis Cycle

The 10-year (average) Boom/Bust Cycle

Plus the other cycles that Andy has identified: the 180-year cycle and 144-year cycle, to name just two.

Without a doubt, we face a time of extreme change. That's why I call this the greatest revolution since the simultaneous emergence of democracy and free-market capitalism.

And though at times it may look and feel like the end of the world, it really isn't. It's just the end of the world as we know it.

And thank God for that! We need change. Desperately.

We won't grow without change and challenge to our status quo! And in the developed world, we can't escape our never-ending demographic trap of lower birth rates. Not unless we innovate big time!

Before we move on to look at two big areas where we'll see massive change in the not-too-distant future . . . and how to profit from all of this . . . humor me with this discussion of another part of the puzzle I believe we'll see. . . .

The Real Network Revolution: Bottom-Up, Not Top-Down

I don't care what Trump promises about bringing manufacturing and good jobs back to America . . . it's not going to happen to any significant degree. And in a worsening economy ahead, it's even less likely!

I've been saying it since my very first bestselling book, *The Roaring 2000s,* in early 1998: it's all about the network revolution that allows political and business institutions to operate from the bottom up, not the top down . . . to leverage the creative and more entrepreneurial capacities of the everyday worker by bringing the information directly to them—including their profitability and each customer they serve—so they can make better decisions and create more profits for you and your company.

And if you don't think it's possible, keep reading. . . .

That's the only way to restore a rising middle class. We need information-enhanced entrepreneurs creating more customized products and services for more defined segments of consumers here and around the world.

Or, as I put it, "Every customer (or small segment) a market, and every employee (or small team) a business."

And here's the result: real-time personalized service at affordable costs. Screw competing with standardized products and services, with their lower-wage, overseas workers, robots, and computers!

Henry Ford was the Steve Jobs of his time. He was an arrogant SOB, but he had a vision in the early 1900s that everyday people could afford his newfangled and expensive cars.

He made this happen by creating the assembly line. That made his everyday workers ten times more productive, which allowed him to raise their wages substantially so they could be the first everyday workers to afford his Model Ts.

Managers I talk to around the country say, "Oh, most people just want to be told what to do and aren't that creative or willing to take risks. That's why we do what we do!"

If that's what you believe, then my answer to you is: You have no vision or understanding of human nature and how it evolves. You're no Henry Ford or Steve Jobs.

Most entrepreneurs I've worked with claim to have vision, but their businesses almost never work out the way they planned, including mine.

But one contemporary who had true vision was Steve Jobs. He saw from the beginning that portable computers, as clunky as his first ones were, would eventually bring power to the people by putting information into their hands.

He, like Ford, saw that the everyday person could rise to higher levels of income and standard of living than anyone thought possible.

Ford and other radical innovators brought the average person out of bare security and survival and into the belonging stage of Maslow's hierarchy of human needs. He helped create the first middle-class society.

Steve Jobs and many others have brought many people out of that belonging stage and into self-esteem and a minority into self-actualization.

It's time that more business and government leaders did the same . . . by bringing information and power to the people instead of running ever more inefficient top-down bureaucracies from the past.

Yes, most people won't take more risks or believe in a new system . . . until they see other people doing it and profiting from it. It's called the S curve of human adoption. Understanding the S curve and what the leading edge is doing today and how it will likely expand to the masses is one of the secrets to vision and forecasting.

Steve Jobs never did customer surveys to see what people wanted. His vision was, essentially, "I will create what you would have really wanted if you only knew it was possible."

And Henry Ford was famous for saying, "If I had asked people what they wanted, they would have said faster horses."

In business, if you just get the best people to follow a new system of innovation, accountability, and profits, and others see it working and making more money . . . they'll follow.

No one wants to miss the boat.

Pardon me, but most managers and supervisors are in the self-esteem phase, and are often in the business of preventing their employees from going past the belonging stage as they treat their employees like children that need to be constantly supervised and told what to do. That's a pity, because they'll never make it to the self-expressive and leadership level of self-actualization if they don't rethink their approach. And if they don't do that, they won't be able to compete with computers, robots, and foreign workers.

Look back at my first chart in the preface. **Human evolution is crystal clear.** It grows toward greater self-expression and creativity and toward more rational or scientific thought.

If you want to manage compliant, bureaucratic employees, move to Afghanistan! There would be a future for you there . . . but not in this revolution coming in the developed world, wherein employees won't even have the choice of being compliant and following the rules. Computers and robots will do that. People will have to get creative!

In the late 1700s, previously compliant British subjects in the United States stood up and said, "No taxation without representation." That caused the greatest political revolution in history until now.

Governments in developed and emerging countries, as well as managers and owners of large and smaller companies, have no idea what's coming in the next several years and the decades beyond.

So if you don't listen to me, your employees might, and then you'll be up the creek without a paddle.

The problem is that everyone is holding on to the old model of top-down control and management as if their lives depended on it.

Their lives DO depend on it . . . but not on the "holding on" part. Instead, they need to let go.

China is going to prove without a doubt that a top-down managed economy doesn't grow as well as a bottom-up, free-market, democratic one. It will see the greatest bubble burst after overbuilding its economy more than any over the past 30 years.

Then there are large and small corporations in business. . . .

Especially bosses, managers, and supervisors who get a kick out of having control over their employees and interfering with the very people who best know what they're doing and truly understand their customers.

The most happening large company I've walked into isn't Apple or Google. It's Bloomberg, where I do media interviews in New York. You walk in and everyone is moving, talking, cooking. There are free drinks and snacks. The place buzzes like nowhere else.

But even these leading-edge companies, from Apple to Google

to Bloomberg, aren't quite the model I see. They're not the Fords or Alfred Sloans of today.

Jack Stack takes that honor.

Jack Stack, whom I'll talk about more below, nailed it when he said, "Nobody knows the job better than the guy who is doing it."

He also said, "If you want employees to act like owners, you should make them owners." He's done that in spades and made an old-line manufacturing company into a large group of blue-collar millionaires.

That's how you make America great again!

Damn, Jack. I would vote for you for president.

If we want a leading-edge businessperson to lead a revolution, it wouldn't be a very successful top-down manager like Donald Trump. It would be people with *real* vision.

But here's the real point at this revolutionary time in history. Essentially, we need to flip our current models on their heads—in everything from work to business to government.

Think about it: Does anything in nature operate from the top down? Is the lion the king of the jungle . . . or just the greatest predator?

Do trees know how to grow by themselves? Yes, but they do better if they get better soil, sunlight, and water—like a good government structure and environment that sets the rules for the game and gets out of the way.

Management in the past and even today only comes from scarce information and the *seeming* lack of natural entrepreneurial instincts. Well, information is no longer scarce, and there's a huge well of natural entrepreneurial instincts to be tapped if management would just get the hell out of the way!

Try going to the kinds of seminars I speak at. There are many people looking to escape the corporate and government world and create or become their own business.

Technologists talk about the automation of most work. As I said early on in this book, most people fear this automation. Really? We should embrace it. Not only does it eventually lead to an improvement in our standard of living, but the automation of management would revolutionize business and free up workers to do what they most want to do . . . what they are going to these seminars for.

So consider this proposition. But I warn you, it's not easy to hear: **Management is the problem, not the solution. . . .**

The automation of management, supervision, and bureaucracy I propose puts the most critical information on the front lines of everyday decision making, such that companies and government institutions can literally operate from the bottom up, in real time, not from the top down in bureaucratic time, with handcuffs that often keep them from doing what their customers really want and need.

And that frees boring managers to become exciting visionaries, leaders, strategists, mentors, and coaches to people rather than merely filling out the high end of the bureaucratic chain of "command and control."

The thing I hate most about customer service is that there almost isn't any anymore. Try to get a customer service agent on the line, even at leading-edge companies like Yahoo or Google. Good luck with that! Only a hacker could get in and find a damn 800 number. They don't want to talk to you. You're a pain in the ass to them!

It's so hard to get a real person when you need one. Companies go out of their way to direct you to automated Web sites and phone message lines that ask you ten questions before you finally give up and say, "I want a representative, dammit!"

Is the result of the great information revolution that we get access to more information and potential products, but no one, no human, who can help us choose the right ones?

I'm a smart and creative person. The reason I started my own business is that I don't want some bureaucratic manager who has no idea of who I am and what I can create telling me what to do.

The direction of the economy in the developed world is simple: real-time, personalized service at affordable prices, delivered by everyday, information-enhanced, entrepreneurial workers who are the best at what they do because they're passionate about it. And you can actually interact with them in some human way! The best part is that you both evolve, in intelligence and relationship, through such interactions.

If you want to order music online, after the automated software recommended some options—which it can be very good at doing—wouldn't you prefer to talk to a real person (even in a chat window) who has the same music interest as you and can help you get the very best options?

Wouldn't you be more loyal to such a company and even pay more for that service?

I know I would.

That's why I pay for a concierge doctor. He can really get to know me and is there whenever I need him. And he's connected to the best specialists, giving me priority in their appointment books!

The best line I ever heard at a speech was that 95 percent of people are a genius at something . . . That's the key insight. We have a guy in Puerto Rico who can fix anything in our house . . . priceless.

So why not develop a bottom-up organization that allows that 95 percent to do what they do best? Enhance them to do that. Measure what they do and what they contribute, and then reward them for that directly.

Why not enhance their skills with your access to other services and enhance their marketing to related customers through your larger network? Reduce their marketing costs and increase their revenue, then split the profits with them?

My company does this all the time. We call it "affiliate marketing."

We have the greatest income inequality since 1929 thanks to this top-down approach and free money from central banks that only allows the rich to speculate more profitably.

But it will soon fail, dramatically.

In fact, it's already failing, with falling real incomes since 2000 and declining labor-force participation with aging and near zero productivity growth.

So what do we do with aging workers?

We make them into part-time or full-time entrepreneurs.

There was a lady on *Shark Tank* who employed women in nursing homes to knit her customized clothing line. It was a win–win for the company and its aging subcontractors.

Hence, a much bigger solution than the new emerging middle-class factory worker of the 1940s will rise. They're the "information-enhanced entrepreneurial worker," and companies of the future will become the "bottom-up network corporation," driven more by customers and frontline workers than by top-down management, with their damn stock options.

Does bottom-up sound like a threat to top-down management of companies or governments?

You bet it does, and the information revolution says it's not just possible—it's inevitable.

To give you a brief example, the new network corporation already exists in the most information-intensive industries, like stock exchanges.

Where's the management of the New York Stock Exchange? It's there, but you don't see it, as you do in most corporations (invisible dark matter again).

Someone rings the bell at 9:30 a.m. and all hell breaks loose.

Is anyone in control? No. Every stock trades, and every trader gets real-time feedback on his or her transactions and profits. Then, at the end of the day, trading closes and the chaos ends (except in futures and overnight markets).

Here's the secret: all the bureaucracy and management is programmed in the real-time, light-speed, computer-driven software!

The result is that the system is driven by the customers or end users, not the back-line bureaucracy. It's totally automated and operates in real time, at customers' beck and call.

This is the automation of management and supervision and accountability. It's coming at office and professional work faster than factory jobs that have already largely been lost. And I'm not dying for a good factory job any more than I yearn to work on a farm.

So, for you top-down managers, you need to be designing the software that will replace you if you want to have a job in the future. You'll have to be leaders and visionaries, not dictators and supervisors!

And it needs to happen now!

But, unfortunately, it won't until you get your asses so kicked that you have to do it to survive. The companies that stick to their mainstream strategy of merely streamlining their top-down bureaucracy will be brought to their knees until they finally realize they can empower their front-line employees or "browsers" to access their back-line experts, products, or "servers" to do what they already know they need to do, in real time, without your !@#$%^& rules and regulations and bureaucracy—as if you know better and need to approve everything.

You're in the way. Get creative about figuring a way to get out of the way!

My message to you—again, with all due respect for your achievements thus far—is that most of you don't know shit, even if you used to be on the front line or the factory line, because you are not there anymore, and the world is changing at light speed, in case you haven't noticed.

And you seem to know better only because you control the best information and don't put it on the front lines, where the people who best know their work and customers, because you want to be in control. You want to be the boss. Again, !@#$ you for that. It shows that you have not moved from the "self-esteem" level of Maslow's hierarchy of needs to the "self-actualization" level, wherein you do what you most value and help others to do the same.

So how do you get to that next level? Empower your best workers to make more decisions and achieve that level of self-esteem, and even better, become self-actualized, creating their own businesses inside the larger company and living their dreams. And that's how you become self-actualized and do something for the greater good than just your own profits. If you do that effectively, you and your company should profit more than ever. Just ask Jack Stack (still ahead). You can see I'm holding him back, but not for long.

If you don't, then you will never have an employee like me who can change the world and create whole new products or services or markets. Because anyone who has any soul or potential creativity would not work for you!

Note that I did create my own company, then expanded it by creating partners who had capacities I did not, and finally partnered with a marketing company that does understand me. It's all about partnerships and fair rewards for measured value added . . . and we have that at Dent Research.

That's the revolution that is coming in business and in governments around the world, starting in developed countries, where we can no longer compete with the lower wages in the rote jobs you managerial morons have created for most of us—in factories and in offices and in the least useful middle management and supervisors who mostly interfere with customers and real workers rather than contribute.

There is no way the already declining middle class of the United States and Europe can compete with lower-wage workers in Asia or anywhere in the emerging world! This is rote work that we once dominated, at high wages that will never be commanded again. And who wants rote, repetitive work anyway?

Anyone can work on most assembly lines. That makes you middle-class at best, and still in the "belonging" phase of Maslow's hierarchy.

So what do the higher-educated, everyday workers in North America and Europe have to offer?

Their education and their right-brain, creative, relational, and entrepreneurial skills!

Have you ever met a creative or humanlike computer? No, I'm sorry, Watson from IBM doesn't qualify . . . yet. Do computers identify new opportunities and ways to test and prove them to new consumers?

Do automated computer systems relate well with customers on a human level?

No!

Do you love your computer like your spouse or best friend or your dog?

Of course not!

So forget the Trump backlash—and global backlash—against trade and foreign competition for lower wages in emerging countries. It's only part of the early stages of this broader revolutionary cycle, not the result or even the conclusion thereof.

The real driver of this network revolution will be computers and artificial intelligence (AI), but not to just eliminate all of our jobs. It's about freeing workers to think and act like entrepreneurs and businesspeople and create higher-value-added products and services—ones that don't compete with the typical standardized products from third-world countries or automated services from computers and software.

We have no other choice. Smart leaders and managers will focus their companies and workers in this direction. Make them human customer service agents and creative entrepreneurs.

Researchers at Oxford estimate that nearly 50 percent of jobs today will be automated by 2040 or so. I tend to agree. Automation has occurred throughout history, but has always created better jobs. Again, would you rather be living in *Little House on the Prairie*?

We're talking robotics in manufacturing and software automation of all types of office and bureaucratic tasks . . . even large parts of what professionals and even doctors do!

Computers are left-brain machines operating at the speed of light! There's no way to compete with them. They are more a threat than foreign workers and immigrants from emerging countries, because they can do both simple and more complex left-brain tasks. That makes innovation, human relations, communication, creativity, and right-brain skills the traits that give us the edge!

Isn't this what increasingly affluent people really want? How about those who are coming up in the emerging world?

I wrote about this dynamic 20 years ago, and I can't believe almost no one in politics or corporate management gets it yet. This should be obvious with current technologies and the leading edge of our best entrepreneurs and workers.

Companies should be turning their best people into entrepreneurs, not marginally more innovative rote workers. A few are, kind of, but most are still not.

As I said in the introduction: Technologies change faster than cultures, and cultures change faster than genes.

But—and this is the critical takeaway here—as AI takes over the mundane and even more complex left-brain jobs, it frees us up to be creative and entrepreneurial.

Think about it: what if every human being were to turn their best expertise and interests into their own business or a business within a larger company, creating ever newer products and services for their customers?

I don't know about you, but I am sick as hell of companies that have taken out the human element, leaving me to deal with automated phone systems, unable to get a real, creative, and friendly human being to help me get what I want and need. Thus far, computers and software have largely "killed" customer service in the name of cutting costs. Instead, the focus should be on creating a higher level of product customization and personalized service at affordable or lower costs.

That would add more value than another assembly-line or office worker!

Don't you want to do business with someone who really understands your needs or provides an essential expertise that you don't have—and locally, if possible?

Of course you do.

Thankfully, Amazon and eBay are already providing large-scale platforms for everyday people to market their products and services with very broad, low-cost communication and efficient delivery systems. They combine the best of the large- and the small-scale through these new Internet networks.

But even better . . .

What if you and/or a small team of people could become your own business within a larger corporation? They would provide the larger-scale marketing or distribution, or even production networks, while you focus on your unique market of customers, knowing them more intimately than anyone else or any computer system.

Your company provides the information to you in real time, so you know what works or doesn't work with your customers, what they will buy or not, when they are likely to need different products or services, how profitable each product or sale is, how profitable each customer is in the entire purchasing history . . . and, most important for accountability and reward systems, how much profit YOU generate for the company.

They measure your direct costs and allocate your indirect overhead so that you're as accountable as a small business . . . with such profitability measurements in real time related to your unique efforts.

You get your fair share of the profits after you compensate the larger system for what they contribute.

Our only way out of the "Asian deflation" in global wages and the inevitable automation of left-brain office and professional work is to become entrepreneurs: creators of new, higher-value-added products and services, what I call "real-time, personalized service."

There is no other way.

Let me return to my example of something I willingly pay substantially more money for: concierge medicine.

A doctor who sees me on short notice, with little or no waiting time, who is connected to the best specialists.

A doctor who treats his clients as a priority . . . who spends the time needed, whether that is shorter (doesn't waste my time) or longer (for something that is important).

That's bottom-up entrepreneurial business.

And the only way to leverage our everyday talents and higher-than-average education is to leverage the very things we have the most interest and knowledge in.

Yes, create a business out of your very own passion!

I know that sounds like advice from a motivational speaker . . . but that is the essence. Anyone will learn faster and better if they're dealing with something they love.

The Internet first decentralized information access through Google and e-mail, and now Twitter and Facebook. This revolutionized communication.

My productivity in economic research has roughly tripled due to such information access.

I used to have two full-time research employees; now I have one half-time researcher . . . and he's more efficient thanks to Google and e-mail.

Yes, over time, that cut a few jobs in my company. But it has created more timely and more affordable research, and as a result, we have many more subscribers and more employees in other areas of the business, focused on marketing and customer service. We have new areas of research that employ more researchers than we used to, and they're more focused in areas they can specialize in and add more value.

The Internet also allows global communication between people of like interests, for more targeted marketing and communication. That creates a whole new means of promoting directly to customized interests.

Energy is next, with the centralized providers orchestrating a decentralized network where we get more of our energy from solar and other local sources and save from the network or sell back to it.

Economist Jeremy Rifkin is the prophet of this "distributed power" revolution.

Emerging countries are also using solar panels in the most remote areas to gain access to basic light and electricity at affordable costs. It may not be fully affordable here yet, but in these remote areas it's a godsend.

That's why I don't believe we'll see $100 oil prices again.

And then there are driverless cars that will revolutionize and economize transportation. Driving is not a high-productivity job unless you're on the Formula One, NASCAR, or IndyCar circuit.

Now that I live in San Juan, Puerto Rico, I drive only about 200 miles a month, as compared with 1,200 when I was in my forties in the United States.

We're already on this road to bottom-up operations and focusing even more on what we do best and love. I love driving, but it's not the best thing for me to focus on. For the world to enjoy any substantial growth again one day, we need to hop aboard this revolution sooner rather than later.

Driving This Entrepreneurial Revolution Forward

America has always been an entrepreneurial nation, a place where a penniless immigrant could rise to the top.

Well, not so much now that the educational establishment has made a college education much more expensive than even our over-inflated healthcare system, whose costs are twice as high as those of most other developed nations. This same problem is keeping our kids and grandkids away from further learning as well!

Now only the most affluent kids can afford a college education. Everyone else ends up with massive student loans that put even buying a house out of reach.

This will change!

Education is an information industry, much as healthcare is. There's no conceivable reason why costs should be going up instead of down. Yet costs are rising rapidly, because this industry has parents by the short and curlies, forcing them to spend most of their money

Figure 8-1: The Three Menacing Inflation Bubbles
College Is By Far the Worst

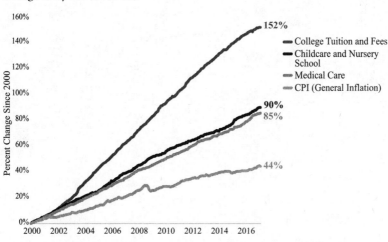

Source: Bureau of Labor Statistics

on lavish campuses, bureaucrats who should be automated, and retirement systems!

The number-one goal of most parents is to give their kids the best education, so that they can excel past them. Yet this is becoming increasingly impossible.

Look at Figure 8-2. The American Dream is fading fast. More and more kids are struggling to surpass their parents' incomes and achievements.

Education could be—and, mark my words, it will be—radically transformed, with limited campuses and real estate and a bigger online presence, where the best experts in the world transmit in real time.

There are live, in-person courses wherein human interaction is critical, and then there are courses that you can log into from anywhere, at any time, when you just need the best content from the best experts anywhere.

I would do this for pennies per student and be happy about it. I

Figure 8-2: Is the American Dream Dead?
Percentage of Children Earning More than Their Parents

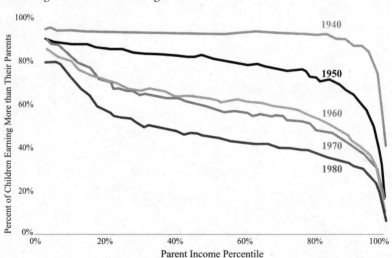

Source: Raj Chetty, *The Fading American Dream: Trends in Absolute Income Mobility Since 1940*

have no doubt every other successful entrepreneur and expert would feel the same.

How could a local professor, however smart, be better than the best experts in the world? How many specialized topics can a limited number of professors master and relate to students?

And don't even get me going on healthcare. The excessive costs there are all about bureaucracy and special interests that could be radically transformed as well. And, after education, what is more information intensive and bureaucratic than healthcare?

Again, software should be all about automating the rote and bureaucratic tasks and making information accessible and customizable in real time. I call this the automation of management and bureaucracy. It's not about the automation of leadership, human relations, and the creative application of products and services to individual needs when they need it.

If we don't kill the education, healthcare, and childcare bubbles, we can't advance our standards of living.

And if we don't create new, higher-value-added jobs from more entrepreneurial instincts, we won't continue to grow beyond our falling standard of living.

"America First!" should instead become "America the Entrepreneurial!"

Isn't that where we lead the world?

Isn't that what Donald Trump seems to be . . . a successful entrepreneur?

Maybe he should step down as president of the United States and be chief entrepreneurial officer.

A Reason to Hate Corporate America

I'll just come out and say it: I've always hated corporate America, despite the fact that I respect what it does.

I worked for a Fortune 100 company for two years before I

entered Harvard Business School, and then I worked at Bain & Company, consulting for Fortune 100 companies after I earned my MBA. I just couldn't deal with the top-down bureaucracy, even when streamlined more and more.

It's just not natural to have your creative talents constrained by a bureaucracy that handcuffs you and stops you from giving customers what they really want—real-time, personalized service (like my concierge doctor)—and would only be productive in an era of scarce information! Times have changed. Information is more abundant than water or air.

Picture this . . .

You are the leader of a small team of people accessing and selling a customized solution to a small segment of customers.

You, not your central systems, are in control of what you can charge and how you combine and customize your products and/or services with real-time information. This empowers you to conduct business profitably, because you can adjust on the fly.

You know the variable costs of each component, so you can know the direct profitability of each sale you make without interference from above.

You also know the indirect or overhead costs that go to your larger company for its centralized services that make you more effective and efficient, such that you know how much you need to sell to cover that every week or month—just like any good small-business owner.

Managing the customer growth and satisfaction through decisions you make every day is the key to your profitability and growth, just as with your own business. You may get a minimal salary, but you advance more on a fair share of the real and measurable profits you make for your company. Like a waiter who gets a lower-than-average wage but makes it up from tips, but with much more direct control and upside potential.

Your job is to find out what each customer really wants and

needs, and then to get creative about combining the best package of products and services at a price they can afford.

You would not likely have such an opportunity without the funding, marketing, distribution, and production capabilities of your larger company. But you know better than they do what your customers really need and want.

And you get a reasonable but fair share of the profits, which are directly measured through your or your small team's efforts through real-time information systems.

This is totally possible with current technologies. Most managers and supervisors simply prefer to boss their people around and have control over them. It helps them feel important.

Supervisors and top-down managers are dead!

Coaches, trainers, and facilitators are what workers need, not second-guessing, pinheaded bureaucrats.

Companies just don't want to share this information with employees, because they're as reluctant to relinquish control as the French nobles before their massacre and the peoples' revolution.

Information systems can today enhance everyday workers and turn them into entrepreneurs and profit creators, not just rote production or office workers.

And they must, because the higher-paying jobs of the past are gone forever.

And workers should worry more about AI and software automation of left-brain tasks than about competing with assembly-line workers in third-world countries or illegal immigrants here.

No tricks in tax cuts or deregulation or trade negotiations will bring these jobs back substantially. The assembly line is very old technology now. It was invented by Henry Ford in 1914. . . .

It's time to move on to something greater. And that is the information-enhanced, entrepreneurial, customizing "monomaniac with a mission."

We need to wake up and become what we are, what computers can likely never become: creative, entrepreneurial, relational human beings.

Such information systems make employees both more accountable for results and more rewardable for their direct contributions. This is a win-win for corporations and employees.

Who needs unions in that scenario? Except to be a funnel for ideas from workers who could create better products and higher profits . . . and make sure they get their fair share of such newly created profits!

Jack Stack's World

Okay, I admit that I have delayed getting to this story so I could keep you reading. But I'll end this chapter with the entrepreneur and author I most admire, and that's saying a lot, with my experience consulting for and studying them.

Let's look at a successful entrepreneur and manager who really gets it: Jack Stack. He wrote one of my favorite books—EVER—called *The Great Game of Business,* way back in 1992, the same time I wrote *The Great Boom Ahead.* (Damn! Being an innovator takes decades to prove out! It's frustrating.)

That book was about how to teach every worker to think like and become a business owner.

As I quoted him earlier, "Nobody knows the job better than the guy who is doing it."

Well, he damn well followed through and proved his concepts in real life.

He took over a failing manufacturing company in Springfield, Missouri, and turned many of its workers into blue-collar millionaires.

Screw slightly higher minimum wages!

Jack Stack has paid out more than $100 million in ownership shares to workers!

His company, SRC Holdings, is wholly owned by his 1,600 employees. They manufacture engines and components for trucks, tractors, and heavy equipment. You know, the type of manufacturing industry where we're losing jobs to foreign competition and automation!

And on top of that, SRC has launched 60 companies, ranging from banking to medical devices to furniture.

Jack's premise is very simple: You can boost performance by making a "game" of tracking and improving key metrics (i.e., real-time information systems) delivered directly to workers.

"If you want employees to act like owners," he says, "you should make them owners."

Taking it even one step closer to complete transparency, the company's financials are available for everyone to see. There's no top-down control and secrecy.

The results, according to Jack's figures, are astounding: "A guy who started here in 1983 making $7.50 an hour has now got $1.2 million." (That's on average, I presume.)

Talk about the American Dream!

Talk about making us great again!

This is the entrepreneurial revolution we need . . . the one we're already on the road toward. It's just that most of corporate America doesn't see it yet.

Jack's secret is not just to reward people for their profit contribution in the "great game of business." It's to put real numbers right in workers' faces so they make better decisions every minute, every day, for every customer.

I would go one step further, and maybe Jack already has. I would give employees a minor share in the overall company, but I would also then use software to measure each individual's or team's contributions after fair overhead allocations and direct costs. This would mean the back-line "servers" have fair revenue recognition of their efforts on behalf of the front-line "browsers" who actually serve the end customers.

Is this not possible in a light-speed world of software and business metrics?

We need more real business leaders and visionaries like Jack Stack, not BS Wall Street leverage artists or old-line corporate managers who merely streamline their top-down management systems while their workers wait for their unfunded retirement and death.

And we need real educators, like Neil deGrasse Tyson, who can make science understandable to everyday people.

Most of all, we need people to love what they do so much that they won't even think of retiring at age 63 or 65 or even 75.

They're so productive and happy that they don't worry about a retirement that doesn't make sense to them anymore, though it's there if they have health challenges.

They're too busy satisfying their customers and creating new businesses to contemplate life without that fulfillment. They're so focused on what they do that they're like the champion basketball player who's totally "in state" and one with his process. They're certainly not bored or waiting to retire and do nothing!

My 500-year cycle says the future is brighter than demographic trends now project. That gives me a clear vision that, first, a revolution in work and retirement is emerging. And, further down the line, we'll see a revolution in how long we live and contribute, to offset the declining birth and demographic trends that otherwise seem irreversible in an ever more affluent and urban world with low birth rates.

But it will be this revolution in work and institutions at all levels that will first regenerate our aging developed countries and then filter down into the faster-growing emerging ones. Emerging countries will always be taking over the "older" technologies and business systems at lower labor costs, which is why we have to focus on the newer ones.

Of course, this process will be painful for many companies and governments for many years ahead. But it will mean the greatest freedom granted to everyday people since the advent of democracy itself.

Now, regarding the greatest top-down bureaucracy of all: government must change, and radically!

22 Government Reforms that Must Happen

Reform #1: The Glass–Steagall Act was repealed during the Clinton administration. After several decades, people had forgotten why it was instated in the first place—to prevent conflicts of interest in banking and financial services that helped create the bubble and Great Depression that followed.

We simply must separate the functions of major financial institutions, placing walls between traditional banking, investment banking, and brokerage services without which we get conflicts of interest with harmful effects for the economy and consumers.

Banks take deposits and lend money. They don't create investment funds or have brokerage accounts.

There should be simple, ironclad rules about reserve ratios for banks, which should be higher—say, 20 percent instead of 10 percent—with appropriate down payments required on loans, like 20 percent.

Income verification is always required, as the banks are really lending consumers' and businesses' money, not their own, and should be responsible fiduciaries of that money.

Investment banks raise money for investment in companies and IPOs. They don't speculate in investments outside of that . . . like Goldman Sachs.

Brokerage firms offer brokerage accounts and financial advice. They don't manage or offer investments. That's a conflict of interest with their customers—to be shoving their own products down customers' throats in the name of objective financial advice.

Seriously!

How can they be unbiased when they're pushing their own investments and funds?

That leaves investment management firms, but they can't give financial advice or offer brokerage accounts. Investments are delivered to end consumers through automated online or human retail brokerage firms.

During this revolution, we'll likely see these distinctions brought back.

Reform #2: Social Security, Medicare, and Medicaid have to change their qualification or retirement ages from 65 to 75 over the next 10 to 20 years, in line with our much longer lives. Thereafter, it should continue to be extended every five years for increased life expectancy in the future.

This will keep consumers in the workforce longer, producing and earning and consuming more, paying into the system longer, and retiring for 12 years, on average, instead of the 22 years they get today. No one should do nothing for 22-plus years! That's enough to kill you from boredom and uselessness.

And this is the only way to preserve such benefits in the future for the time you do need to wind down your life and deal with health challenges.

The present system isn't even remotely viable, given the slowdown ahead and the increased pressure on the system as baby boomers squeeze through it and our economy slows in the years and even decades ahead as compared with the past, according to my Four Fundamentals.

Reform #3: The government should actively encourage and reward restructuring of consumer and business debt and return to "mark to market" rules for loans. Such a new approach to debt deleveraging would be taking a cue from the very successful Chapter 11 process in the private sector.

The normal Chapter 7 bankruptcy process just sells the assets of a failing company to pay off the creditors but typically results in fire sales and low levels of payback.

Chapter 11 is allowed for companies that are viable if they can reduce their debt and costs. This process protects the company from creditors for a while and allows it to sell off assets at better-than-fire-sale prices, cut costs, and renegotiate with creditors . . . all of which most often yields a win–win for all parties.

The Great Depression was like a Chapter 7 debt deleveraging for the economy. Not the best way to approach a failing economy.

As this revolution unfolds and we see a financial crisis between now and 2020, the government could choose to work with the banks to implement more of a Chapter 11 restructuring of debt so that fewer banks and companies would have to fail altogether.

Debt has been accumulated way beyond present and future needs. Writing such debts down would give great long-term relief to consumers and businesses, which would help offset the natural demographic slowdown.

In the 1930s and '40s, private debt went from 180 percent of GDP (in 1929) down to 60 percent (shortly after World War II). That's the very purpose of deflation and depressions: to deleverage debt and financial bubbles.

Reform #4: We can't return to the gold standard, for countless reasons—many of which I wrote about in my e-book *How to Survive (and Thrive) during the Great Gold Bust Ahead*. But we absolutely need ironclad standards regulating how much debt can grow versus GDP!

Debt should be allowed to grow modestly more than GDP, in line with rising incomes and creditworthiness.

And debt should be allowed to grow a bit more when larger percentages of consumers are in their prime home-buying and debt-acquiring years, between the ages of 27 and 41. This is what happened between 1988 and 2001, and it was totally predictable based on demographic data.

However, today it's not the case at all.

What needs to happen is that the Federal Reserve should curb excessive debt by raising reserve requirements or absolute limits when debt exceeded such GDP-related and demographic targets.

The best solution here would be the emergence on a large scale of the Bitcoin-like blockchain technologies, such that some of these companies could become highly efficient new creators of money and currency. But that would occur only in response to real transaction needs, not from governments trying to cheat and overstimulate their economies, cover up debt failures, and lower their export costs by devaluing their currencies.

Reform #5: Special-interest lobbying should simply be banned. No more. Ever. Again! It's unbelievably corrupting to the political system. In fact, it's been the very worst assault on democracy and free-market competition.

If Congress needs studies on the impacts of a political issue or a bill, it should employ an independent firm to do so, with federal, state, or local governments covering the cost. Companies can send their analysis, but they can't spend money pushing or entertaining or bribing lawmakers.

Reform #6: Campaign finance should be reformed such that there are clear limits on personal donations, to restore democracy (just like each person gets an equal vote).

Corporations should no longer be treated as individuals, per the Supreme Court decision in 2015. This would create very clear limits for corporate donations as well, possibly scaled somewhat by profit levels. No more billionaires like the Koch brothers deciding who gets to run for president or Congress in their party. (They vetoed Romney in the 2016 primary.)

Reform #7: The political system should be as neutral as possible relative to economic policies. There should be no subsidies for debt, like the mortgage deduction.

Capital gains shouldn't be taxed at preferential rates, except possibly for new ventures and IPOs that actually create new jobs. Holding an already issued stock for one year does little or nothing for job creation and shouldn't enjoy any favor.

Financial transactions should be taxed at low rates to hit the most affluent more.

Taxing investments is a better way to hit the rich than dramatically taxing higher incomes. That just funds countless tax lawyers and accountants who game the system, only complicating business and decision making further and adding costs. And it can work against innovation incentives to a degree.

Let businesses and consumers make better decisions based on market rates and feedback, not on tax advantages and endless incentives from governments to support this or that special interest or goal.

Municipalities shouldn't be tax-exempt on their bond interest. Corporations and municipalities should be allowed to deduct interest as a cost of doing business, like everything else.

And, again, no lobbying by corporations and special interests to influence political decisions and laws. Deductions for charitable contributions should be much more narrowly defined in terms of things governments would do with tax money, like help the poor, rather than people's own religious or personal dreams.

Better yet, they could be eliminated altogether.

Reform #8: The Federal Reserve shouldn't set short-term interest rates. They can be lowered temporarily only in emergencies, defined as recessions with greater than 10 percent unemployment or some-thing like that.

Quantitative easing to directly inject liquidity and to impact longer-term rates should be allowed for only short periods of time—one year, maximum—in response to recessions with greater than 10 percent unemployment.

It shouldn't become a semi-permanent policy that totally per-verts markets and investments and prevents needed rebalancing, debt deleveraging, and innovation, as was the case between 2008 and 2016 in the United States.

Reform #9: Instead of endlessly complex pollution regulations, we need to simply set a fair and statistically determined tax on carbon and other pollutants that reflect actual down-the-line costs to the economy. Then let businesses make better decisions about how they minimize their carbon footprint rather than having detailed specs and bureaucracy for everything companies and consumers do.

Use those tax revenues to counter such pollution and global warming. If the taxes are too onerous, then normal income and sales taxes could be cut to help offset them.

Total taxes could stay near the same, while businesses and con-sumers would have incentives to make better decisions for the econ-omy on energy use and pollution factors, with less bureaucracy and complexity.

Reform #10: A very basic level of Medicare needs to be determined that is universal, establishing a one-payer system. Restrictions need to be put on government-funded operations and care for people who have limited life expectancy—of, say, less than one year. Above that, people can choose to pay for higher private insurance.

Estimates are that up to 50 percent of healthcare costs are paid in the last year of life. That is an unfair burden on younger people.

Individuals can make their own choices above that for private insurance or funding, including care in the restricted last year of life or whatever period is determined to be optimal.

Our healthcare costs are roughly double those of other developed countries, and our life expectancy is one of the lowest.

The private sector has simply failed here, largely due to special interests and lobbying that have created so many hidden costs, bureaucracy, and unjustifiable advantages.

Reform #11: Hedging for businesses should be allowed through leveraged futures and the like but should not be encouraged for use in speculation.

There should be much stricter limits on margin debt, with either no leverage or two-to-one leverage at most, except for legitimate hedgers protecting downside risks.

Warnings about opening trading accounts should be as strong as those on cigarettes.

Reform #12: Credit default swaps should be eliminated or much more restricted. They are designed to be insurance for downside risk in financial assets, but there's no collateral, so it's not real insurance.

Collateral should be defined and required for credit default swaps that are allowed.

Reform #13: The federal budget must be balanced over rolling five-year periods.

At least modest surpluses should be mandated in times when economic growth is averaging 2 percent or higher.

Deficits should be allowed in recessionary times only to the extent that they are covered by surpluses accrued in the past, plus a maximum of 3 percent or so of GDP in recessionary years. Social programs like welfare should not be allowed to become permanent.

And if someone cannot get a job, they should at least do some public service to compensate.

The United States also cannot continue to police the world and subsidize military spending of our allies.

Reform #14: Trade deficits should also be balanced over rolling five-year periods. No country should be allowed to run endless trade deficits.

Reform #15: The education system must be reformed to reduce excessive real estate costs. This can happen through greater use of online teaching where appropriate, and live teaching only where necessary.

Teachers should take on the role of helping students identify their greatest aptitudes and interests, and design their curriculum accordingly, i.e., customizing them to individual needs.

Tenure has to be reformed and/or abolished.

Universities should sell excess real estate and facilities to businesses and research firms and/or conduct paid research for them to reduce tuition fees.

Reform #16: Political campaigns should be shorter—between six weeks and three months, instead of the typical one to two years. As it currently stands, it wastes resources and takes lawmakers' attention off of making laws effectively.

Reform #17: There needs to be simple but effective regulation of advertising. There are too many exaggerated, unproven claims and too much money spent on appealing to people's subconscious desire for "heaven on earth."

Advertising and marketing should be educational and help consumers make better decisions, not manipulative and misleading, as, sorry to say, most are.

Reform #18: Rewards for damages in business, healthcare, and so on should be limited to real damages and not "winning the lottery."

No matter how good a business or a doctor is, there will always be mistakes. Even our genes have mutations, and Xerox machines fail here and there.

Occasional failures should be expected and tolerated more by the system.

Excessive failures or irresponsible conduct should be punished to the full extent of the law, but it shouldn't be a case of awarding people multi-million-dollar settlements for vague "damages" or unquantifiable "pain and suffering."

Reform #19: Illegal immigration should be stopped to the extent possible (something President Trump is trying to accomplish, although I don't agree with how he's going about it).

Already present illegals should have something like two years to apply and qualify for residency or citizenship, or be deported. Simply sending 11 million–plus immigrants back is impossible, unbelievably costly, and very disruptive to businesses and families—sorry, Trump!

Such a mass deportation would cause a deep recession from the lost spending and lost production of such workers.

Like Australia and Canada, we should target the skills we want and need, and then favor for entry those immigrants who possess such credentials. We should encourage highly educated foreign students to stay, not put quotas on them. And there are lower skills that we need as well, so this does not mean cutting large numbers of legal immigrants as Trump has proposed.

In the future, children of illegal immigrants should not be automatically naturalized. They have to apply like anyone else. That creates too big an incentive for continued illegal immigration.

Reform #20: If there is one thing that deserves subsidies, it's childcare. Countries like France and Sweden have found that reducing childcare costs does more for the economy than liberal maternity leave or tax credits for having kids. When kids cost more than $250,000 to raise, what does a $5,000 tax credit matter?

This is the greatest challenge for working mothers and their conflict between work and having kids.

Childcare costs, like healthcare and education, are insanely high in the United States. This needs to change.

Reform #21: Hackers should be treated like the "terrorists" they are. They pose a much greater threat than global and internal terrorists by threatening the Internet and communications and transactions systems that we all have come to depend on. They treat this like a game—it should be a very serious crime, with much stronger enforcement and penalties. Otherwise we could see a major breakdown of the system at some point.

Reform #22: The secretary of state and the president of the United States should push much harder for free-trade rules globally, but these rules must have teeth and be enforceable.

Countries like Japan shouldn't be able to manipulate their currency and purposefully push it down to make their exports more competitive—that is cheating. Countries like China and India shouldn't be able to pollute to massively higher levels to save costs—that is cheating.

Being poor should not be an excuse for excessive polluting and not recycling your waste.

Pirating software and technology is cheating.

If you don't play by the rules, you don't get to play the game and your trading rights are restricted, or even eliminated.

I'm again talking about simple rules, not a new global bureaucracy!

And some economist has to come up with a better way of settling trade imbalances.

Floating exchange rates can make a good company uncompetitive overnight or make a country more expensive to visit for no good reason. More stable, large-scale, bottom-up, digital currencies could emerge to address this need.

To summarize, regulations should be simple rules of the game that keep competition fair and communications open and honest. They shouldn't be endlessly detailed and onerous.

Set simple rules and guidelines, tax pollutants, and let businesses and consumers make better decisions.

And then let the courts settle the fine lines of disputes when necessary, with stronger laws to counter frivolous lawsuits that exploit and jam up the system.

Said a simpler way: It's time that central banks, lobbyists, politicians, and governments get out of the way and let our economy follow its natural course. . . .

A course that leads us right into the jaws of a necessary financial crisis and deleveraging after the greatest debt and financial bubble in history, and beyond that a revolution greater than the emergence of democracy itself.

It's all about designing systems to take out the bureaucracy and allow businesses and governments to deliver real-time, personalized service at affordable prices and to organize around your customers, not your back-line BS bureaucracy.

It's ultimately about operating from the bottom up, not the top down. . . .

That's the real revolution.

And that requires the automation of management and the empowerment of the front-line workers with the information they need to satisfy their customers without idiotic supervisors!

But the real bottom line for governments in the free world during this revolution is this: Special interests have taken over democracy, with large corporations and the top 0.1 to 1 percent enjoying undue influence to further their own interests. That has to stop. No more lobbyists or lobbying. No more big donations to campaigns. Donations should be limited to $1,000 or something like that.

Central banks have overwhelmed free markets by trying to create an economy that never has a recession and never has to rebalance excesses of the past. In doing so, they've created greater bubbles that benefit the same top 1 percent who massively outperformed, just like in the Roaring Twenties, and have contributed to the excessive special interests' impact. That, too, must stop. And I think that it will when this totally artificial, third, extreme bubble crashes, between late 2017 and early 2020-plus.

I would encourage voters to never trust central banks again, as they learned not to trust the aristocracies that controlled most Western economies into the 1700s.

The truth is that we don't need central banks, except in emergencies, for short-term liquidity. They should never be allowed to create money at will or manipulate the economy or free markets again.

It is the very marriage of democracy and free-market capitalism that has made us so unbelievably rich since the late 1700s. The information revolution can amplify that if we don't keep killing the "golden goose."

But we do need to address the slowing demographic trends as the massive baby boom generation ages, and we do need to find a way to restructure our massive debt, which is still mostly private . . . as would a business in a Chapter 11 debt reorganization.

Our governments could help facilitate that by assisting only the banks that actually write down debts in this next financial crisis, rather than endlessly printing money to cover over such debts and losses.

That means many banks and businesses will still go under, but the numbers won't be as extreme as in the national Chapter 7 crisis of the 1930s.

It's time to take our medicine and move on to the next spring season, unlike Japan has done. It has proven that 20 years of more stimulus and debt does not cure the addiction, but has only made it worse. And Japan has worse to come.

China will, when it falls, finally prove once and for all that top-down governments that expand at will only get more inefficient and more in debt . . . and fall harder.

Bubbles always burst, and we're near the top of the greatest global bubble in modern history, led by China.

PART II

The Invisible Yet Blatant Bubble

CHAPTER 9

There's No Bubble Here?!

Stocks are more overvalued today than they were in 2000, at the peak of the dot-com bubble. Anyone who can't see that is blind!

Harry Dent

THE CHEERLEADERS ARE BOUNCING AROUND, waving pom-poms, and chanting:

No bubble!
No bubble!
No. NO. Bubble!

Janet Yellen's one of them.

So is Warren Buffett, the Oracle of Omaha, who said earlier this year on *Squawk Box*, "We are not in bubble territory!"

They should be shouting a different chant . . .

We're number one . . .
Can't be number two . . .
And we're going to beat . . .
The whoopsie out of you!

When this bubble bursts—and we ARE in a bubble . . . and it

WILL burst—it's going to absolutely beat the whoopsie out of those ignoring the obvious.

Economist Robert Shiller developed the best valuation indicator thus far. The Nobel laureate's cyclically adjusted price-earnings ratio is known as the Shiller P/E, or CAPE.

Shiller's CAPE shows that we are clearly in bubble territory, yet even he doubts it . . . eventually everyone joins the bubblemania!

He uses the average of the past ten years' earnings to smooth out wild fluctuations near tops and when earnings suddenly crash in major recessions or depressions. This makes the model more reliable than the simple price-to-earnings ratio (P/E).

Only a blind person couldn't see that we're deep in danger territory!

We've gone higher only twice before, and there are specific reasons for that, which I'll explore shortly.

But just look at this chart. . . .

Figure 9-1: Present Stock Valuations Approaching 1929 Peak
Shiller's Ten-Year Adjusted Price-to-Earnings Ratio

Source: Robert Shiller's 10-Year Cyclically Adjusted Price-to-Earnings Ratio, Dent Research

We saw peaks in 1902 (22.9), 1929 (32.6), 1937 (22.2), 1966 (23.9), 2000 (44.2), and 2007 (27.5).

Now we're at 29.3 and rising, with likely another 10 percent coming in the "Trump rally," which is based on the totally false hope that anything could create 3 to 4 percent growth again in an aging and massively over-indebted country.

That's higher than all but two previous peaks . . . and nearly as high as the one in 1929.

By the time this Trump rally tops out later this year, we'll likely be right at that 1929 peak.

So, by saying that we're not in a bubble, are the experts insinuating that 1929 wasn't a bubble?

That the 90 percent crash, the greatest in U.S. history, was just bad luck . . . a "black swan"?

It certainly seems that way, but then again, most people can see a bubble only with 20/20 hindsight.

That's because, as I explain in *The Sale of a Lifetime,* most people don't *want* to see a bubble. They want to believe they've found heaven and can stay there forever. They want to continue getting something for nothing while their stocks and home prices rise irrationally.

And most people don't understand the cycles that lead to bubbles.

But when you take off the blinders, it's easy to spot how deep in the whoopsies we are!

Nothing is more predictable than major bubbles. The hard part is predicting when the irrationality will finally end and burst. The most likely time, as of the writing of this book, would be in the classic crash season—around late October—of 2017.

Yes, P/E ratios were much higher in 1999, but that was during a time when my four key cycles were all moving up together. Moving into the next greatest peak into 1929, only three were moving up together.

Between 1995 and early 2000, the U.S. economy was at its best.

The baby boomers were in their peak spending acceleration. All was well (relatively speaking) around the world geopolitically, and the Internet was soaring into the mainstream, juicing productivity—just as autos had in the Roaring Twenties.

Today we are in exactly the opposite position.

As I explained in chapter 5, since 2014, those four key cycles have pointed down. This means that ratios at the levels we're seeing in 2017 are even more dangerous than those we saw in 2000. I'll briefly explain in a moment, but let's get back to Shiller. . . .

Shiller is the only mainstream economist I respect and follow. (Lacy Hunt is my favorite, but he's too realistic and contrarian to be called mainstream.)

Besides his CAPE indicator, he was the first to adjust U.S. home prices for inflation and demonstrate, once and for all, that it is a non-appreciating asset in real terms.

Real estate, as he proved, is *not* the great investment most assume it is. (Neither is gold, but at least you can garner rent or save rent from owning real estate.)

People mistakenly formed the idea that real estate was the ultimate investment because we've lived in unique times, when the first middle-class generation (the Bob Hopers) who could more broadly afford homes boosted home buying after World War II. They could also afford mortgages, thanks to the GI Bill.

The greatest inflation surge in modern history followed, a result of the baby boomers' joining the workforce (as I explained in chapter 7). And real estate correlates directly to inflation, which Shiller proved.

The biggest generation in history, baby boomers went on a massive home-buying spree in unprecedented numbers. All of this lifted home prices to the moon, ending in the greatest bubble in history, between early 2000 and early 2006.

But those good old days are gone.

The boomers are shuffling off into the sunset, and real estate prices will never again enjoy the explosion they did between 1983 and 2005. How can they, when we'll have increasingly more diers than buyers into the early 2040s?

As I discuss in chapter 3 of *The Demographic Cliff*, two simple charts—Shiller's inflation-adjusted home prices back to 1890 and my "net demand" (peak buyers at age 41 minus diers at age 79)—will tell you more about real estate trends than the rest of economic research combined.

But I digress. . . . We'll talk real estate in chapter 11.

Pundits also use Shiller's CAPE indicator. But they're using it to say that we're not in bubble territory yet because we're not remotely close to the 44.2 peak of 2000.

This just reveals their lack of research and deeper understanding of cycles.

Shiller's CAPE is higher today than it was at four major peaks—1902, 1937, 1966, and 2007. After each of those tops, stock investors were mauled. Yet those peaks ranged between only 22 and 24.

The lofty 32.6 peak of 1929 was just slightly higher than today's 29.3. And, like I said, I think we could get as high as that 1929 level before the wheels come off this bus for good.

If you look at the simple P/E, it's easy to see why Shiller adjusts the earnings for cyclicality. If you don't, such an indicator is largely useless. It's higher near the end of a crash, as in 2009 (again, due to the sudden crash in earnings), than at the top, when you need the warning.

See for yourself (Figure 9-2). . . .

There was a series of peaks, between 22 and 23, in the 1920s, '30s, and '40s—all lower than where we now sit, at 29.3. But those peaks came when earnings were crashing, as during 1920–22 and 1930–33!

In late 1929, when the crash started, the indicator was at a mere 18.

So stocks are not overvalued now at 29?!

Clearly the "experts" are bubble blind . . . and cycle blind to boot. . . .

Figure 9-2: The Traditional Price-to-Earnings Ratio
Often Rendered Useless by Extreme Earnings Gyrations

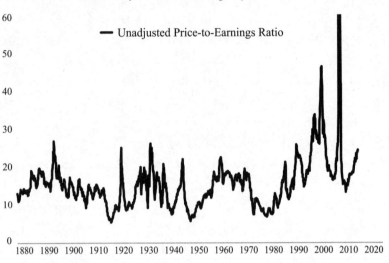

Source: www.econ.yale.edu/~shiller/data.htm

The Difference Cycles Make

Remember my Four Fundamentals (from chapter 5)? Here's that chart again (Figure 9-3). . . .

Let's do a quick comparison, using these four cycles, of the 1925–29 bubble, the tech bubble of 1995 to early 2000—which the "experts" are using as evidence that we're nowhere near any danger zone right now—and the current bubble.

The 45-year Innovation Cycle peaked in 1920, precisely with the peak of the railroad industry. It then turned down into 1942.

The 39-year Generational Spending Wave pointed up strongly into late 1929, with a massive generation of immigrants. Then it crashed and had a secondary high, from demographic trends again, in 1937, before crashing once more.

The 34-year Geopolitical Cycle turned up in 1915 and peaked in 1930, converging with demographic trends through late 1929.

The 10-year Boom/Bust Cycle turned up in late 1923 and peaked

Figure 9-3: Hierarchy of the Four Fundamentals
Developed Countries

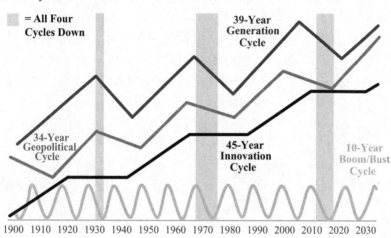

Source: Dent Research

in late 1929. Then it crashed into late 1933, the depths of the Great
Depression.

So three of my four key indicators converged in an upward arc
from late 1923 into late 1929. The actual bubble phase was late 1924
through late 1929.

All four of them headed downward simultaneously from late
1930 into 1933. At the peak, the Shiller CAPE indicator reached an
unprecedented 32.6, while the normal P/E ratio hit only 18 at the top
and then spiked up to 27 when earnings suddenly crashed!

These four cycles converged again from late 1988 into early
2000, wherein we saw the greatest stock bubble since the Roaring
Twenties.

The Generational Spending Wave turned up from late 1982
through late 2007.

The 45-year Innovation Cycle turned positive from late 1988
through 2010.

The Geopolitical Cycle headed up from late 1982 into 2001 (with
9/11 as its first warning bell).

And the Boom/Bust Cycle was up from August 2009 (when the Great Recession bottomed) until February 2014 and has pointed down since then, with a bottom projected around early 2020.

All four cycles were heading up—together—into early 2000.

This put the tech bubble in the most favorable period in history, even more so than the Roaring Twenties bubble, the greatest before it.

That's why we witnessed the highest-ever valuations.

It was baked into the cycles cake.

But all four cycles have been in their negative turn since early 2014, and those trends will persist until early 2020.

The impact of the Geopolitical Cycle on stocks alone is to halve valuations at its bottom compared with its top.

Based on this cycle, high P/E ratios of 22 to 24 would be more normal at this point, with dot-com-era peak ratios of 44.2 unattainable.

We're already at 29.3. But, again, we'll likely see that ratio 10 percent or so higher before this crazy bubble and blow-off Trump rally finally peaks.

It's a very different world today than it was in the 2000s.

There should be no comparison to that early 2000 peak and its valuation levels. Our economy isn't even half as good as it was back then.

It's like comparing diamonds to cut glass.

I often show this chart to prove that we're in a bubble today, no matter what those cheerleaders try to convince us of.

The Economic Fall Bubble Boom Season is where bubbles come, once in a lifetime due to falling inflation and interest rates, killer technologies moving mainstream, and the strongest demographic trends that are often enhanced by openness to immigration. The boom since late 1982 has seen four bubbles and crashes—more than any boom in history, and with each successive crash being deeper than the last. The greatest one is just ahead, into the full-on Economic Winter Season.

This chart shows that the recent one, since early 2009, tops them all—in pure point terms as well as based on percentage gains. Look at the S&P 500 in the current bubble and compare it with that index during the tech bubble, which everyone agrees was a bubble.

See for yourself how this bubble is longer, more stretched, and just as steep!

Also notice that each successive crash has been deeper: 40 percent after 1987, 51 percent after 2000, 56 percent after 2007. So don't you think this final and most dramatic bubble will see a bigger crash?

If you can't see that this is a bubble, you might literally be blind.

It's not only the longest bubble in the series of four bubbles since the 1983 Economic Fall bubble boom commenced, but it's by far the largest point gain and, just recently, the greatest percentage gain.

By the time this irrational and final blow-off phase of the Trump rally peaks later in 2017, it will be off the charts . . . with valuations closer to 1929.

You don't want to be holding stocks in such a scenario. Period.

Figure 9-4: This Isn't a Bubble? The Fourth and Largest Since 1983. Dow Jones Industrial Average

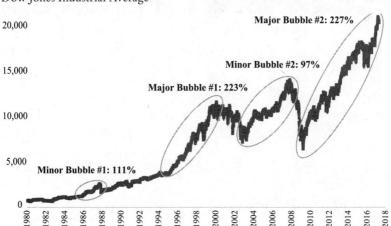

Source: Yahoo! Finance

As Different as Night and Day

The so-called experts' inability to see the bubble we're clearly in comes down to a lack of understanding (and maybe even a lack of appreciation) of how different our economy is today from that of the late 1990s and early 2000, when the dot-com bubble peaked at record valuations.

I found this great summary, courtesy of Michael Lebowitz of 720 Global, on how different our economy and earnings growth really has been in recent years.

Look at the differences between the 1995–99 boom and 2012–16! GDP growth was 4.08 percent from 1995 to 1999.

From 2012 into 2016, it was just 1.9 percent—less than half.

Estimates for 2017 put it at near 2 percent.

Five-year earnings growth was 7.53 percent between 1995 and 1999.

Figure 9-5: We Were in Better Shape During the Dot-Com Bubble
A Broad Range of Economic Comparisons

Indicator	1995–1999	2012–2016
GDP Growth	4.08%	1.90%
GDP Trend	2.30%	1.80%
Productivity Growth	1.84%	0.49%
Federal Debt (trillions)	$5.36	$17.47
Federal Debt, % of GDP	60.23%	101.40%
Personal/Corporate Debt (trillions)	$15.49	$41.11
Personal/Corporate Debt, % of GDP	156.09%	220.13%
Federal Deficit, % of GDP	-0.33%	-3.29%
10-Year U.S. Treasury Yield	6.05%	2.13%
Federal Funds Rate	5.38%	0.18%
S&P 500 3-Year Earnings Growth	7.53%	-3.84%
S&P 500 5-Year Earnings Growth	9.50%	0.49%
S&P 500 10-Year Earnings Growth	7.74%	0.89%

Source: 720 Global

Between 2012 and 2016, it was *minus* 3.84 percent! Five-year growth was 9.50 percent, as compared with 0.49 percent! How could a stock market have such high valuations with such low earnings growth?

Our federal debt is now $20 trillion, versus $5.36 trillion in 1999, while deficits are 3.29 percent of GDP, versus 0.33 percent in the earlier period.

And then there's productivity!

Between 1995 and 1999, it was at 1.84 percent.

By 2016, it was limping along at 0.49 percent!

With further retirements and aging ahead, I think it's heading to zero or lower.

This clearly is not the same economy we enjoyed back in the late 1990s. Valuations today cannot reasonably or rationally be compared with those back then. Ratios of 44.2 times earnings were extreme but possible back then. Not today!

There's another way to look at this. . . .

Here's a chart that adjusts the CAPE ratios for GDP growth trends.

Figure 9-6: Stock Valuations Versus GDP Growth Higher than Ever
Ten-Year CAPE Average to Ten-Year Real GDP Growth

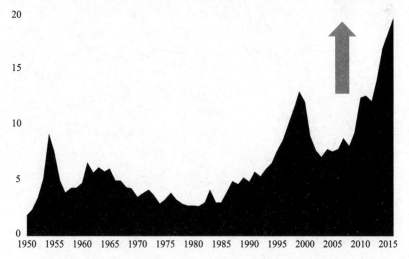

Source: 720 Global; www.econ.yale.edu/~shiller/data.htm; St. Louis Federal Reserve

The picture is clear: P/E ratios are higher than ever, much higher than in 1999 if you adjust for lower growth and economic momentum.

And if that's not proof enough, there's another valuation indicator I like. This one's from John Hussman, an excellent analyst.

Also known as the Warren Buffett valuation indicator, it compares the expected ten-year average return given the current measure of total market valuation of publicly traded corporations as a percentage of GDP.

This indicator shows that, without my projections of falling demographic, innovation, and geopolitical trends, if you buy stocks at today's very high valuations, you should expect 1.5 percent average annual losses over the next decade. That will only increase to 3 to 5 percent average annual losses if stocks advance another 5 to 10 percent, as I expect they will by around late October of 2017.

Why take the risks in such an overvalued market with rising volatility?

Figure 9-7: Expected Ten-Year Returns
Market Valuation Versus S&P Ten-Year Average Annual Return

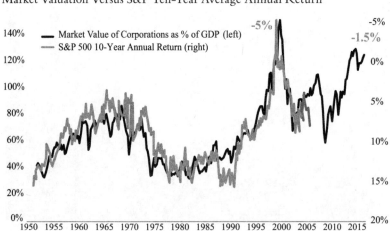

Source: Bloomberg, St. Louis Federal Reserve, Hussman Funds

The very low or negative returns aren't worth it!

I expect stocks to do worse than this, given the rare downward convergence of my four key economic indicators and the unprecedented debt and asset bubbles that must and will burst.

This indicator and others Hussman studies clearly show that you shouldn't take any unnecessary risks in this market.

The Next Boom Will Be Nothing Like the Last One

I called the 1983–2007 boom the greatest in modern history, because it was generated by the largest generational and demographic surge, and it was augmented by powerful Internet and portable-computing technologies (which were like the modern-day printing press).

My three longer-term cycles converged between late 1988 and early 2000. Two of the three converged from late 1982 into 2007.

The sunspot cycle oscillates more often and spends more of its time on the downside, but it chimed in from mid-1986 through early 2000, and again from late 2009 through early 2014.

Projecting these Four Fundamentals, I see demographic trends globally diverging, with most developed countries pointing down for as long as we can see and all emerging countries except China pointing up into at least 2040. Some, like the sub-Saharan Africa nations, keep going up into as late as 2100. The largest up-and-comer, India, points up into around 2065 and peaks around the same time that the collective emerging world does.

The 45-year Innovation Cycle points down from late 2010 into mid-2032. That's a long time before it turns up around 2055.

That's when we will likely see the first stage of what I call the Aging Revolution, where we start to live longer (to as late as 120) and our workforce cycle stretches from 43 years (ages 20 to 63) to 80-plus (ages 22 to 102-plus).

That increased life span would reverse the ever-growing demographic black hole of lower-than-replacement birth rates. Just retiring at age 75 today, in line with our already higher life expectancies, would make a big difference in demographic cycles.

But here's a big difference: The 34-year Geopolitical Cycle largely runs counter to the Innovation Cycle. It turns up in early 2020 and points up into around 2036, then turns down again into around 2053. The 45-year Innovation Cycle points down into 2032 and then turns up into 2055—almost perfectly opposite. We won't see the convergence of cycles that we saw from late 1988 through early 2000, and less so from late 1982 through late 2007, at least not for many decades.

The Generational Spending Wave in the United States turns up in two waves for the millennials: the first from early 2023 into late 2036, the second from early 2044 into around 2056.

The three longer-term cycles converge only between mid-2032 and late 2036, and between 2052 and 2055—a few brief periods.

The second wave of demographic spending trends takes the United States no higher than the first wave, adjusted for inflation, and the first wave takes us no higher than the peak of the baby boom wave. So be on notice that the 2023–36 boom should be stronger than the 2044–56 boom to follow, and that we may not see the Dow higher than 22,000 again, adjusted for inflation.

Dave Okenquist and I have made estimates of birth rates and immigration trends that are lower than the mindless straight-line projections pumped out by mainstream "experts." We take into account predictable cyclical downtrends, especially the demographic ones, which everyone else ignores. I predicted, in advance of the 2007 top, that births and immigration would decline. They did, and they'll decline even more when this bubble finally bursts.

All of this shows us that the next depression is due to be at its worst between the late 2060s and the mid-2070s, and we'll have declining birth rates and immigration trends after 2007 to thank for that.

The most dynamic parts of Asia—from India to Southeast Asia— will be on a demographic decline by then as well, and will mature in urbanization, which creates the greatest productivity growth.

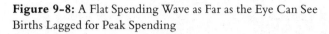

Figure 9-8: A Flat Spending Wave as Far as the Eye Can See
Births Lagged for Peak Spending

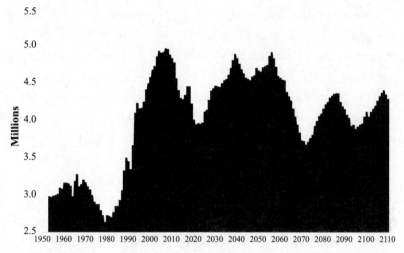

Source: Dent Research, U.S. Census Bureau, Bloomberg

The world economy will literally move sideways between the 2020s and the 2070s as this great revolution plays out.

Only after that will we see another "great" global boom more like the one from 1983 to 2007.

This period, from the 2020s through the 2070s, will likely end up being similar to 1720–87, when European stocks saw a 67-year sideways or bear market. Only this one will be livelier, briefly just coming into its peaks around 2036 and 2056.

Where the world will be more expansive will be in India and Southeast Asia. There will be another great commodity boom, driven more by the demographics and urbanization of emerging countries that are more commodity-intensive. I will discuss these two powerful trends in chapters 17 and 18.

Unfortunately, most of us today will be dead before much of this unfolds, so what do we do NOW? First, we understand how bad this could get. . . .

A World of Hurt

The Trump rally that started in early November 2016 very likely represents the final orgasm in a rare series of bubbles, the last and most extreme, made possible only by endless government QE and stimulus.

This fourth and final stock bubble in this Economic Winter Season has grown exponentially, as all bubbles do before they burst (just look back at Figure 9-4). It's larger in both point terms and percentage gains than the unprecedented 1995–2000 tech- and Internet-driven bubble!

And first crashes are typically 40 percent–plus within two and a half months, on the way down to 80 percent–plus, as my bubble model shows (more on this in the next chapter). This has been the case in most of the strong stock bubbles, like 1929, 1989 (Japan), 2000, and 2015 (China). That's why it's better to get out a bit early than late.

Let's break this down into the key markets and look at the possible future we face. . . .

The NASDAQ

Potential Loss = 88 Percent

The NASDAQ was bubbling the most as I wrote this in May 2017. It was thanks largely to just five FAANG stocks: Facebook, Apple, Amazon, Netflix, and Google (they were driving the S&P 500 up as well).

If I make that sound like a problem, it's because it is. These are great companies, but so were General Motors and General Electric before the Great Depression.

Every time just a handful of companies have driven the market like this, the bubble has burst.

Figure 9-9: NASDAQ Is Bubbling the Most, as in 1995–2000

NASDAQ 100

Source: Yahoo! Finance

Every. Time.

The dot-com bubble took the NASDAQ from 800 to 5,050. That was a 6.3-times gain in just over five years. Crazy!

Then we had a long correction (a classic a-b-c) into early 2009. The index ultimately lost 78 percent during this time.

The next wave up to new highs looks like it'll peak around 6,500 to 6,600 and then experience its first crash starting by late October. That jolt could see the index lose close to 40 percent.

The ultimate support for the NASDAQ is between the late 1994 low of 800 and the early 2009 low of 1,100. That means it could lose 83 to 88 percent before all is said and done and this crash has wrapped up. Recall that the Dow lost 90 percent between late 1929 and late 1932.

Small Caps: Signaling the Top

Small-cap stocks tend to do the best in a strong boom, because the smart money invests there to grab the bigger gains, and it takes more

Figure 9-10: Small Caps Starting to Underperform—Sign of a Top?

Source: Yahoo! Finance

sophistication to do that! So when the smart money starts to exit, the small caps tend to lead on the way down! It's a telltale sign!

The top in stocks on May 17, 2017, didn't see new highs for the Russell 2000 (the index that tracks small caps). That could be the first sign of an important divergence for this bubble since March 2009.

This is the chart I follow closely because I'm looking for a classic divergence between large- and small-cap stocks in the final rally of this bubble, as occurred in the tops in the early 2000s and late 2007.

If the Russell 2000 moves sideways for a while and then doesn't make a new high on the next sharp move, that would signal that this bubble is done. The same thing happened between August and October 2007 in the previous top.

The Dow Jones

Potential Loss = 75 to 83 Percent

Here's the Dow megaphone chart. The logic is simple and obvious—although no Wall Street experts talk about it.

Each of the past three bubbles has made new highs, only for those peaks to be followed by new lower lows.

The projected low for the Dow is around 5,500, or more than 75 percent below the projected highs of between 22,000 and 23,000 just ahead. If it returns to its bubble origin in late 1994, to around 3,800—which, as I'll show in the next chapter, is typical—the loss would be 83 percent.

Figure 9-11: The Third and Final Dow Bubble Will Burst!
Megaphone Pattern, Dow Jones, Log Scale

Source: Yahoo! Finance

S&P 500

Potential Loss = 83 Percent

Finally, here's the S&P 500, the best summary chart for the U.S. economy.

It looks like a final, fifth wave will peak around 2,600 or a bit higher.

The first support is the 2009 low of 642. That's 75 percent down, just like the Dow. The ultimate support is at the beginning of the bubble, in December 1994. That means the S&P 500 could lose as much as 83 percent by the time the crash is over.

Figure 9-12: S&P 500 Headed from 2,500+ to as Low as 442 (That's 83 Percent)
S&P 500

Source: Yahoo! Finance

CHAPTER 10

The Model That Politicians and Investors Desperately Need

Bubbles are just like orgasms. This makes them predictable, as Masters and Johnson would say.

Harry Dent

OBVIOUSLY, WE'RE IN A BUBBLE. (If you skipped chapter 9, go back and read it now.) And if you really want an education on bubbles, get my last book, *The Sale of a Lifetime*, or check out my Web site, dentresources.com.

The cycles have brought us here.

Central bankers' and politicians' follies have aggravated the situation and created a third, totally artificial bubble in stocks that is more extreme than ever, and a second bubble in real estate.

And the experts don't seem to see or understand any of it.

When this bubble bursts, I'm willing to bet you they'll cry, "Black swan!"

They're idiots!

This bubble burst, and all those that have come before and will come after, are totally predictable. And I've created the prototype that helps us see how these events will most likely unfold, years in advance.

It's my bubble model.

Before I detail this model for you, I will say that, while inflating and deflating bubbles are easy to predict, nailing down the precise day and time the chaos will begin is near impossible, due to the extreme irrationality at the top.

Think of it like this . . .

If you keep dropping one grain of sand at a time onto the floor, a mound will build. It will get steeper and steeper until it looks like a Hershey's Kiss (a clear sign of a bubble in its late stage). That's when you know that an avalanche or crash is coming. That's easy to predict.

But there will be literally just one single grain of sand that will suddenly cause the mound to collapse.

Predicting that *one single grain of sand* is just NOT possible.

But, working with Andy now, and using this bubble model, we can get as close to it as possible, dammit. Our best guess, as of early August, the time of this writing . . .

Mid- to late October.

When it comes to bubbles, especially in stocks, it's easier to see the downside risks and roughly how long it will take a bubble to unwind once it has built exponentially and is in the orgasmic final bubble stage.

And *this* is what we want to know about, because it's how we avoid the pandemonium and financial injuries that are inevitable when the sky falls.

I've said it thousands of times in my previous books, in my newsletters, in my speeches, but I'll say it again: bubbles don't correct.

They crash and burn.

If you try to time the peak to the day, you'll lose, because the first rapid crash can see as high as 50 percent of the total crash occur in just a matter of months.

Even the few people who see bubbles rarely see the extent of the downside risks.

They think that such bubbles in financial-asset values can plane out for a while or correct 20 percent to 50 percent, like what you see during normal longer-term bull markets. That NEVER happens!

That's what makes my bubble model so vital!

It works around five key principles. . . .

Key Principle #1: Bubbles begin when stocks (or any financial asset) start growing faster than the more linear or fundamental trends, most often well after the bottom of the last major correction or crash.

As this trend builds, investors increasingly buy . . . just because a market is going up faster than usual, for a long enough period of time to give them confidence in their decision.

Greed and speculation start to take hold.

Fundamentals fly the coop.

I call this point the bubble origin, and I'll show ahead why that's important.

Key Principle #2: Bubbles then build exponentially for several years—typically five to six years in stocks and often longer in real estate.

Key Principle #3: The greater the bubble, the greater the burst.

Bubbles vary in intensity, which determines both their height and how big their crash. I calculate the Bubble Intensity by taking the "times gain"—how much it increased in value, expressed as a ratio (instead of a percentage)—and dividing that by the length of time from origin to peak.

So, for example, if a bubble took five years to triple from bottom to top (a 3.0-times gain), the Bubble Intensity is 0.6.

This allows me to compare bubbles in different asset sectors with historical ones, especially if their durations differ.

Key Principle #4: Bubbles then burst, typically twice as fast as they build, and more so with stocks than with commodities or real estate, which take about the same time to burst as they do to build.

The typical stock bubble is about five to six years in length, with a 2.5- to 3-year crash after the peak. This was the case with the stock bubbles in the late Roaring Twenties in the United States, the Japan Nikkei bubble in the 1980s, and tech stocks in the latter 1990s.

The typical real estate bubble is roughly six to ten years, taking about as long to unwind, because property is far less liquid than stocks and people have more of an emotional stake because they live there.

Key Principle #5: Most important, bubbles tend to go back to where they started, at what I refer to above as the bubble origin. Sometimes they won't quite make it all the way down. Other times they'll drop even lower.

That's why it's so important to identify where a bubble started. That is your best estimate of your downside potential—and it will scare the crap out of you, as it should!

Knowing these five principles, along with several other factors, gives us a good idea of where the crash will end and how far it's likely to go down.

At this point, I need to take you on a quick, and important, detour. . . .

How Simple Linear Trends Always Go Exponential

My first principle of bubbles is that all long-term growth is exponential, not linear. Then I say that when we get an exponential trend from the nearer term fundamental linear trend, *that's* the bubble origin.

Sounds a little contradictory, I'll admit. But it's not.

The best and easiest way to think about this is with the principle of compound interest or growth.

If you take a constant 3 percent growth rate, which is apparently linear, and compound that growth—which means that 1 percent becomes 1.03 percent and then 1.06 percent, and so on—that seemingly linear trend becomes exponential over time. That 3 percent trend is building on an increasingly larger base, like that mound of sand being built one grain at a time.

Your experience in investing is *linear* if you withdraw your gains every year and spend them. If you reinvest them, they ultimately become *exponential*.

That's why systematic saving is so important to building wealth over the longer term.

That's why you can become wealthy if you just invest consistently from a young age and then reinvest those gains and dividends.

Knowledge and evolution are also exponential in the long-term.

They build on themselves and compound naturally. The more knowledge grows, the more it builds on itself.

Ultimately, it comes down to perspective. If you look at the horizon when both your feet are planted firmly on the ground, the earth looks flat. Go up just a hundred miles and immediately you can see the earth's curve.

Look at a trend close up and it'll appear to be linear.

Step away and take a longer-term view and you'll see that it's actually exponential (and cyclical).

When bubbles pop up in the late stages of a long-term growth trend, they're simply reflecting the late and extreme stages of such compounded and exponential growth.

This always comes in the Economic Fall Season (or peak) of any four-stage cycle . . . like the colors of leaves morphing to their greatest beauty before they die in winter.

So when the seemingly linear trend of 7 percent real stock growth shifts gears and races to 15 or 20 percent–plus, you know it's nearing the end.

With all that being said, let's return to the point of this chapter: my bubble model.

Creating the Baselines

My model starts with the male orgasm chart from Masters and Johnson. I explained extensively in *The Sale of a Lifetime* why I use this chart as a guide to seeing and predicting bubbles, but for those who haven't read my last book, I'll quickly explain.

Quite simply, financial bubbles are exactly like orgasms. I can put the scientifically documented male orgasm chart over any major market chart and tell whether it's a bubble or just a normal healthy bull market (like 1942–68).

See for yourself . . .

After a bubble has begun to form, I draw a trend line through the linear fundamental trend going back to the last bottom. Where the markets first diverge above those trends—and keep diverging exponentially—is the bubble origin.

The bubble accelerates into the last blow-off, and that's when we know the peak is getting close. (We saw this clearly from late 1998 to early 2000, in the dramatic tech bubble, and from early 2016 into

Figure 10-1: Bubble Model for Stocks
Masters and Johnson Sexual Response Cycle: Male

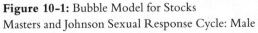
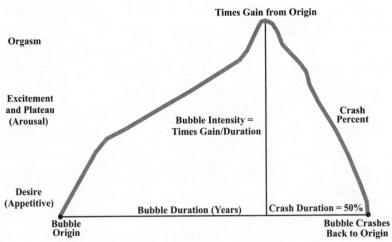

Source: Dent Research

2017 in this one.) The Trump rally from November 2016 into 2017 looks very much like that final blow-off rally and top.

As that top approaches, I can calculate the intensity of the bubble and compare it with other current or past bubbles.

Long before the actual top, I know the downside potential, because the sector should return at least near the bubble origin.

Once the bubble starts to burst—and it typically does so violently, with 30 to 50 percent of the total decline occurring in the first sharp crash in just 2–3 months—I can estimate about how long the overall crash will take by calculating the time it took to rise from the bubble origin to the peak and then taking 50 percent off that.

That's why calculating the bubble origin is *more important* than just looking at the last long-term low before the bull market began.

It's important to note, though, that this calculation is for stocks only. (It's a bit different for commodities and real estate.)

And it's really that simple.

The Model in Action

The Japanese stock market enjoyed the first major baby boom bubble from late 1984 through late 1989. Then it crashed dramatically into late 1992, just as the rest of the world was starting to live large through the greatest boom in modern history.

I alone predicted that bubble crash back in 1988–89, in my presentations and my first book, *Our Power to Predict.*

Here's that Nikkei bubble chart again, but this time with my bubble model applied (see page over). . . .

I went back several years and drew that fundamental trend line. This showed me that the Nikkei started going exponential from around late 1984, when the index was at about 8,000. That was the bubble origin.

It then exploded into the very end of 1989, reaching 39,000.

That gives it a gain of 4.4 times.

Figure 10-2: Japan Nikkei Bubble and Burst: Late 1984 to Mid-1992

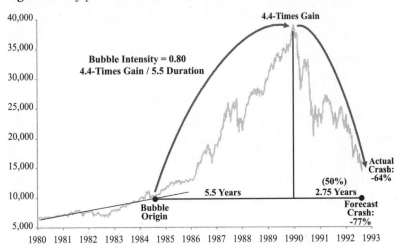

Source: Bloomberg, Dent Research

The bubble lasted 5.5 years and had an intensity rating of 0.8, a bit higher than average for stocks.

My model forecast that the crash would have lasted 2.75 years, with a 77 percent decline.

The actual first extended crash saw a loss of 64 percent but was very close to the model's time estimate, in late 1992.

The reason the crash was a bit less intense than expected was because the rest of the world was recovering from the 1990–91 recession and was beginning the greatest stock boom in history—as I also predicted back in 1988–89.

The first, very sharp crash saw a 31 percent decline in less than three months, declaring that a top had finally occurred. After a brief bounce, the market went down 49 percent in just the first eight months.

Again, *that's* why you get out a bit early!

The crash lasted 2.75 years—in this case, exactly 50 percent of the 5.5-year rise—and first bottomed 64 percent down in July 1992, just above the bubble origin.

The ultimate low (thus far)—down 80 percent, at just 7,600—came in early 2003, when Japan's demographic trends were at their worst.

Eventually this bubble *did* erase all of its gains and go back to the bubble origin.

Looking at the most prominent stock bubbles in modern history in the table below, you can see we get dynamics and parameters similar to those of the Nikkei bubble.

Stock crashes are both more rapid and predictable, because investors can panic much faster than they can with real estate, which is far less liquid, and people most often live in it.

The major bubble preceding the Nikkei collapse was the infamous Roaring Twenties stock bubble that peaked in September 1929, a moment in history we are all too familiar with as the eve of the Great Depression.

Its bubble origin date was very late 1924, and it peaked in late 1929.

It saw a 3.8-times gain in just five years, with a Bubble Intensity of 0.78 (similar to Japan's bubble).

My model projected that the crash would last 2.5 years and see losses of as much as 74 percent, but the actual crash was worse, as the whole world collapsed together, unlike with Japan's great crash!

By July 1932, the Dow had lost 89 percent.

Figure 10-3: Table of Stock Bubbles Past and Present

Bubble	Start	Bubble Duration	Times Gain	Bubble Intensity	Crash Duration	Crash Severity
Nikkei, 1989	1984	5.5 Years	4.4	0.80	2.75 Years	-64%
Dow, 1929	1924	4.9 Years	3.8	0.78	2.5 Years	-89%
NASDAQ, 2000	1995	5.3 Years	6.8	1.3	2.6 Years	-78%
Shanghai, 2007	2006	1.75 Years	5.2	3.0	0.9 Years	-72%
Biotech, 2015	2011	3.75 Years	4.2	1.12	1.9 Years	-75%
S&P 500, 2017	2009	8.4 Years (Est.)	4.0	0.48	4.2 Years	-83%*

* Estimated by Model

Source: Dent Research, Bloomberg

The NASDAQ bubble of 2000 had its bubble origin in very late 1994. It peaked in early March of 2000, building over 5.2 years.

The gain was a whopping 6.8 times, so it had a Bubble Intensity of 1.31—the highest major developed-country stock bubble in modern history. No wonder the P/E was so extreme!

The bubble took exactly half the time to unwind, losing 78 percent. (My model projected an 85 percent loss.)

Over in China, the Shanghai Composite saw the most dramatic short-term bubble from very late 2005 into October 2007. It had a 5.2-times gain in just two years and a Bubble Intensity off the charts, at 3.0. That's the highest I've ever seen!

The crash bottomed in early November of 2008 at 72 percent, only slightly above my forecast target of 81 percent down. That is still very close for a forecast of such a volatile event. And the timing was right on: two years up, one year down.

Then came the second bubble in the NASDAQ: biotech.

It took 3.75 years to create a 4.2-times gain into mid-2015.

Its Bubble Intensity was 1.12, nearly as high as the first NASDAQ bubble.

Its initial crash saw losses of 40 percent in the first 2.5 months—the classic sign of a bubble beginning to burst and yet more evidence for why you should get out a bit early rather than later.

The S&P 500 is the best reflection of the U.S. economy—the best house in a bad neighborhood globally. It looks to Andy and me as though it will most likely peak around mid- to late October, but of course, that's just our best guess (though likely a good one).

Assuming that date for a peak, with a top at around 2,600, this index will see its third and final bubble origin in early March 2009, enjoying a 4-times gain. Its Bubble Intensity will be at a more typical 0.48.

The first bubble was the most dynamic. Every one since then has been less intense, given slower demographic and technological trends, not to mention steadily worsening geopolitical trends. The current bubble is the worst because it's totally artificial, driven by zero-percent interest rates and endless QE.

My model here projects an 83 percent crash in late 2022. That's perfectly in line with my Generational Spending Wave turning up again longer-term in 2023. But most of the damage should be seen by early 2020, when my four fundamental cycles still point down together.

I would expect the S&P 500 (and the Dow) to be down around 75 percent by then and down 83 percent by late 2022. To go back to the original bubble origin in late 1994, the S&P would have to fall to 450 and the Dow to 3,800 . . . Do you want to sit through that scenario?

Commodity Bubbles: The Drama Queens

Commodities have more extreme bubbles and crashes.

They often collapse faster during the initial burst.

They're more likely to bottom at the bubble origin or lower.

And there is more variation between different sectors, making an apples-to-apples comparison essential.

Because of this, commodity bubbles are perhaps hardest to predict—that's why the best traders are commodity traders!

Look at the broader commodity bubble in the chart on the next page.

The Thomson Reuters/CoreCommodity CRB Index (TR/CC CRB Index) is the most basic commodities index. Just look at the bubble from around late 2003 into early 2008! Over 6.4 years, it went up 3.1 times, with an intensity of 0.48.

And look at that first dramatic burst!

The index lost 58 percent and in just eight months, from March 2008 to November 2008. That's just 12 percent of the time it took the bubble to build!

The low thus far has already been minus 67 percent, and should be lower still into 2018 or later. I'm talking down a total of 74 percent or more.

Figure 10-4: Global Commodities Bubble, TR/CC CRB Index

Source: Bloomberg, Dent Research

Commodities were among the first to crash in this global bubble environment, and they'll likely be the first to bottom as well. It's likely to be an earlier rally in the emerging countries, with their strong demographics (outside of China), that lifts commodities out of their nosedive.

But note that people always claim that I'm being extreme in my downside forecasts. That's not because I'm bearish by nature; it's because I understand bubbles. I was also more bullish than almost anyone for most of my career, because I understood the magnitude of the baby boom generation, and I understood that you get bubbles in the Fall Season's boom.

Oil's bubble and crash was the most extreme of the lot, going from $32 in late 2004 to $147 in mid-2008 (just 3.6 years) and then crashing back down to $32 in just 4.5 months.

I had *never* seen a bubble crash that hard and fast until oil's spectacular display!

Oil advanced 5.4 times in a short period, so its Bubble Intensity was 1.13—very high.

Then it crashed 79 percent in just 4.5 months. Holy crap. You wouldn't have wanted to get out of that one a little late!

Oil is likely to bottom somewhere between $8 and $20 by late 2018 (or maybe as late as early 2020). That will mean an 86 to 95 percent decline from its peak of $147 in mid-2008.

However, typical commodity bubbles are more like real estate bubbles and tend to take about the same amount of time to reach their ultimate bottom as it took the bubble to build. (I'll talk about real estate in the next chapter.)

I summarize some of the other key commodity bubbles in the table below, but note that commodity bubbles are more likely to vary from the model estimates for both time and severity of the crash.

Copper is the more typical industrial metal that follows the economy, because it goes into so many different products.

Its bubble origin was in mid-2003, and it peaked in early 2011, with a 4.6-times gain and an intensity of 0.59 over 7.75 years. It's already been down 56 percent at worst, in early 2016.

My model projects that copper's crash will continue into around late 2019 or early 2020, ultimately losing as much as 84 percent from its peak. Commodities could peak earlier, given how much most have already come down.

Then we come to one of the areas of greatest interest: gold.

Figure 10-5: Commodity Bubbles: Past and Present

Bubble	Start	Bubble Duration	Times Gain	Bubble Intensity	Crash Duration	Crash Severity
CRB, 2008	2002	6.4 Years	3.1	0.48	7.6 Years	-79%
Copper, 2011	2003	7.75 Years	4.6	0.59	7.75 Years	-77%
Oil, 2008	2003	4.8 Years	5.4	1.13	7.6 Years	-88%
Gold, 2011	2005	6.25 Years	3.5	0.56	6.25 Years	-77%*
Iron ore, 2011	2007	3.25 Years	4.1	1.26	4.5 Years or 7.9 Years	-88%*
Corn, 2012	2006	6 Years	3.3	0.55	6 Years	-70%*

*Estimated by Model

Source: Dent Research, Bloomberg

First, gold, at its core, is a commodity. The greatest consumers are the two countries with the largest populations: China and India!

Second, gold has been in a bubble, like all other commodities.

The last time gold bubbled was into early 1980, along with the broader commodity sector, and then it crashed first into 1986 and ultimately bottomed between 1998 and 2001.

Third, gold correlates most with inflation, as commodities in general do. It is NOT a safe place to be during deflationary times, which we face ahead.

Gold's latest bubble origin started around mid-2005, when the yellow metal was close to $450. (Its ultimate low was $250, back in 2001.) The most likely target would be $450 by early 2020, and perhaps sooner.

From 2005, though, it went up 3.5 times over 6.25 years into late 2011, giving it a Bubble Intensity of 0.56. That's a bigger bubble than stocks saw. (From the 2001 low, gold went up 7.7 times.)

Gold has already been down as much as 46 percent in early 2016, despite the greatest money-printing spree in history. At the $450 target that would represent a 77 percent crash from its September 2011 high of $1,934.

The commodity bubble with the most extreme Bubble Intensity and most persistent crash is iron ore.

That bubble started in late 2007 and exploded into early 2011, with a higher intensity than oil, at a whopping 1.26. That was a 3.25-times gain in just 4.5 years.

Of course there would be a big crash.

It's already lost as much as 78 percent by early 2016. It could lose as much as 88 percent by late 2018 or early 2020 at the latest. Here's a bubble that clearly shows that crashes like 80 percent are to be expected when a bubble bursts. It's not outrageous. Commodities are showing us what is likely to happen to other volatile markets like stocks.

And, finally, corn.

Figure 10-6: The Corn Bubble

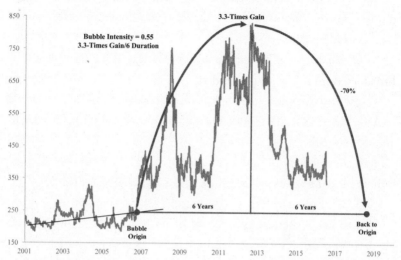

Source: Bloomberg, Dent Research

I keep hearing people say that the one thing people can't stop doing in a downturn is eating, so there's little downside in agricultural commodities.

Well, tell that to corn prices!

In six years, corn bubbled up 3.3 times into late 2012, and it has crashed 63 percent already.

It's likely headed lower, down a total of 70 to 80 percent in the years ahead, especially with sunspot cycles suggesting a bout of cooling into late 2019 or early 2020.

And So...

Major stock bubbles tend to come every 60 to 80 years, in line with the average human lifetime. Commodity bubbles rise into the high point of the 29-to-30-year Commodity Cycle. And real estate bubbles come on the 80/84-year Four-Season Economic Cycle, but real estate also has its own 18-year cycle.

We're in the twilight of the greatest and most pervasive bubble in modern history. Commodities burst first, and then real estate in elective areas follow suit.

This third major bubble in stocks is last, and it's set to burst by late 2017.

Now just imagine how much more effective politicians, world leaders, business leaders, and central bankers would be if they knew about this stuff.

All they need is an understanding of all the cycles at play, and my bubble model prototype, and they could actually be useful.

A man can dream!

Of course, there was one sector I didn't talk about in this chapter—possibly the one of most interest to everyone—but before we get into that, Andy has some details to share about how we can fine-tune our forecasts. . . .

CHAPTER 11

Missing Links from Past Financial Crises

The simplest way to forecast is to look for the birthdays.

Andrew Pancholi

BY NOW YOU SHOULD SEE how the macro cycles repeat, often with incredible accuracy.

However, as a trader and investor, you still could lose your shirt if you're a few weeks or even a few days out. Knowing when the big cycles come in is useful, but clearly you need to be able to fine-tune this information.

That's where I come in.

Forecasting shorter-term cycles is a completely different kettle of fish from working with the macro ones.

The simplest way to forecast involves looking at anniversary dates, or "birthdays." You'd be surprised at how often markets make highs and lows on the birthday of the previous year or on the birthday of a previous cycle high or low.

For example, take the dates of October 4 and 5. They are the birthdays of some interesting events. Looking at the U.S. markets, we see . . .

- The 1931 market had its annual low.
- The 1974 market had its annual low.

- The 1979 market had its annual high.
- It was the beginning of the 1987 crash.
- The 1992 market had its annual low.
- The 2011 market had its annual low.
- And the 2012 market had its annual high.

There are some dates in the yearly calendar that occur more often than others, defying all statistical probability. October 4 and 5 are two such dates.

If we apply this type of information to the cycles that we watched for potential turning points for autumn 2017, they include:

- 90 years ago, in 1927, the market reached a high on October 3 (just one day off the time window above!) and sold off into October 24.
- 60 years ago, in 1957, the market reached a high on July 16, and the final low came on October 22.
- 30 years ago, in 1987, the market reached a high on August 25, then a secondary high on October 2, and the final low came on October 20.

Can you see how closely these three thirty-year cycles correlate?

If we were to subtract the 20-year cycle from 2017, then we'd see that the market sold off sharply into October 28, 1997.

In other words, four of my major recurring cycles made significant lows between October 20 and October 28.

However, it's not as easy as all that.

There is a whole series of dynamic and static cycles. That means the cycles are of differing lengths and vary within each set.

This makes the task far more complex than simply looking at linear time-cycle repetition—or static sequences.

Another factor that comes into play is proportionality.

Every market has its own DNA, but it changes and mutates with time. That's why we sometimes see long bull markets and at other times we see short ones.

I get all of this information from my proprietary Profit Finding Oracle system (PFO) in *The Market Timing Report* software suite. It enables us to identify high-probability turning-point days well in advance.

We do it by distilling macro events down from yearly to monthly to weekly to daily (and potentially even hourly) cycles.

The cycles are resolved into histograms, and trend changes are possible where spikes occur. These spikes are marked by the vertical lines in this chart.

And as you can see to the right of this chart, these histograms can forecast into the future. Those are longer-range cycles.

The bottom line is that whenever we see a significant peak in the histogram, we know a turn is coming. Somehow, in some way, the market will be impacted.

Figure 11-1: Histogram Peaks Coincide with Market Turns
S&P 500

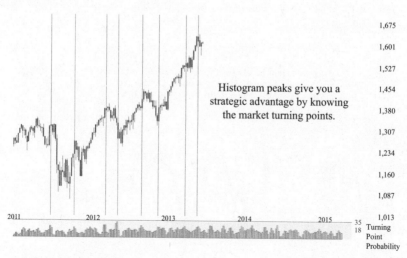

Source: markettimingreport.com

This is incredibly valuable information. Because we know where the future turning points are, we know when the market trend is likely to change.

But how do we know if a turning point is going to be positive or negative?

Quite simply, if you know the direction of the market as it moves into a histogram spike period, it'll most likely reverse course.

In other words, if the market is trending up into a turning point, then it'll likely roll over, and vice versa!

This isn't just a hypothesis. This has worked time and again since I created it.

We identified the exact high for the euro in May 2014, the collapse of crude oil, and the swing highs and lows shown on the S&P 500 chart in the figure below.

But that's not all. We can then take this several stages further by adding different layers, which also help us identify when the major and minor cycles align.

Figure 11-2: My System Found Nearly Every Turning Point
S&P 500 Index

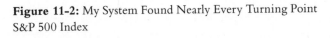

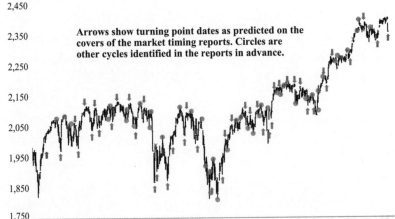

Source: markettimingreport.com

Figure 11-3: The Triple Overlay Cycle Stack Euro/U.S. Dollar

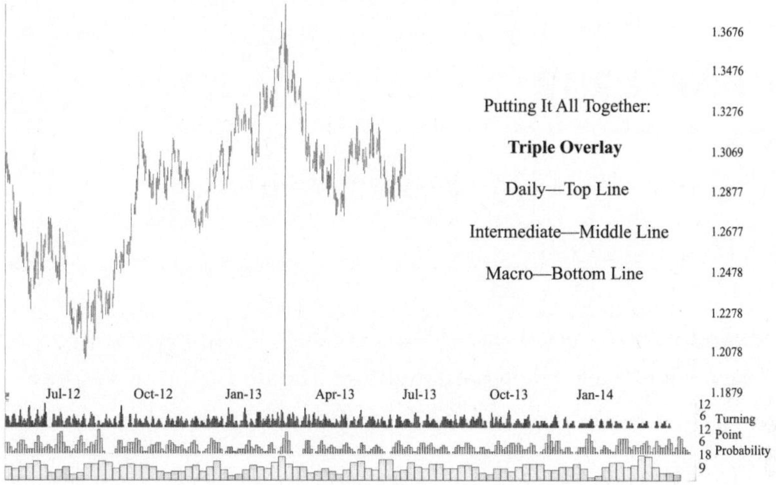

Source: markettimingreport.com

In the chart of the euro against the U.S. dollar, you can see how three different cycle sets are used.

The bottom line of histograms shows the longer-term cycles. These are the major turning points in the market. The two layers above that identify the shorter-term cycles through two different algorithm sets. The vertical red line shows where the different sets all line up. This coincides with a major high in the market.

The software creates the histograms in advance. This enables us to get a handle on what's coming up and how we can fine-tune the forecast to the day.

Let's look at what's coming up over the next few years. But remember that these cycles are always provisional and are updated as each time window approaches. With that health warning in mind, Harry will start with real estate.

CHAPTER 12

The Modern-Day Mount Vesuvius in Real Estate

When this insane real estate bubble blows, it's the everyday, hardworking folk who'll be slaughtered again. . . . But guess who owns the most real estate? That top 0.1 to 10 percent.

Harry Dent

SADLY, it's not only the stock market bubble that the "experts" and people in general seem to be missing. Real estate has reinflated back into bubble territory as well. . . . And in many countries, like China and Canada, it's gone to insane new highs.

It's mind-blowing how people can deny what's right in front of them.

A husband gets caught cheating on camera, but when confronted with the video footage, he denies it was him—like the famous South African rugby player Joost van der Westhuizen, who denied that the man having sex with a prostitute in the grainy video was him.

Or a politician gets caught doing something illegal—like Marion Barry being filmed smoking crack and then responding, "Allegedly smoking crack!"

Or a president denying he's deployed troops to a region—like Vladimir Putin saying there is no Russian army in the Ukraine when there are men in green (clearly the Russian army) killing thousands of Ukrainians.

Or . . . that the new real estate bar—of $250 million—is not indicative of a new bubble.

It's a bubble, dammit!

And people are going to get slaughtered when it bursts. Rich people the most, but everyday people as well, just as in the 2008 financial crisis.

I wrote an article for *Economy & Markets* in April 2017 headlined "The $1 Billion Bargain."

The coolest house I ever saw, I said, isn't a house. It's Antilia . . . a 27-story skyscraper in Mumbai.

Mukesh Ambani, chairman of the second-largest oil and gas company in India, Reliance Industries, built it for a cool $1 billion. It's a 27-story skyscraper in the heart of the hottest city in their country. It has six levels just for parking! And three helipads.

Man! Imagine the parties you could throw there! In a city where there's no parking anywhere, anytime.

For a billion dollars, Antilia is actually more of a bargain.

It's 400,000 square feet of living space in the best part of one of the largest and most densely populated cities in the world. When you break that down, it works out to just $2,500 a square foot.

Compare that with the top penthouses on Central Park these days.

In 2012, the most expensive was the 6,744 square feet at 15 Central Park West. It cost Sandy Weill, former chief of Citibank, $13,049 a square foot.

The first condo to break the $100 million mark, in 2015, was at One57, in midtown Manhattan. It cost $9,136 per square foot.

As I was writing this book, the leading-edge penthouse at the newest 220 Central Park South was being offered at $250 million, for 23,000 square feet. For four floors and 16 bedrooms in the hottest part of Manhattan, you need only fork over $10,870 per square foot.

We whisked by the $200 million mark without blinking.

Yet buyers think you can never go wrong buying the most pres-
tigious properties in the hottest cities?! History proves otherwise.

I spell these bargains *b-u-b-b-l-e*!

Of course, it can't just stop there.

Beverly Hills won't be outdone!

A 53,000-square-foot property with vineyards was listed for
$195 million. Hey, that's only $3,679 per square foot more in the
countryside.

And a listing in Bel-Air just came up for a whopping $250
million!

There must be some kind of elite rich-guy club that stipulates
you can join only if you buy a home for at least a quarter of a billion
dollars.

And guess what the developer had to say about this new listing?

"Why would a billionaire pay $220 million for a yacht, and not
that or more for his house?"

That's bubble logic if I've ever heard it. A yacht moves; a house
doesn't. And I wouldn't touch that $220 million yacht with a ten-foot
pole. Yachts will be selling for pennies on the dollar in the years
ahead, as will this house.

That $250 million house is 38,000 square feet. It has 12 bed-
rooms, 21 bathrooms (rich people must need to pee more from all the
champagne they drink—the house has five bars), three kitchens, a four-
lane bowling alley, an 85-foot infinity pool with an outdoor pop-up
theater-size movie screen, and an indoor 40-seat movie theater . . . and,
of course, a helipad on top.

At $6,578 a square foot, this is very likely the highest price ever
asked for a suburban mansion.

Personally, I'd take the $2,500-per-square-foot skyscraper in
Mumbai over any of these U.S. bubble homes. It's a bargain in bubble
land . . . yet still likely to decline in value in the coming years first.

But, then, I can see this bubble, while apparently it's invisible to
anyone else.

The high end is clearly going totally nuts, and such scenarios have never ended well.

When I was looking at moving back to Miami from Tampa in 2016, high-end condos that had been going for nearly $1,000 a square foot in 2007 were now going for $2,000. Some were as high as $4,000.

That's double (and then some)!

And there were more cranes in Miami in 2016 than anywhere I've seen in the United States. Even more than I saw there in 2006 and '07.

The Final Blow-Off

The luxury market in Manhattan is seeing average sales of more than $9 million recently, as this next chart shows.

The last significant bottom in this market came back in late 2001. I have a test for real estate based on my bubble principles and prices tending to crash back to their bubble origin. This isn't perfect, but it's the best indicator of what your downside potential is.

Figure 12-1: Manhattan Real Estate Bubbles to New Highs

Source: millersamuel.com

It's simple: Find out what your real estate was worth at the beginning of January 2000.

That simple indicator would suggest that your downside risk on a $9.4 million condo today in Manhattan would be about 73 percent! My worst-case scenario would be 77 percent, and the (less likely) best case would be 48 percent.

Do you think all-knowing rich people in New York believe such a crash could possibly happen in the "greatest city in the world"? Of course they don't. They're wrong.

The first wave up peaked in late 2000, and then there was a minor two-wave fall into late 2001. Then there was a sharp advance into late 2008.

It seems that when the stock market started to crash heavily in 2008, investors switched over to real estate in Manhattan.

Not for long, though.

The market fell sharply into early 2009.

It has been in a final blow-off fifth-wave move ever since, with recent prices hitting $9.3 million on average while the billionaires fight over $100 million–plus condos.

Since late 2001, luxury prices have advanced by 4.4 times over 16 years. That's more than in Sydney, Australia!

Prices have moved up by 2.07 times, or 107 percent, since early 2009 alone, with most of that coming after 2012.

This kind of price acceleration won't continue for much longer. Not with the tsunami of cycles crashing over us and the revolution under way.

And there are so many potential sparks that can ignite the implosion of this and the stock market that it's just a disaster waiting to happen. I'll tell you of at least six possible triggers in the next chapter.

To summarize again: The best-case scenario for the luxury real estate sector is that prices fall back to the 2009 low, around $4.8 million. That's a loss of 48 percent.

The worst-case scenario is that they fall back to the late 2001 low, near $2.1 million, shedding 77 percent. (Later in this chapter, I'll explain how I can be so precise with these forecasts.)

Of course, only a small percentage of Americans live in these luxury houses and condos. So what about "normal" America?

Get Your Hard Hat On

The high-end markets tend to bubble up the most and then collapse the fastest. Manhattan in the 1930s is the prime example: Real estate dropped 61 percent, more than twice what the average home in America lost, at 26 percent! Then it took until 1954—21 years—to get back to the bubble highs, while middle-class homes had reinflated by 1940.

Still, average Americans took it in the shorts when prices fell. And nothing has changed today!

Demographia has some of the broadest global data and uses the median-home-price-to-median-income index to give a better picture of the wider U.S. real estate markets around the globe.

If we look through this lens, the usual suspects come up as having the greatest bubbles:

- China
- New Zealand
- Australia
- Canada
- the UK

But the United States and Japan are absent from that list, even though California is home to the most overvalued properties in the United States.

That's because both have already seen significant bubble bursts, especially Japan in the 1990s.

In fact, Japan's residential real estate is still down between 60 and 67 percent (depending on which measures you use), with commercial real estate still down closer to 80 percent. And it's *still* a bit overvalued when compared with more normal levels of three times income.

As far as the United States is concerned, real estate took a beating from early 2006 to late 2012, but since then it has slowly trended back up into bubble territory. Only this time, it's not a countrywide phenomenon. Like in a popcorn popper, certain areas have bubbled up again sharply, while others remain more subdued.

We're on the cusp of the bubble areas imploding. The trick is to know whether you're in one of those areas or not.

The most expensive homes, of course, are in China.

It's important to note on this chart that these valuation measures are much lower than the average, because they don't include the high-end markets. Normal valuations in Hong Kong, covering all levels of property, are closer to 36 times income.

Yet, looking at median home price versus median income, it's still a whopping 18 times.

Figure 12-2: Housing Affordability Around the World
Median Multiple (Median Home Price to Median Income)

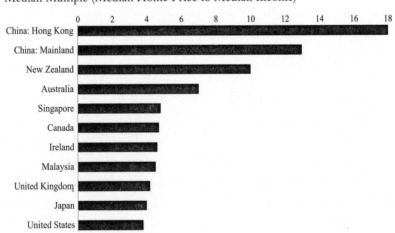

Source: 13th Annual Demographia International Housing Affordability Survey, 2017; Demographia

How many everyday people can afford that?

None, of course.

Only wealthier foreigners or speculators can pay those prices. And it's the cities that attract the affluent and the foreign buyers laundering money out of their countries that have more expensive real estate.

On the mainland, it's a little better. Buyers need to pay only 12.8 times their income to become proud homeowners.

That means someone with a typical $10,000-per-year income is paying $128,000 for a condo in the city. The equivalent in the United States would be someone who earns a typical income of $60,000 per year paying $768,000 for a house.

Does that sound sustainable to you?

It absolutely doesn't to me!

Who's next in bubbly prices?

New Zealand, thanks to pricey Auckland. The rest of the country has more sheep than people. Yet it comes in at around ten times.

Australia comes in at seven times income, but it's the most expensive at the extremes.

Then we have three English-speaking countries that boast home prices of around five times income: Singapore, Canada, and Ireland.

Ireland took a hit in the 2008 crisis, but Singapore and Canada didn't.

Singapore has taken a hit since 2016, but only because it put a 16 percent surcharge on foreign buyers. If they flip their real estate within one year of buying it, they're smacked with another 12 percent. If they flip after two years, they must swallow another 16 percent "tax."

Malaysia and the UK come in at closer to 4.5 times income, but, of course, that doesn't include London, which is high on the list of global city bubbles.

The good old U.S. of A. comes in at the most affordable. On average, it costs us just 3.9 times our income to buy a home. Of course, this doesn't apply in the bubbliest cities, which really are the fly in this real estate bubble soup. . . .

The Most Expensive Cities in China and English-Speaking Countries

When you look at average home prices to average income, the valuations are much more extreme as the higher end dominates, especially in a bubble. Beijing tops the charts in this category. It boasts home prices 33.8 times income! Only Hong Kong is higher at 36 times.

It's no wonder the Chinese living there either must own a small

Figure 12-3: Average Home Prices to Income, Globally—Off the Charts

City	Average	Median
Hong Kong	36.2	18.0
Beijing	33.8	14.5
Shanghai	32.6	14.0
London	27.8	8.5
Singapore	21.6	4.8
Vancouver	13.1	11.8
New York City	12.9	5.7
Sydney	12.4	12.2
San Francisco	12.1	9.3
Auckland	10.1	10.0
Honolulu	10.0	9.4
Toronto	8.5	7.7
Melbourne	7.6	9.5
Miami	6.6	6.1
Seattle	6.0	5.5
Los Angeles	5.7	9.3
Denver	4.1	5.4
Tampa	3.8	4.1
Chicago	3.6	3.8
Atlanta	2.7	3.1
Phoenix	2.4	4.1
Dallas	2.3	3.7

Source: 13th Annual Demographia International Housing Affordability Survey, 2017; Demographia

box, with room for nothing more than a bed . . . or they must commute.

Shanghai comes next, with real estate prices at 32.6 times income (on average).

As with Hong Kong and London, the average is much higher than the everyday valuations, thanks to super-affluent speculation and foreign buying. In China's case, it's a result of the rich speculating.

Real estate in Shenzhen, the more industrial city outside Hong Kong, is priced even higher.

Sydney comes next, as I would expect, at 12.2 times.

Vancouver is close behind at 11.8.

Auckland real estate costs 10 times income.

Melbourne real estate sits at 9.5 . . .

Honolulu at 9.4 . . .

And Los Angeles and San Francisco are both at 9.3.

San Francisco is another city that attracts the uber-rich and foreign buyers, with an average valuation at 12.1, similar to Sydney.

London has the highest average price to income, at a whopping 27.8. Yet its median comes in at 8.5, lower than San Francisco.

Toronto and Miami round out the other expensive cities, at 7.7 and 6.1, respectively.

New York's average valuation is a more reasonable 5.7, while its average is 13.0—higher than San Francisco or Sydney, but much lower than London.

Singapore is another city that has a low median ratio of 4.8, but a sky-high average of 21.6. That's why Singapore had to slap on such an aggressive foreign-buyer tax in 2015.

So that's where to look for the bursts in the next real estate crash. It'll come from those cities where foreign buyers and wealthy speculators have driven prices to the extremes, specifically Hong Kong, London, Singapore, Manhattan (as opposed to broader New York), Vancouver, San Francisco, and Sydney.

On the flip side, the most affordable large cities in the United States are Atlanta, with valuations at 3.1 times income, Dallas at 3.7, Chicago at 3.8, and Tampa and Phoenix, both at 4.1. These are cities where everyday people can still (barely) afford houses.

Declines in those areas should be less severe but still substantial.

Let's apply the bubble model I discussed in the previous chapter to this real estate beast. . . .

Applying the Bubble Model: Three Key Cities as Examples

As I explained in chapter 11, with stocks, bubbles tend to burst in half the time it took them to build exponentially. Real estate is different. Property-price bubbles take about the same time to burst as they did to build. That's because real estate is harder to sell, and many owners live or work in it, so they're emotionally attached. They won't dump it as fast as they will a stock.

Stock bubbles also tend to crash back to where the bubble started, while real estate holds up a little better, retracing only 85 percent of the bubble.

Let's look at the San Francisco bubble to illustrate (Figure 12-4). . . .

The City by the Bay is not only one of the bubbliest cities in the United States, but also an example of a double bubble, where current prices are now significantly higher than in the first one . . . which makes it more overvalued than ever.

But what's less clear is whether it will correct toward its original bubble origin or back toward the lows of the last bubble burst.

Either way, it'll be painful!

When charting out a bubble, I always start with calculating the rough bubble origin. That's where prices start to accelerate beyond the natural trends.

For San Francisco, I place this around mid-1997.

Figure 12-4: Double Bubble in San Francisco

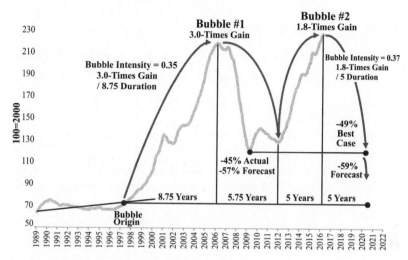

Source: St. Louis Federal Reserve, S&P/Case-Shiller

    The first bubble accelerated into a peak in early 2006. It was longer than most in the United States, lasting 8.75 years.

    To get the Bubble Intensity, I divide the times gain, in this case 3.0 times, by the duration, 8.75 years. That gives me a medium Bubble Intensity of 0.35.

    In this case, the bubble model would have forecast a decline of 58 percent, but we saw prices drop only 45 percent . . . and in a shorter amount of time than normal: just three years, into early 2009.

    Why did it happen that way?

    Because this was a very buoyant area with strong job growth and foreign buying. That stopped the first bubble from deflating properly . . . AND set the second bubble in motion in early 2012. That has lasted five years thus far and looks close to peaking.

    But double bubbles aren't common, and that makes them less predictable.

    Using my bubble model, my best-case scenario is that San Francisco crashes back down to that early 2009 low, which means property

Figure 12-5: Sydney Advances 3.1 Times since Early 2001

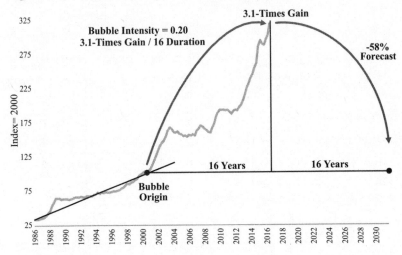

Source: Australia Bureau of Statistics, Dent Research

prices will lose 49 percent from the time we penned this book. If they rise further, real estate owners face greater than 50 percent losses!

The worst-case scenario is that prices fall back to the initial bubble origin from back in 1997. That would be a 68 percent to 72 percent punch in the gut (although I think this is unlikely).

Another good illustration of my bubble model at work in real estate in Australia.

Sydney has a classic five-wave advance that looks close to peaking.

Every time I speak there, the local economists and journalists attack me viciously when I tell them they're on the verge of a crushing real estate collapse.

But when I last spoke there, in late May of 2017, more experts admitted that the country definitely has a bubble. Now it's a question of *when* it will burst and how much it'll hurt.

Sydney's real estate bubble began to inflate exponentially in 2001. It's taken 16 years to advance 3.1 times. That's not as high an intensity as other bubble cities, like London. But, like San Francisco, Sydney was already expensive, and this bubble has built over a longer time frame, as have those in Melbourne and Brisbane and other major cities. Perth has already seen declines of as much as 50 percent on the high end, with the iron ore and commodity bubbles collapsing and Australia's declining trade with China depressing total exports.

My model suggests that Sydney real estate will experience a long slide into 2032–33. That's 16 years of decline if it peaks later in 2017.

However, I have a hard time believing that, because Australia's demographics are the most favorable in the developed world.

When I apply my diers-versus-buyers model to Australia, it peaks around now and falls into 2022, then rises back near these levels into 2026 before declining again into around 2043.

Note that Australia's net demand never turns negative, as has happened for years in Japan and will occur from 2028 to 2039 in the United States. It just drops from a double peak of around 1.25 million a year down to 700,000, or 44 percent.

Sydney property prices will more likely crash by about 53 percent into the early 2020s (going back to early 2006 lows), or 58 percent if I strictly apply the 85 percent bubble-retracement rule.

Figure 12-6: Australia Net Housing Demand
Peak Buyers (40–44) Minus Diers (80–84)

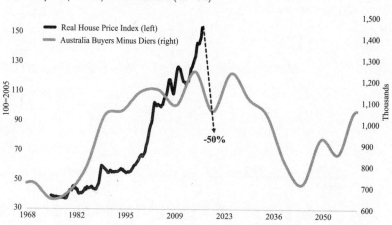

Source: United Nations Population Division, Dallas Federal Reserve

Then it will bounce back for several years, but it's unlikely to ever get back to its current highs.

From the late 2020s forward, it could decline once more and for years after that.

Australia, and Sydney in particular, has another unique attribute: a high concentration of Chinese buying.

When the Chinese bubble bursts, it'll wallop Australia's export economy as well as its real estate market. But those Chinese buyers may well continue to launder money via places like Australia when their bubble first bursts—until the Chinese government is forced to clamp down on such practices . . . and they'll have to at some point.

Vancouver and Toronto are the bubbliest cities in Canada, a country that never had a serious correction like the United States. Vancouver's chart is very much like Sydney's, and it's due to crash by 55 to 60 percent. And it, too, has slapped on a hefty foreign surcharge to start putting the brakes on foreign and Chinese buying.

That brings us to the mother of all bubbles. . . .

Shanghai real estate prices have soared by 8.7 times since 2001!

Figure 12-7: Shanghai, the Mother of All Bubbles: 8.7 Times

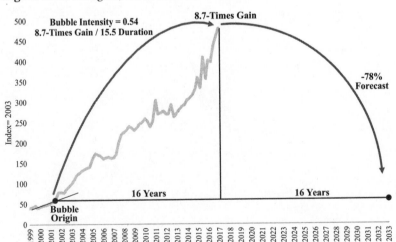

Source: China Real Estate Index Systems, Bloomberg, Dent Research

They now stand to lose almost 80 percent. That's off the charts for real estate, but it's totally in line with the intensity and extremes of its real estate bubble, even while as many as 27 percent of the condos in major cities are vacant.

This bubble originated at the same time as the one in Sydney, in mid-2001.

The 8.7-times gain gives this a high Bubble Intensity of 0.54.

Based on these numbers, and the fact that China has overbuilt its infrastructure and real estate capacity out by 10 to 15 years, I expect prices in Shanghai to take 16-odd years to hit bottom before they start to advance again.

This long and deep decline, not only in Shanghai but all across China, will weigh heavily on Australia's real estate markets at first, and all of Asia, despite Australia's strong demographics in the decades ahead.

My bubble model suggests that the Queen of the Orient could witness a crushing 78 percent loss, perhaps as much as 85 percent if prices go all the way back to the 2001 origin.

The best case (though I don't see it as likely) would be a decline back to the late 2012 low, or a 47 percent decline. That's still major for a country where 75 percent of net worth is in real estate, as compared with 27 percent in the United States.

Prices are up 1.88 times, or 88 percent, in just 3.5 years since 2012. That's crazy!

But that's the key here: When things get as insane as they have in China, you know the bubble peak is close. When even Australian economists finally start to admit that they have a bubble, it's probably closer still.

Finally, the U.S. real estate bubble took a little more than six years to deflate, from early 2006 into mid-2012, with the worst losses felt in 2008–09.

We face a similar scenario ahead: a crash from late 2017 well into 2023, with the worst hitting in 2018 and 2019.

Last time, the overall crash was 34 percent in the United States—but as much as 52 percent in Miami.

This time, the model projects a 50 percent crash at best, and at worst a 63 percent loss. Oh, this is going to hurt, with more homes underwater.

In short, when this modern-day Mount Vesuvius blows, it'll decimate all the cities that have taken up root at its base, and it'll likely take six years or more, into 2023 or so.

Review your real estate holdings and consider what you really love and/or whether it's strategic to your life. Get rid of everything else now, before the wheels come off this bus. Remember, real estate becomes agonizingly illiquid, fast!

I'm down to owning just one property on an island. Otherwise I lease or rent.

Use January 2000 as a most likely future valuation for your properties, and use 1996 as the worst-case scenario . . . then decide if you love it that much! You'll likely be shocked when you look at your potential downside.

With all this talk of bubbles bursting, let's turn our attention to the big question: What could set this disaster in motion?

CHAPTER 13

The Six Bubble Busters

China's downturn will be like an elephant falling from an airplane!

Harry Dent

AS WE'VE DISCUSSED, cycles are leading us into a time of revolution, chaos, and change. In the short term, that's a very bad thing. But in the long-term, it's like a big cleansing that leads to the next spring season. Stock markets are more overvalued than they were at the end of 1999, when we saw the highest P/E ratios in U.S. history. Even Robert Shiller's superior, cyclically adjusted CAPE shows this.

But that begs the question "Why?"

Why are stocks so high when there's nothing to support them?

Economic and earnings growth are much lower in this recovery since 2012. Earnings growth has even been negative at times in recent years. Why are stocks still going up? Because they're in a bubble, and government-created interest rates, short- and long-term, are the lowest in history, rewarding such speculation.

Yes, interest rates are the lowest in history, mostly due to artificial stimulus and government bond buying.

Debt levels are much higher, especially now at the government level, thanks to their idiotic, desperate, endless stimulus programs.

And by the first quarter of 2017, we were nowhere near the ideal

3 to 4 percent growth. In fact, first-quarter growth came in at a paltry 0.7 percent on an annualized basis.

President Trump promised he'd get America back to sustainable 3 to 4 percent growth. It'll never happen . . . ever again! Not during his presidency or in our lifetime. No matter how much fiscal stimulus and tax cutting is implemented, declining demographic trends and unprecedented debt will make it impossible.

Japan is living proof that we can't beat the demographic wave downward. It has thrown more stimulus at the problem than any country in the world. Yet still, 20 years later, it has near-zero growth, with zero productivity and low inflation.

In short, this situation is untenable. All we need is a trigger to start the avalanche. Lucky for us (ha!), we have six!

Here they are . . .

Bubble Buster #1: President Donald Trump!

The man's a live wire! A walking time bomb.

Although Republicans finally have a president with majorities in both houses of Congress, they're not a united party. Most didn't want Donald in the White House! Now that he's there, they're often fighting him right alongside the Democrats.

He faces insurmountable resistance to his pro-business reforms, his immigration policies, his tax overhaul schemes, and his healthcare reform plans.

His promise of 3 to 4 percent growth is unachievable and demographically impossible. Period. When the markets realize that, they'll crash.

The truth is that Trump brilliantly won an election he wasn't favored to win, but he walked into the office at the worst time possible.

And he's become a national security threat with his flapping lips, facing the threat of impeachment. (Andy actually has a histogram that suggests Trump might be assassinated or forced to leave office in late 2017.)

The problem is that greater debt and deficits from fiscal stimulus and pro-business policies like tax cuts conflict with the constantly rising debt ceiling.

The federal debt has doubled every two administrations (every eight years) since George W. Bush's presidency in 2001.

It went from $5 trillion to $10 trillion under Bush.

It went from $10 trillion to $20 trillion under Obama.

With the worst of our Economic Winter Season ahead, any major tax cuts would push the debt from $20 trillion to $40 trillion (if Trump survives two terms, which I highly doubt!).

Any misstep Trump makes is a potential trigger.

Then there's this: by late 2017, the "strong" job growth we've enjoyed since 2012 will very likely suddenly falter and disappear.

Bubble Buster #2: Job Growth

We've been creating 200,000 or so jobs a month regularly since 2012.

But what economists won't admit or just don't understand is that the workforce in the United States has barely expanded since 2007 and will decline in the next several years. This is a big deal and a ceiling on future job growth, even if the economy doesn't crash, as we predict.

In aging societies—and this is the case in almost all developed countries—baby boomers are draining out of the workforce, which eventually contracts it.

And, of course, this is predictable, as I explained in chapter 6. The baby boomer Spending Wave peaked between 1983 and 2007 (as they reached age 46).

Their retirement wave started in 2000 and continues into 2026, assuming present average retirement trends with a retirement age of

63—though that will likely stretch out a bit as boomers realize they can't afford to retire in a bad economy. This has already occurred in Japan to a degree.

And what happens when this outsize generation starts dying, from 2017 into 2044?! That'll kill the real estate market (diers are sellers) and population and workforce growth. But that's a story for another day.

The simple truth is that, in this highly stimulated, zero-interest-rate, and QE-driven economy, we've merely been hiring back the workers we lost in the 2008–09 Great Recession. Painfully slowly as well, at just near 2 percent growth rates.

By June 2017, we were approaching full employment again, with unemployment numbers coming in as low as 4.5 percent. At some point, there will be no jobs left to be had. That means either late-stage inflation (which is typical in most boom cycles) to bid retiring workers to come back in, or just no growth. Neither scenario is good for the economy.

My point is that it's demographically impossible to sustain growth of 200,000 jobs a month . . . unless we increase the retirement age to 75. Try running on that platform as a politician! Although that will become a reality when the economy collapses and we all realize we're bankrupt . . . and that retirement for 22 years on the dole is impossible (as many labor unions are having to concede).

This is why I think that job growth could suddenly slow down by the second half of 2017. I'm talking a drop to just 50,000 jobs a month or lower, not 200,000.

That would be a cold slap of reality to the face of Wall Street!

This next chart shows the rebuilding of the workforce into 2017 back to 2008 levels. We are back at full employment, and the future looks rather flat!

It also shows how natural workforce growth (20-year-olds entering versus 63-year-olds retiring) will actually shrink into 2023–24.

And then it grows at only 0.2 percent a year for decades after that. That's just 25,000 jobs a month.

Figure 13-1: Workforce Growth with Projection at Full Employment
U.S. Civilian Employment and Projections

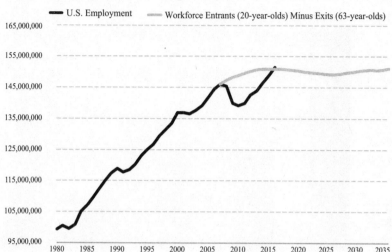

Source: St. Louis Federal Reserve, U.S. Census Bureau, National Center for Health Statistics,
Dent Research

Bubble Buster #3: Greece and Italy

When Greece first defaulted in 2010 and threatened to leave the
euro, the issue wasn't so much about that tiny country, but that other
nations in Southern Europe might follow.

Well, Greece has debt payments due to the European Central
Bank and the International Monetary Fund (and others) in July 2017.
It cannot pay!

This will raise the bigger issue of Italy.

Italy has 18 percent nonperforming or bad bank loans. Ten percent is typically bankrupt!

Only Greece and Cyprus have a higher percentage of nonperforming or bad bank loans, but neither of those countries is big enough
to torpedo the euro.

The following chart shows that Italy has the greatest number of
bad bank loans in the entire eurozone—30 percent of the zone's total.

Figure 13-2: Italy Dominates Bad Loans in Eurozone
Member Share of EU Nonperforming Loans, 2016 Q3

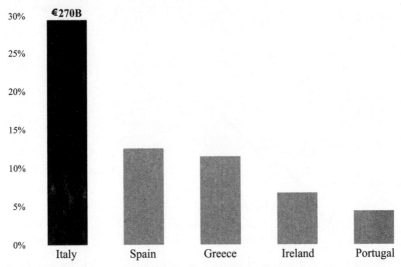

Source: European Banking Authority Risk Dashboard, 2016 Q3

This a default waiting to happen! It's also a huge incentive for the Boot of Europe to leave the euro and the eurozone.

As Iceland did (and came out the better for it), Italy could leave the euro, devalue its currency to stimulate exports, and default on all foreign loans—from banks *and* governments.

The price, as Iceland knows, would be high consumer inflation from greater import costs and the loss of access to future credit.

But there's a bigger problem: TARGET2 loans, owed largely to the central bank of Germany.

Europe's powerhouse (supposedly) has been floating the central banks of its major export partners in Southern Europe, just to keep them buying.

This is idiocy. It's essentially extending credit to less creditworthy customers so they don't lose the sale—never mind that they'll likely be unable to pay.

Figure 13-3: Italy Accounts for Half the TARGET2 Loans from Germany
Select TARGET2 Balances in the Eurozone

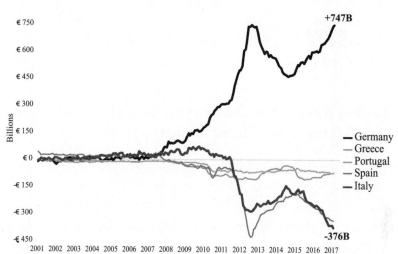

Source: European Central Bank, eurocrisismonitor.com

Germany is owed $747 billion, mostly from Italy and Spain!

Italy's tab is nearly half of that, at $376 billion.

If Italy leaves the euro and the eurozone, it could default on that debt immediately.

Then there are the foreign-bank loans to Italy . . .

They total around $550 billion—$280 billion of which is from France alone, with $80 billion from Germany.

Adding that up, Italy could default on more than $900 billion in foreign debts if it left the euro and the eurozone. That's the biggest incentive I've ever seen!

And Italy is only second to Greece, with 47 percent of its population in polls saying they don't favor the euro, against only 43 percent favoring it. Fifty-three percent of the Greek population isn't in favor of the euro. They may vote to exit the euro, even after all the bailouts they've gotten.

But Italy could easily be next, and the loss of Prime Minister

Matteo Renzi on his reform referendum was the first sign of a potential Italian exit.

This is likely to be the most damaging bubble buster of them all.

Meanwhile, there's another event that hasn't received as much notice as it should.

Bubble Buster #4: The Dissolution of the Union— Blue States Start Threatening to Leave

Shortly after Trump became president, a petition was taken up in California to secede from the United States. The Yes California campaign needed just 576,000 signatures to put on the ballot in November 2018 a vote for California to declare that the United States is not the law of the land. Then it wanted to put on the ballot in 2019 a vote to actually leave the Union and become its own country.

With almost 40 million people calling the state home, and Trump's impulse control of a grease fire, that would have been easy.

California leaving the United States would be like France leaving the eurozone!

However, that petition has died out, because the founder decided he wanted to live in Russia for the rest of his life. Maybe he was planted from Russia to disrupt the U.S. political system.

Still, the threat and the issue behind the petition remains, as I explained in chapter 4.

Major countries and regions are breaking down into more religiously and culturally compatible units, in a backlash against globalization that is shaping up to be a megatrend for the next few decades.

Trump's election started the red-state/blue-state civil war and has accelerated polarization between the two groups.

The United States could break into a number of blue or red zones in the years to come, just as Europe could break into northern and southern zones and China could break into an affluent urban coastal zone and a rural interior zone.

Such events will shatter investor confidence and bring this aging bubble down in flames!

It was the red states that were seceding in the Civil War. But since the Republicans are more in control, it makes more sense that blue states would consider leaving and possibly forming their own political and trading zones.

That's the paradox: The more Trump and the Republicans succeed in passing their ultraconservative and regressive agendas, the more the blue states could threaten to bolt. The obvious blue regions are the West Coast, the Northeast, and the Upper Midwest.

Bubble Buster #5: Seasonal Trends and Potential Turning Points

Then there's Andy!

He has his biggest turning points on his models for stocks in Europe and the United States popping up in mid- to late October 2017.

Figure 13-4: October 2017 Is the Largest Turning Point Since 2001 S&P 500

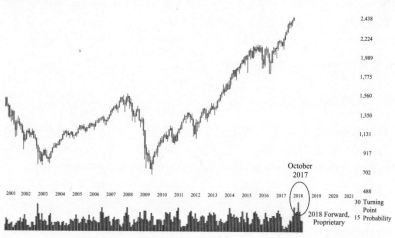

Source: cycleanalysis.com

By our calculations, by late August we could see an intermediate top, with something like a 10 percent correction into September. Then a final bubble surge into mid- to late October. But we'll see when the turning points play out. . . . That's the value of Andy's newsletter (markettimingreport.com).

Then, the past history of bubbles says, there would be a high chance for a first dramatic and sharp crash that sees 30 to 50 percent down in just a few months. We see a topping process between late July and late December 2017, before a major crash begins.

Seasonal trends, particularly in crash years, tend to hit in the July–November period, especially August–October. That's another reason that we could see a peak and a sharp crash at least begin in this time frame if this bubble is finally about to burst. Although July through November is typically the more likely time frame for a major crash, Andy's model suggests we're more likely to see it between late October

Figure 13-5: Major Bubbles Tend to Crash 40 Percent in 2.5 Months Panics and Sharp Short-Term Crashes

Stock Index	Crash Severity	Duration	Calendar Months
1907 Dow	-36%	4.25 Months	July–November
1929 Dow	-49%	2.5 Months	September–November
1937 Dow	-41%	3.3 Months	August–November
1987 Dow	-41%	1.9 Months	August–October
1990 Nikkei	-28%	3.1 Months	January–April
1997 Hong Kong	-48%	2.75 Months	August–October
2000 NASDAQ	-41%	2.5 Months	March–May
2000 NASDAQ Internet	-50%	2.75 Months	March–May
2000 NASDAQ Biotech	-50%	1.5 Months	March–April
2008 Dow	-37%	2.75 Months	September–November
2015 Shanghai Comp.	-43%	2.5 Months	June–August
2015 NASDAQ Biotech	-29%	1 Month	July–August
Average:	-41%	2.57 Months	July–November typical

Source: Dent Research, Bloomberg

and late January. Major long-term tops, like 1929 in the United States or 1989 in Japan, tend to come between September and December.

Look at this chart. It highlights the major crash years, when markets saw exceptionally sharp crashes in very short periods.

Notice how they tended to concentrate in this July–November time frame.

Bubbles burst suddenly and sharply. This one could be the worst, after being stretched longer and further than any past bubble.

Note not only the typical 30 to 50 percent crashes in two to three months. Also note that, outside of the tech-bubble burst, which included the biotech and Internet sectors, most of those sharp crashes occurred in the July–November time frame.

And let's not forget China . . . the ultimate bubble buster.

Bubble Buster #6: China

It wasn't enough the Soviet Union proved that centralized planning doesn't outperform bottom-up free-market economies with democracy as a balance.

It wasn't enough that all the dictatorships around the world, with their high corruption, prove the same, especially in the Middle East and Africa, and even Latin America.

No! It was China that had to take this model all the way and try to prove that if you sneaked some capitalism in there but still kept government in absolute control, you could create a communist utopia . . .

The smog choking the country is the first clue it's not working! The 16.4-times debt increase since 2000 is the next clue.

The dead giveaway is the massive overbuilding of everything: condos, infrastructure, office buildings, malls, railways, industrial capacity.

How does a non-elected government keep its people happy?

It creates "endless" jobs and wage growth through rapid urbanization and overbuilding everything . . . of course!

Free markets can go nuts at times, but ultimately, a discipline toward efficiency always ensues.

Not in China, where there are neither free markets nor democracy.

The way to get rich in China is to become cozy with the local communist party boss who hands out all the building contracts and government-guaranteed loans.

It's an oligarchy like Russia. It's just incorporated capitalism a little better and spent less on wasteful military expenditures than its neighbor to the north and west.

I've said it over and over: China will be the final proof that top-down planning and bureaucracy doesn't beat bottom-up, free-market capitalism and democracy—despite the obvious flaws of those two opposite systems. Their opposite characters are their very strength. Capitalism rewards individual contribution and merit. Democracy includes everyone in the system and aligns the troops with the generals.

When people look at China today, they see the best and brightest starting up multi-million-dollar companies. They don't see the everyday person living in the interior who survives on $2,000 a year and calls a shoebox condo home. The masses endure long commutes and suffer the effects of high pollution, traffic, and unaffordable real estate costs.

That's why the massive force of rural migrant workers in more urban areas (where they're not registered citizens) recently peaked at 253 million. And that's why they've finally started moving back to their rural areas. Since 2014, 7 million Chinese have gone back home to the rice paddies.

This chart should send chills down the spines of the top-down communist planners in China! It counters their core growth strategy . . . of overbuilding infrastructure for nobody, assuming they will come in the future. Now they are *really* not coming!

China's total workforce is the first in the entire emerging world to peak and decline since 2011 (the gray bars).

Figure 13-6: China's Urban Migrant Workers Go Back Home
Following China's Workforce, the Migrant Population Begins to Fall

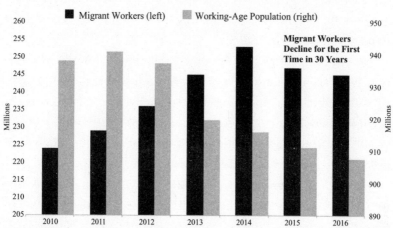

Source: China National Bureau of Statistics

So how does the country grow at 8 to 12 percent, with a declining workforce?

It keeps moving more people into urban areas, a move that typically triples their income.

And *that* has been China's top-down strategy.

It keeps overbuilding everything to attract more rural migrants to work and/or move into cities. It provides jobs for today and assumes that the stuff it's building for no one will eventually be needed by future rural migrants into cities.

But this overbuilding has now reached epic proportions, with cities built for a million people standing largely empty.

The largest mall in the world was turned into a tourist attraction because there were no retail clients. It was built in the middle of nowhere, for no one, so businesses didn't want to lease space.

An estimated 27 percent of condos are empty in major cities! This from an independent survey that measures condos and houses finished and hooked up to electricity. No electrical use means they're empty!

You can never listen to the official statistics from China, but in this case they're all we have. They're contrived and manipulated to keep confidence in the bubble going. . . . Sound like central bank strategies everywhere else?

By my estimates, China has now built enough overall infrastructure, housing, and industrial capacity for 10 to 12 years. The problem is, with migration trends reversing, there will be fewer people to occupy and make use of these increasingly empty structures.

That's all fine and frightening. But what's the "bubble buster" event that could shake out the markets?

An urban migration revolt! After three decades of massive rural-to-urban migration, the unregistered, second-class citizens are voluntarily going back home. You can see this back in Figure 13-6.

This is the death knell for the bubble of the top-down, over-building strategy in China.

As I've said for years, when the China bubble bursts, it'll be like an elephant falling from the sky.

Anyone who says there will be a soft landing in China is 100 percent detached from reality! Anyone who thinks a top-down government can better plan growth than the free markets, which are much more accountable to reality, needs to go live in Russia. You and vodka will become best friends so you can drown your misery.

Since mid-2015, China's stock market has foretold a broader crash and real estate bubble burst ahead. This next chart shows how its first dramatic bubble peaked in late 2007 and crashed 70 percent in one year!

Yes, up 6.2 times in two years and then down 70 percent in one year. . . . That is a bubble!

Then there was the second bubble, stimulated by more government overbuilding and a 16-times increase in debt since 2000. It mutated again between mid-2014 and mid-2015. Then it crashed 43 percent in just 2.5 months.

Why? The top-down government was trying to shift speculation

Figure 13-7: The Next Shoe About to Drop in China
The Twin Bubble Bursts in China, Shanghai Composite

Source: Yahoo! Finance

back into stocks instead of real estate. . . . Sound like a good strategy? Nope.

There has been a "dead cat" bounce ever since, only it's been fueled by the government buying its own market to prop it up. That's like the $4.5 trillion QE that created a measly 2 percent growth in GDP in the United States . . . and less in Europe and Japan.

Such a strategy won't succeed for much longer.

Mark my words: there's another crash coming in China's stock market, one that will take it down 84 percent or so from its 2007 top, to hit the 1,000 level on the Shanghai Composite, and possibly lower.

That will start a domino effect that will finally cause the great China real estate bubble to burst more dramatically than that of any other country in the world as the most affluent investors finally start to question real estate values, as they should. This will suddenly destroy wealth and send a tsunami of real estate crashes to crush all the English-speaking cities where the rich Chinese have laundered their money.

And recall that the Chinese have 75 percent of their wealth in real estate—much more than in stocks, and far more than other major countries, where it's normally more like 27 to 40 percent.

It's game over when the great China bubble crashes and there's no amount of global QE and BS stimulus that will counter that mega-trend!

What to Do

With all of that said, my advice to you is to get out of the markets now—both stock and real estate, if you're investing without a strategy, or if you're simply buying and holding as your stockbroker is telling you to do.

With the speed at which the wheels could come off these buses, you'd be better off leaving the show a bit early, especially by mid- to late October 2017, when Andy's and my cycles only turn down more aggressively.

Remember, when stock market bubbles burst, they tend to lose close to 40 percent in just months. When real estate bubbles burst, your property becomes an anchor around your neck as it becomes illiquid, unlike stocks or commodities. It also often has major debt attached to it.

But don't abandon the markets altogether. There are incredible opportunities to make money during this crisis and after. Your best bet is to find a proven, time-tested strategy and stick with it. We have several to offer any level and risk orientation of investor. You can find the details at dentresources.com.

Buy-and-hold strategies have endured painful volatility since March 2000. They'll continue to suffer even more until at least late 2022.

You need to choose safe asset strategies and proven trading systems that can excel in up and down markets . . . because we'll continue to see both ahead, but with more volatility and more downside than upside.

You're going to hate most stockbrokers and financial advisers in the years ahead.

In part III, I'll detail several of the opportunities so you can start preparing now.

Before we do that, though, let's get specific with some key markets. Then Andy has some more timing details for you.

CHAPTER 14

When You Put It That Way...

When you see the cycles that are converging into late 2017, you'll realize that this book you're reading is probably your saving grace!

Andrew Pancholi

BY THE END OF THIS CHAPTER, not only will you know and understand why the period from late 2017 to early 2020 is likely to be one of the most critical in the world financial markets; you'll also know some of the key time windows when trend changes are highly likely to take place.

First, here's an interesting factoid. The Decennial Cycle was first documented by Edgar Lawrence Smith, in his 1939 book *Tides in the Affairs of Men*.

In what was really only a study of 40 to 50 years of stock market data, Smith found that years ending in 3, 7, and 0 were often down years. Years ending in 5, 8, and 9 were generally advancing years.

His research was based on optimism and pessimism in human beings and how weather, sunspots, and radiation affect their thought processes.

Ned Davis came to a similar 10-year cycle conclusion with his study of stock markets over 100 years. It's just that we now have a better, more variable scientific cycle to predict that through sunspots.

Well, the fact that 2017 ends in 7 means it could be one of the most bearish years in the Decennial Cycle, as was 1987. We're very susceptible to change this year, which I'll talk about more in a minute.

First, though, know that the real secret to forecasting lies in super-long-term cycles, and it's all about knowing where to look.

I keep a series of crisis matrices that list all the significant economic occurrences that I can find. Then I analyze these events to unearth the critical cycles.

Let's begin with the 72-year cycle, which starts with the 1929 Wall Street crash.

As you know, the crash was preceded by the greatest boom of the first half of the 20th century.

America could do no wrong. Neither could most of the Western world.

Skyscrapers sprang up all around New York. Automobiles were in vogue in urban areas.

And during the latter stages of the rampant boom, everyone was in on the stock market game. Even the shoeshine boy was recommending stock picks to his clients. (Sound familiar to anything we're seeing today?) That was the tip-off to Joseph Kennedy to sell his stocks.

Subtracting 72 years from 1929, we arrive in 1857.

That year saw one of the first modern-day financial crises to hit the globe (as I mentioned in chapter 2). By then the world was interconnected. This meant that the stage was set for a domino-effect collapse to unfold. And it did.

In America, the railroad boom was going bust for the first time. Railroad stocks peaked in July 1857 and then, in August, the Ohio Life Insurance and Trust Company failed, triggering a financial panic.

The United Kingdom was going through a currency crisis. The government of Prime Minister Lord Palmerston effectively violated the UK's banking laws by not keeping the appropriate gold and silver reserves, as had been decreed.

And the nation had lost its edge in global domination due to the advancement of transportation, in particular steamships. She was not used to so much competition.

These two superpowers sucked the rest of the world into the vortex.

During the course of the next few years, the American stock market declined 62 percent.

Seventy-two years later, we experienced the Great Depression.

Seventy-two years after that was 2001.

Most of the equity markets began peaking in 2000, and, of course, 2001 saw the infamous attack upon the Twin Towers on September 11.

The tech bubble had started in 1995.

The stock market was on fire.

Mobile phones, personal computers, the Internet—you name it—were all the rage. Within five years, what began as a novelty had turned into a must-have!

But by the end of the century, the steam had run out.

(Incidentally, the last five years of the previous two centuries, from 1795 to 1800 and from 1895 to 1900, saw major stock market booms.)

Doubling the 72-year sequence gives us 144 years. This is the period, as you have just seen, from 1857 to 2001.

The 144-year cycle is as important as the 72-year one. . . .

Abhor 144?

Take the inflationary crises of 1720, for example. That was the year that saw the South Sea and Mississippi Bubbles burst!

Adding 144 years brings us to 1864, a year that saw a massive thrust up in the commodity markets.

Most of America was fighting the Civil War, there was no one tilling the land, and cotton was desperately needed for uniforms. Supplies of commodities were low, and demand was sky-high.

Such was the magnitude of the price surge that cotton, which had been trading at between $0.02 and $0.03 per pound, hit a price of $1.89 on August 23, 1864. That's a 60-to-90-fold increase in a matter of months.

Add 144 years to 1864 and we're in 2008. Ring any bells? That was the year the commodity boom made its most recent long-term top on a 30-year cycle!

Then there's the 100-year cycle, what Harry refers to as the Centurial Cycle . . .

The Power of 100

The year 1907 saw the Rich Man's Panic.

Economic uncertainty came in after the 1906 San Francisco earthquake. By 1907, credit had dried up. Otto and Augustus Heinze had attempted to corner the copper market. They failed dramatically.

By October, panic had set in. The market plunged 50 percent from the highs of the previous year and would head much lower still.

Once again there were runs on banks and many failures. Confidence in the financial system was severely shaken. Interestingly, J. P. Morgan himself was called in to help stabilize the markets with his vast wealth.

Well, skip 100 years forward and it was 2007, the year of the global financial crisis. A whole series of challenges, including the implosion of CDOs (collateralized debt obligations) and CDSs (credit default swaps), led to a massive collapse.

Interestingly, the government called on certain institutions to assist with the bailout, but this time JPMorgan Chase, the "too big to fail" bank named partly for the old Wall Street titan, was on the wrong side.

As you can see, history repeats pretty much exactly . . . and right on schedule.

But let us take the sequence a little further and look at the midpoints of the 100-year cycle.

Risky 50

Starting in 2007, if we go back 50 years, we find ourselves in 1957. That year, the market sold off over several months due to a general economic rundown caused partly by the saturation of the automobile market.

By 1958 the world was in depression again, thanks to the policies of President Eisenhower and his government, which included raising interest rates.

Go back another 50 years and we end up in 1907. We've already talked about the Rich Man's Panic, which was also known as the Knickerbocker Crisis.

Back another 50 years and we see something really interesting . . . This takes us to 1857!

We've already seen this in the 72-year cycle AND the 100-year cycle. That's why it was such an important economic turning point.

Something similar is happening in 2017 (more on this shortly).

Fifty years before 1857 takes us to 1807, when the United States enacted the Embargo Act, to supposedly disengage from European hostilities. American vessels were prevented from trading in any foreign port.

This act stressed the U.S. economy immensely.

Once again, you can see that this is another cycle that works like clockwork.

There's one more cycle set that's critical to our future. It revolves around the 90-year cycle and its midpoint of 45 years. The 90-year cycle represents two 45-year Innovation Cycles that Harry documents.

A perfect example of this is Brexit.

Britain went to the polls on June 23, 2016. We all know the outcome of that referendum.

I'd forewarned people that the UK leaving the eurozone was a distinct possibility, because the most telling cycle was the recurrence of the 45-year cycle. This time it was TO THE DAY!!

On June 23, 1971, Geoffrey Rippon, the UK government's chief negotiator, reported to Parliament, saying, "We have a very satisfactory deal."

Up until this the point, the French had been blocking Britain from joining the European Economic Community, as it was known then.

Pro-marketeers cheered. Anti-marketeers groaned. The rest just lost the will to live!

But what's interesting is that it was EXACTLY 45 years—to the day—that Britain voted.

Coincidence? No!

You see, 45 years prior to 1971, on June 10, 1926, Spain withdrew from the League of Nations (a similar kind of body to the EU, in a broad sense), in protest of Germany being allowed to join.

The recurring theme: European polarization!

Doubling that 45-year cycle, we head back to the 1929 crash.

Going back 90 years from that point takes us to 1839, which was, again, a year of crisis.

Going forward from 1929, we reach . . . 2019!

We can expect a serious correction then, after most of Harry's cycles point to a first dramatic crisis from late 2017 into early 2020 or so.

Adding 45 years to 1929 gives us 1974. The Western world had been brought to its knees by the Arab oil crisis and the dramatic 1973–74 stock crash.

This was a major turning point.

The crisis itself began in October 1973, when OPEC launched an embargo against the United States, the United Kingdom, Japan, Canada, and the Netherlands, in response to supportive American action for Israel during the Yom Kippur War.

However, the recovery since then has extended to the present day. In fact, we can argue that 1974 saw the genesis of the present bull market.

That gives us ominous signs for 2019.

Before 2019, though, there's 2017 to contend with. . . .

What's About to Happen

As we already know, years ending in 7 are very susceptible to corrections, and my research shows that pretty much every year ending in 7 in the 20th and 21st centuries had a major pullback.

The fall of 2017 is exactly 10 years on from late 2007, and 30 years past late 1987 on the 30-year Commodity Cycle.

From the high in 2007 to the eventual low in 2009, the markets declined more than 50 percent. The market declined 50 percent during the 1907 Rich Man's Panic.

The time cycle repeats!

The price-drop percentages repeat!!

The further back we go in terms of cycles, and the longer these cycles are, the more significant they become.

So let's look at the long-range cycles weaving together and coming to a head in 2017.

It starts in 1837. That was 180 years ago.

If you're wondering why I chose the number 180, it's because 10-, 20-, 30-, and 60-year cycles are of utmost importance in financial markets. One hundred and eighty years is a multiple of all of these, as well as the 90- and 45-year cycles that we have already talked about.

In 1837, there was a crash and subsequent recession that led into a depression. The roots of that crisis went all the way back to 1819, if not earlier.

Andrew Jackson, Old Hickory, had been vehemently opposed to the chartering of the Second Bank of the United States. A libertarian Jacksonian movement sprung up, favoring free trade and very much against the way the bank had been operating.

In 1832, the bank's charter came up for renewal. Jackson was president and did everything in his power to ensure that the bank didn't continue. One of his reasons was that he believed that powerful outsiders, like the Rothschilds, controlled the bank.

He ran for reelection under the slogan "Jackson and No Bank." He wanted to regain control of the American monetary system to benefit the people of the land.

As soon he was reelected, he withdrew government funds and placed them into state banks, with the intention of putting monies under Democratic control. This was where the plan backfired.

These regional banks didn't regulate credit correctly. In fact, they abused their lending powers by not maintaining specie (i.e., money in the form of coins rather than notes), creating yet another bubble.

Loan money was very cheap.

Chicago and the surrounding regions were the main focus for development. Both railroads and canals were being built at a great pace so that the Midwest could be connected to the Great Lakes and all the way to the Atlantic by way of the Saint Lawrence Seaway.

Property prices rose exponentially, and what followed was a huge land speculation crisis.

In 1836, the U.S. Treasury Department was forced to issue a circular announcing that only gold and silver pieces would be redeemable on payment for public lands. This precipitated the Panic of 1837, which began on May 10.

The ensuing depression lasted six years, with more than 600 banks closing.

This was exacerbated by a rapid decline in commodity prices.

Meanwhile, in Europe in 1837, Great Britain had also rapidly reined in lending.

The consequences were severe. Confidence fell in both the currency system and the economy.

By the early 1840s, American stock prices were down 74 percent from the highs of the previous decade. A serious depression had kicked in. More than 850 American banks failed, and Chicago's overnight boom turned into a 90 percent–plus collapse in real estate prices.

This long-term scenario is similar to where we find ourselves in 2017.

2017

Thus far, we've discussed the 10-year cycle and the 180-year cycle as being relevant to 2017. And we've looked at the historical importance of the 144-year cycle. When we apply this latter cycle to 2017, it takes us back to 1873.

That fateful year saw multiple panics break out around the globe.

In Europe, crisis broke out in Vienna and spread across the continent.

The United States had been in a Reconstruction-era bubble period.

Silver was demonetized.

The Jay Cooke crisis took place. This was when the man widely recognized as America's first major investment banker was forced into bankruptcy as the railroad expansion began to falter yet again, and he was unable to sell the bonds it held in the Northern Pacific Railway. Jay Cooke & Company declared bankruptcy on September 18, 1873.

Two days later, on September 20, the New York Stock Exchange closed for ten days.

This panic developed into a depression that lasted six years in the United States. America readopted the gold standard in 1879, boosting the recovery.

In Europe, the effects were far greater . . .

The railroad expansion was vast as the various countries merged their tracks together. This bubble burst with gusto.

Britain saw worsening economic conditions that lasted nearly twenty years. This was termed the Great Depression (not to be confused with the worldwide 1930s event that goes by the same name).

(Note that if we add about 60 years to the 1873 crisis, we arrive at that Great Depression of the 1930s! This is an example of the Kondratieff wave in action.)

Furthermore, if we add 100 years to 1873, we arrive at the Arab oil crisis in 1973–74, which, in turn, spawned a major recession in both Britain and America.

(Forgive me if I seem a little repetitive in detailing some of these years, but I'm sure you see why it's important.)

The UK went on what was known as the "three-day week," during which electricity was guaranteed for only three working days in the week.

TV stations were made to stop transmitting at an early hour. This was because most power was generated by coal-fired power stations and it was scarce.

British miners went on strike, heightening the issues of the oil crisis. This was the flavor of the mid-1970s.

About 100 years earlier, the United States had been plagued by coal-miner strikes.

Figure 14-1: 1917
Dow Jones Industrial Average

Source: markettimingreport.com, Bloomberg

Returning to the 1930s Depression and adding half the Populist Movement Cycle, or 40 to 42 years, also takes us to 1974.

This is how precise the timing of economic events can be!

You'll recall how the 100-year cycle helped us forecast the 2007–08 global financial crisis. So let's consider its relevance to 2017.

Heading back to 1917, the globe was in the penultimate year of the First World War. While wars are generally good for economic production, due to the high demand for arms, none of the parties had anticipated that this war would go on for so long. A major high came into place across the stock markets in autumn 1917, and we saw a 45 percent correction that lasted a year (see Figure 14-1).

The next cycle that's coming into play is that of 90 years. This takes us back to 1927 (see Figure 14-2).

During that time, we saw a somewhat smaller pullback in what was the biggest and most aggressive bull market to date. This was due mainly to the last part of the Florida land speculation boom, which just ran out of steam. There had been much fraudulent activity, too.

Figure 14-2: 1927
Dow Jones Industrial Average

Source: markettimingreport.com, Bloomberg

Figure 14–3: 1957

Dow Jones Industrial Average

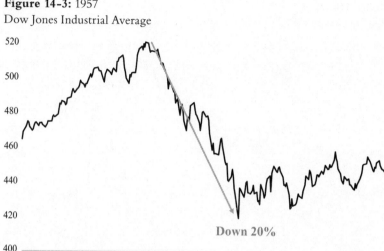

Down 20%

Source: markettimingreport.com, Bloomberg

Heading back 60 years takes us to 1957 (see Figure 14-3).

The U.S. market sold off steadily as industrial production peaked.

The mass market for automobiles reached saturation level.

There was a series of strikes and labor-relations issues.

Some of you will recall the 1987 crash. At the time, it was seen as the sharpest financial meltdown ever as it occurred largely in two weeks, and much of that in one day.

Well, 2017 is exactly 30 years on from this date.

Back then, the market sold off 37 percent. The market dropped 23 percent on Black Monday, October 19, alone.

Some saw it as a technical correction, and some also make the case that derivatives trading and computer-system trading, both of which were in relative infancy compared with the present day, were major factors in this event.

What's interesting, though, is that the UK, which was badly hit by the crash, was experiencing severe weather. A hurricane had swept through the south of England.

England is rarely hit by hurricanes!

Figure 14-4: 1987
Dow Jones Industrial Average

Source: markettimingreport.com, Bloomberg

It had rained heavily before the hurricane, so the ground was sodden. Many trees fell, bringing down huge numbers of power and telephone lines with them. Communications were greatly hampered, and all travel stopped.

I recall being on my way to the airport to catch a flight that evening. It was otherworldly.

There were no other cars out on the road. A solitary policeman took refuge in the doorway of a shop.

My car was blown around by the crazy wind.

I was within three miles of the airport when the road I was on became completely blocked by a massive tree. I had no choice but to turn around and try an alternate route.

At this point I wondered if we'd make the flight. I backtracked half a mile before my path was blocked again, by another tree that had come down just minutes earlier.

I was trapped, and trees that had stood for hundreds of years were coming down left, right, and center!

I survived the night in the car, trapped amid a falling forest! (This was well before the days of mobile phones!)

I tell you this story for two reasons. First, on a practical level, due to the infrastructure damage, very few people went into their offices the day after the storm. This meant that the volume of trading was very light on the Friday before the crash. This may have allowed the computer models to take over.

Second, extreme market behavior often coincides with extreme weather conditions. Just some food for thought!

The 30-year cycle is a strong one, and we must keep it on our radar.

If we were to look back 20 years, 1997 saw the Asian financial crisis, which led to a temporary suspension of trading on the New York Stock Exchange.

During July 1997, the Thai government was unable to support its currency, due to lack of reserves, and the baht collapsed. This exacerbated the economic conditions in Thailand, which was already pretty much bankrupt and unable to meet her financial obligations.

Figure 14-5: 1997
Dow Jones Industrial Average

Source: markettimingreport.com, Bloomberg

Indonesia and South Korea were deeply affected, as were most of the Southeast Asian nations.

This event was so severe, it brought a temporary break to the massive tech rally of the late 1990s.

The 20-year cycle is also important. Don't be surprised if we see a crisis with origins in the Far East in late 2017.

Bringing It All Together

That's a lot of information to process, so let's summarize:

- 2017 is a year ending in 7.
- It's 180 years from the 1837 Panic, which had its roots in Chicago. That's a big one. A massive depression from 1835 to 1843, followed by a relapse into 1857.
- It's 144 years from the 1873 Jay Cooke investment bank collapse and the great railroad panic and depression.
- The 100-year supercycle runs from 1917 to 2017. In late 1917, it resulted in a hefty sell-off.
- The 90-year cycle takes us back to a pause in the rampant bull market of the Roaring Twenties.
- The 60-year cycle from 1957 saw a significant sell-off as automobile manufacturing peaked, and as it appears to be occurring in 2017, as Harry's demographic trends would also have forecast.
- The 30-year cycle takes us all the way back to the 1987 crash.
- The 20-year cycle takes us back to the Asian financial crisis from 1997 into 2002.
- And the 10-year cycle takes us back to the global financial crisis after 2007.

I get chills every time I see that summary. Don't you?!

As you can see, the longer-term cycles have a great economic impact. History clearly repeats itself in the financial markets.

But that list isn't all of it!

There's a smaller cycle of 18.6 years—the business cycle that impacts America. It peaked around May 2017 and has more to do with real estate.

As you can see, 2017 is a critical year and has a huge set of cycle culminations, especially from August forward! That makes the book you hold in your hands now critical to your survival and prosperity, not just through 2017 and the aftermath but through the other challenging years ahead. . . .

2019

The year 2019 sees the reappearance of one of the biggest cycles in a long time: a 90-year cycle from the 1929 crash and a 45-year cycle from the 1974 low. Hence, this is likely to be one of the worst years coming up, along with late 2017.

It will also be 100 years on from the 1919 oil panic.

These are major.

September 3, 1929, saw the final top of a bull market that lasted more than eight years.

The 1920s saw a postwar boom. Automobile ownership was rising, and technology was flourishing—especially the radio. RCA was one of the glamour stocks of the decade.

Aviation was set to grow and challenge the railroads.

As I've already said, skyscrapers were springing up in New York and Chicago.

Silent movies would soon become a thing of the past, following the release of the first talkie, *The Jazz Singer,* in October 1927.

By the beginning of 1929, pretty much everybody was playing the stock market. Everyone was an expert on stock picking. Bucket shops had sprung up, making it easy to invest on margin.

But people were ignorant of the past.

They didn't know about the 72-year cycle that was about to hit them. (We've already talked about 1857.)

They hadn't noted the 10-year cycle from 1919 or the 20-year cycle from 1909, not to mention the 90-year cycle going back to the depression of 1839.

There were so many cycles coming together, it defies belief.

Guess what?

The year 2019 ties into the majority of cycles that triggered the 1929 crash! So be alert for a major stock market event in 2019, especially the latter part of the year.

It's also important to note that 2019 is 45 years on from the Arab oil crisis and the major inflationary recession that took place then.

The 30-year cycle from 1989 marks a critical point in the history of Japanese finance. The Nikkei 225 reached an all-time high in December of that year. This high has never been beaten, and the Japanese recession since is well documented.

I would expect gold to come under the spotlight during 2019 and into 2020 as well, likely a long-term bottom and a huge investment opportunity. . . . But, again, we'll see when these cycles unfold more predictably. Harry is looking for a possible major bottom in emerging countries and commodity prices by late 2019 or early 2020.

Back in 1869, 150 years ago, President Ulysses S. Grant decided to sell gold reserves to pay off debts arising from the Civil War. James Fisk and Jay Gould had a ploy to corner the gold market. Their operations led to a significant rise in the price of gold. However, on September 24, 1869—Black Friday—their corner collapsed, and the price of gold came crashing down.

During the depression of 1884, huge amounts of gold left America and flowed to Europe. This was three cycles of 45 years back from 2019.

Forty-five years ago, in 1974, gold peaked in response to global geopolitical instability.

Heading back to 1979, on two 20-year cycles or four Decennial Cycles, we see that the Hunt brothers attempted to corner the silver market, which went on to peak in March 1980. Gold rose in tandem, making a major high.

They were thwarted in the final stages by a sudden change in margining requirements, and again the price of the metals came crashing down.

All of this is to tell you that 2019 has all the makings for potentially large moves in the precious metals markets at the same time as a major stock market crisis.

2020

The most important cycle that comes out in 2020 is a 300-year one. While you may not think it's relevant to go so far back, it's perhaps the most important boom and bust that has ever taken place. So we can learn a lot from it to secure our own financial future.

I'm talking, of course, about the 1720 Mississippi land bubble in France and the South Sea Bubble in England!

And John Law, the first central banker in France, funded the country's growing debts after wars with England through a totally artificial bubble in Louisiana swampland, selling acreage to high-end investors at low, government-induced interest rates. Near-free money, easy credit, and endless potential in swampland . . . a perfect bubble. And it was the first and most extreme in stock history. Sound familiar to today, with central banks goosing up everything with endless money printing and near-zero interest rates and guarantees of everything from bank accounts to mortgages?

England had a similar strategy of selling off its ownership in the South Sea Company to pay off its debts, and the greatest stock sell-off in history ensued in both stock market bubbles, from 1720 into 1722 . . . the first great stock bubble, following the equally dramatic tulip bubble in futures, in the early 1600s.

And it illustrates how human behavior never changes.

But there are also other cycles . . .

Ten years back from 2020 takes us to 2010. Many of the commodity markets had a second peak that year. This means that gold and silver could see big moves.

The 72-year cycle saw a commodity price peak at the end of World War II.

Twenty years back from 2020 takes us to the end of the tech-stock boom on the NASDAQ.

What I find particularly fascinating when I study our crisis matrix is that all of the other cycles we look at to ascertain what will happen in 2020 show either depression or recession. This is a direct consequence of the events of the previous few years.

Both 1840 and 1870 had recessions, as did 1920 and 1930. The same is true for 1960 and 1970.

This is very telling.

If we are indeed to see a major economic downturn in 2020, that would validate the notion that we're about to see some major financial challenges during the years 2017 to 2019.

How to Profit from the Greatest Revolution and Financial Crisis Since the Late 1700s

CHAPTER 15

The Two Safe Havens in Winter

This is about how well you want to sleep at night, while still being in the game to make money.

Harry Dent

PROBABLY THE MOST IMPORTANT RULE in the entire world of money is: Don't fight the Fed.

It doesn't matter if you're Bill Gates or Homer Simpson; resistance is futile.

The Fed will always have more money than you, because they're the guys who *print* it. So betting against the Fed is a bad, bad idea. Many a trader has tried it. . . . At some point, they probably weren't solvent enough to try it again. I, too, have been humbled by them, predicting that this bubble could peak and then watching as central banks just keep goosing it up higher. They're sowing the seeds of their own death, but I'm still taking it in the nuts!

These days, "Don't fight the Fed" sounds a little provincial. It's a big world out there, and the Fed isn't the only central bank in town. The European Central Bank, the Bank of Japan, and the People's Bank of China all carry similar clout on their own home turf. You fight them at your own peril. And you certainly don't want to buy what they're selling.

The U.S. Federal Reserve has been less aggressive in stimulus policies than these other central banks lately, making us the best house in a bad neighborhood. And that's why the dollar has been one of the safe havens, as I'll discuss ahead.

Yet many foolish investors are buying what these central banks are selling. And it's setting up a potential Fixed Income Trade of the Decade.

I wrote about the possibility of this opportunity in my last book, *The Sale of a Lifetime*. It's still in the cards, and one of only two safe havens you'll have in the financial crises and revolution ahead.

As I said in chapter 13, there are many triggers for the next global crash and financial crisis. What I didn't mention was the stealth trigger gathering steam right under unsuspecting noses: the devastation of emerging markets.

Now understand that emerging markets will be our next boomers (as I'll explain in chapter 16), but first they've got a problem in their leading nation. . . .

After decades of China overbuilding everything and sucking up the world's commodities like an industrial-strength vacuum to keep up the illusion of insatiable growth and remain the export machine to the world, any slowdown there puts the hurt on emerging markets.

Their exports of commodities and everything else suffer, which zings the profitability of their companies and takes a wrecking ball to their stock markets and economies. Fewer exports means less capital coming in and slower growth of foreign exchange reserves (from trade surpluses).

There's no doubt that China's gears are no longer spinning at the rate they once did. And with each report showing slowing out of China, emerging markets take a punch to the gut, as do commodities.

There's also the problem of their currencies. They're unstable due to their export and economic weakness. When their currencies take a dive, they sell their foreign exchange reserves (FX) to defend themselves.

Because 62 percent of foreign central bank reserves are held in

U.S. dollar securities—and the dollar has been the world's strongest major currency—it makes sense to unload dollars the most.

And that means U.S. Treasury (and agency) securities are perpetually on the chopping block.

That's where the Fixed Income Trade of the Decade opportunity potentially lies.

The Fixed Income Trade of the Decade

Selling Treasury bonds puts downward pressure on their price and upward pressure on yields. As low as U.S. Treasuries have gotten (1.36 percent on the 10-year Treasury note in January 2014), their yields can go still lower, for many reasons . . . but mostly because of the deeper trends toward deflation in this Economic Winter Season, when QE and fiscal stimulus plans finally fail.

During 2016, foreign central banks went from buying as much as $231 billion a year to selling $397 billion—a $628 billion shift!

Add to that the fact that the Fed stopped buying $1 trillion worth of U.S. Treasuries per year, and our government bond market shrank by $1.6 trillion in the past two years.

Under these circumstances, Treasury rates are likely to rise initially, despite economic slowing and the deflationary trends at play around the globe right now.

All it takes for bond prices to crash and bond yields to rise sharply is a temporary liquidity crisis. While debt held at the Fed on behalf of foreign central banks is once again high (at the time of this writing), any bump in the road could reverse this situation once again.

When that happens, you'll be able to enter the Fixed Income Trade of the Decade.

Get in when bond prices are at their lowest and you'll secure the highest, safest yields available.

This is like getting that car you've always wanted but couldn't afford because the price just wasn't right. Really, we couldn't ask for

Figure 15-1: The Sell-Off
Central Bank Purchase of U.S. Treasuries

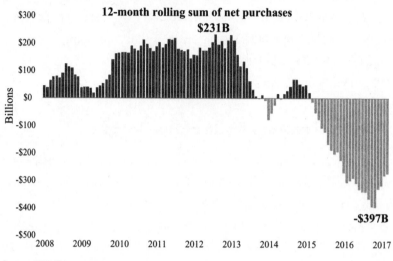

Source: U.S. Treasury

a more perfect setup than the one likely to open up before us just ahead.

A word of warning, though: I'm not saying to buy Treasuries right now. It's too early. But I AM saying you should get ready to back the truck up, because when the time comes, you're going to want to load it up and then come back for more.

When the time is right, corporate AAA bonds will also be seen as a safe haven and will appreciate in value, while junk bonds will suffer major defaults.

Why U.S. Treasuries and Corporate AAAs Could Soon Be Dirt Cheap

Emerging countries are desperate to keep their currencies stable. After all, a weaker currency makes their exports more competitive.

The problem is that currencies aren't valued in isolation. They're valued as compared with another currency. Thus, a weak yuan or peso or rand invariably means a strong U.S. dollar.

And that's actually *bad* for these guys. After all, commodities are priced in dollars, so a strong dollar means weak commodity prices . . . which erodes the value of exports.

Besides that, a declining currency causes inflation to rise sharply (due to rising import costs), and that's a problem for emerging countries (including the big boys of China, Brazil, and India).

Inflation also raises their domestic and government borrowing costs by causing bond yields to rise. And since they've borrowed like crazy since 2008, they must protect themselves from being squashed like a bug by their ballooning debt!

So emerging-country central banks find themselves forced into selling Treasuries—an action that could accelerate in the months ahead.

But know this: this potential spike in rates leading to the Fixed Income Trade of the Decade is a relatively short-term play. I don't expect it to last any longer than several months. Longer-term, deflation is still the trend, and deflation means a strong dollar, high bond prices, and extremely low interest rates across the yield curve.

So think of this bond-market rout as an anomaly to take advantage of in the near term, not a trend reversal back up in rates as many expect. Falling Treasury (and corporate AAA) bond yields still have years to run, despite most analysts and economists assuming bond yields may have bottomed in 2015. They don't see deflation coming like we do.

But mark my words: the bond market is likely to get smacked temporarily before it leverages the de-leveraging of the Economic Winter Season. I'm convinced of this because of several important trends in play. . . .

1. The bursting emerging-market debt bubble.
2. The bursting emerging-market currency bubble.

3. Who holds U.S. Treasuries now.

4. Continued declines in commodity prices.

5. And the warning from the T-Bond Channel.

Let's look at each of these in more detail. . . .

The Impact of the Emerging-Market Debt Bubble

The global debt bubble since 2008 has been concentrated in emerging-market debt, especially China.

Global debt grew by $57 trillion to $199 trillion between 2008 and 2014, according to McKinsey. It's got to be well over $215 trillion or higher by now. Most of that debt occurred in emerging countries, because developed countries have already reached their peak debt capacity.

Total emerging-market corporate debt alone rose from $3.2 trillion in 2003 to $26 trillion in 2016. Much of that was denominated in U.S. dollar loans and bonds.

This dollar-denominated foreign borrowing has risen from $2 trillion in 1995 to $10.5 trillion in 2016. That's an increase of 5.3 times.

And about half of it accounts for total emerging-market corporate borrowing. For some perspective, that's about half the size of the U.S. banking system and half as much as corporations have borrowed in total in the United States.

Think of it this way: we now have a *global* U.S. dollar debt that does nothing for our economy.

In late 2008, when Lehman Brothers collapsed, the Fed not only had to bail out the U.S. economy with massive QE and other measures, but it also had to extend $1 trillion in U.S. dollar swaps to provide liquidity for foreign banks dealing in U.S. dollar debt to fend off a liquidity crisis overseas.

What if the next crisis, with the much higher dollar-denominated

Figure 15-2: The Rise of Overseas Dollar Borrowing

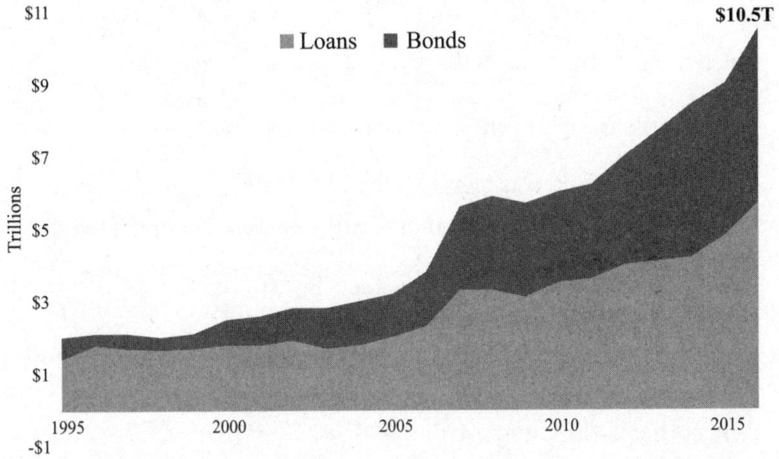

Source: "Feeling Green," *The Economist,* March 21, 2015

foreign debt, required as much as $2 trillion in such liquidity? Can the Fed bail out our economy *and* the foreign markets, too?

Unlikely.

Congress didn't like the last foreign liquidity extension, so any new one could be blocked or stalled—especially now with a Republican Congress.

This has implications for the broader global financial crisis just ahead, but there's a clear and direct threat for the issue I'm discussing here. That is, without such liquidity, foreigners—especially central banks—would be forced to sell their Treasury bonds at lower and lower prices.

Why Only 59.8 Percent of the Treasury Market Is At Risk

Then there's the bubble in emerging-market foreign exchange holdings since 2000.

FX holdings grew from $802 billion in 2001 to nearly $8.06 trillion in mid-2014. By the end of 2016, they stood at $10.79 trillion. That's more than 13 times the growth rate in 13 years.

Just look at this chart, which shows the proportion of U.S. Treasuries held by foreigners.

Emerging markets have taken the largest slice of the foreign holdings, growing from $0.3 trillion to $3 trillion, or a whopping ten times.

It's estimated that more than 80 percent of these emerging-market holdings are at central banks, not with private investors.

This is important because it's China and other emerging-country central banks that will be the big sellers of Treasuries.

If we break this down further, in the below chart you see that, out of $19.9 trillion of U.S. Treasuries, $5.6 trillion (27.9 percent) are held by Social Security and Medicare, and $2.4 trillion (12.3 percent) by the Federal Reserve.

The U.S. government controls 40.2 percent of its own Treasuries. It just holds them. It doesn't trade or sell them. That means that only 59.8 percent are tradable.

Figure 15–3: Emerging-Market Central Banks Are Growing Players in Treasury Market

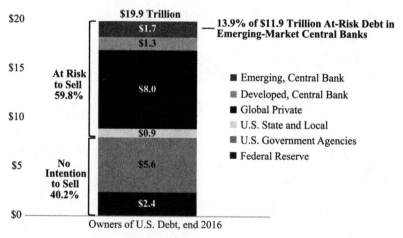

Owners of U.S. Debt, end 2016

Source: U.S. Treasury

Of that, emerging-market central banks are 22.7 percent of the market.

That's substantial, especially when they herd to buy Treasuries together when their currencies are rising, and then sell together when their currencies and exports are falling.

The $8 trillion held by real investors makes up 40 percent of the $20 trillion total in U.S. public debt. . . . Normal free market investors aren't driving this market.

Early in the next financial crisis, it will be private investors and emerging-market central bank selling that will create a spike in yields.

Who's Going to Buy When the Selling Accelerates?

Another trend that has me expecting this Fixed Income Trade of the Decade to become available by late 2017 or early 2018 is the inventory of U.S. Treasuries held by brokers and dealers.

As the Federal Reserve and government agencies have accumulated so much of the total stock of U.S. sovereign bonds, brokers and dealers have held less as a percentage of the bonds outstanding. After all, they need less when the Fed is dominating the market.

This next chart shows that the ratio of their inventory of bonds to the total marketable securities has fallen dramatically, from a ratio of 0.19 down to 0.04. That's a decline of 78 percent!

This raises the question: Who is going to be on the buying side when investors and emerging-market central banks are selling in droves?

Thus far, global private investors have picked up the slack, essentially buying what the emerging-market central banks are selling.

Could this continue indefinitely?

Anything is possible, but I wouldn't bet on it.

Emerging-market selling is accelerating, and it won't take much in an illiquid market like this for supply to completely overwhelm

Figure 15-4: Dealers Are Holding Fewer Treasuries

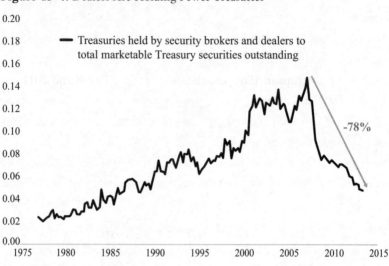

Source: Deutsche Bank; "About Liquidity," *Business Insider,* October 10, 2015

demand from the private sector—especially if something goes wrong in the world.

When there's strong selling in a less liquid market, bond prices will fall more, which will make their yields rise faster and higher than they otherwise would.

But let me reiterate: This will be a shorter-term crisis, not a long-term one. This opportunity to get in on the Fixed Income Trade of the Decade is likely only a short-lived one, so you must prepare now and be ready to pounce when the time comes.

Emerging countries won't be able to sell off their foreign exchange reserves forever. They'll do it only after their governments have tried the quick fixes first. But this crisis is too big to fix, and they'll have to stop selling Treasuries soon enough, if they don't run out of them first.

There's also the fact that commodity prices have been collapsing since mid-2008.

Their decline worsened in early 2011, due to China's increased slowing. At the bottom of it all, this is what's hurting the foreign exchange and emerging-market debt bubbles the most.

Why Commodity Prices Will Make Matters Worse

The Commodity Cycle runs very close to 30 years. And it tops like clockwork—1920 and a double top in 1949 and 1951 are perfect examples. So are the tops in 1980 and the double top in 2008 and 2011.

But the bottoms are much more varied.

The last cycle peaked in 1980 and bottomed between 1998 and 2001. The current cycle peaked in June 2008, dominated by the severe crash in oil and energy. Then industrial commodities and precious metals peaked in April 2011. It's been downhill since then.

Oil was down 80 percent at its worst point in late 2008. Iron ore and coal have been down more than 79 percent recently. Silver fell 70 percent. Even gold, the great crisis metal (ha!), has been down 45 percent.

At this rate, the Commodity Cycle could easily bottom just after the next crisis—sometime in 2018, or early 2020 at the latest. But even if it doesn't, 90 percent or more of the damage is likely to be done by then.

Figure 15-5: 30-Year Commodity Cycle: Greatest Surge Ahead

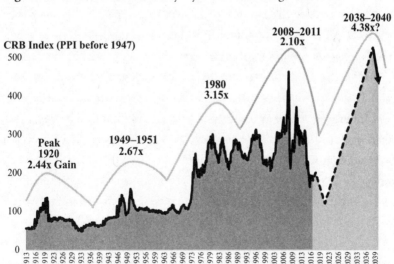

Source: Dent Research, Bloomberg

This continued decline will preserve downward pressure on emerging-market exports, stocks, economies, and currencies. That means this vicious cycle of selling foreign exchange reserves to support currencies and stimulate economies will roll round and round until it simply can't go on any longer.

On that note, if the commodities cycle *does* bottom in 2018, that would create a great long-term buying opportunity in both commodities and in emerging-country stocks (which I'll talk about later). We won't see such an opportunity come to developed-country stocks until early 2020 into late 2022.

The final nail in the coffin is my T-Bond Channel . . .

Watch for a Potential Short-Term Spike in Rates

I've used this tool for more than a decade now.

Ten-year Treasury yields have traded in a channel downward since 1989. The previous cycle saw a bottom in December 2008 at 2.03 percent, and a top around 4 percent into mid-2009, but that didn't test the top of the channel.

What makes this tool particularly useful is that, if you buy bonds when they approach the top of this yield channel and sell them when they approach the bottom, you'll very likely score a win each time.

It last tested the bottom trend line of this channel in July 2012, at 1.39 percent, and then first rallied to 3.04 percent into December 2013. Most of that was in just a matter of months. Yields went back down to 1.36 percent in January 2015 and appear to be rallying upward again, with rates hitting 2.62 percent in late 2016. They back off to 2.12 percent into 2017. One more spike and we get near the top of this channel at 3.0 percent to 3.1 percent.

If that occurs, that's when I will be telling my subscribers to load up on 30-year Treasuries and AAA corporate bonds to play the deflation phase of debt and bubble deleveraging in the years ahead. With the storm clouds darkening over emerging markets, that makes this the high-quality fixed income buy of this decade. That would imply yields of 3.6 percent–plus on 30-year Treasuries.

To take advantage, here's what I want you to do. . . .

Action to take: When the time is right—and I'll give you the green light for this one in my newsletter—buy as many 30-year Treasuries as you can get your hands on. Or buy AAA-rated corporate 20-year bonds.

Again, I suggest the longer-term bonds, because they'll benefit more from the deflationary slide with 10-year Treasuries reaching 1 percent, or a good bit lower, and 30-year Treasuries reaching 1.6 percent or lower.

You'll also get the highest yield on the 30-year bonds: 3.6 percent–plus if the 10-year goes to near 3.1 percent. And they'll appreciate more when rates start falling later in 2018 and likely well into 2020-plus.

So many investors cry to me about how they're depending on their high-dividend blue-chip stocks to retire and live on.

My response is always the same: That's a mistake.

You're going to pay a heavy price when stocks decline by as much as 80 percent before this crisis is over.

Figure 15-6: 10-Year U.S. Treasury Yields—Spike Before Dive?

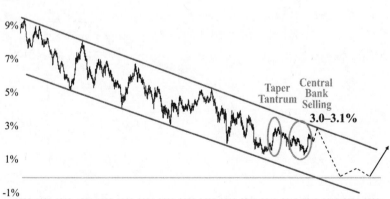

Source: Yahoo! Finance

Is it worth taking that kind of risk for a 2 to 3 percent dividend for the next several years? I don't think it is.

And how many stocks give you a 3 to 3.6 percent dividend compared with the 30-year Treasury?

Stocks did the worst of any asset class in the Great Depression of the 1930s. Even blue chips like the Dow were off 89 percent at their worst point, in late 1932. And they took 23 years to get back to late 1929 prices. Commodities were also down for a long time and were slow to come back. So was real estate, which lost 26 percent during that crisis and will be down much worse this time around.

Yet, while everything was cratering and asset allocation and diversification were proving to be of little use, long-term Treasury bonds and AAA corporate bonds roughly doubled in value including interest in the 1930s.

Long-term Treasuries almost doubled in the wrenching decade of the 1930s, while AAA corporates a little more than doubled when you count the steady interest.

If you're going to be a passive investor, make this Fixed Income Trade of the Decade.

Figure 15-7: High-Quality Bonds Did Best Through the Great Depression

Source: Global Financial Data

Use this likely spike into late 2017 or early 2018 to buy long-term 30-year Treasuries and AAA corporate bonds. You'll get interest higher than from most stock dividends, sleep better at night again, and get some healthy capital appreciation.

Of course, there's a chance I could be wrong. What then?

What if, by some miracle, demand from the private sector accelerates enough to soak up all the excess supply from central bank dumping?

That is the beauty of this scenario.

Given how low yields are today, we're not really risking anything by staying out of 30-year Treasuries for now. At current prices, the 30-year Treasury yields a pathetic 2.2 percent.

If we don't get back near the top of this T-Bond Channel, I'll still recommend buying 30-year Treasuries and AAA corporate bonds for the more conservative side of your asset allocation in this Economic Winter Season.

Most analysts think the bond bubble and rally is over. I see it as the last to rally, because it is the only major sector favored by deflation, other than the good old U.S. dollar.

Speaking of which, the dollar is the second safe haven . . . not gold.

Gold went up in the early stages of the last crisis, with investors expecting money printing to follow. But what happened instead was the meltdown of our financial institutions.

When such deflationary trends set in, much like in the early 1930s, gold collapsed. It lost 33 percent, and silver lost 50 percent.

But guess what spiked up in that crisis?

You got it: the U.S. dollar.

It rose 27 percent.

It was the other safe haven, along with the highest-quality bonds and cash.

The dollar has seen a massive fall versus our key trading partners since 1985.

Figure 15-8: U.S. Undervalued after 58 Percent Devaluation in Boom
U.S. Dollar Index (DXY)

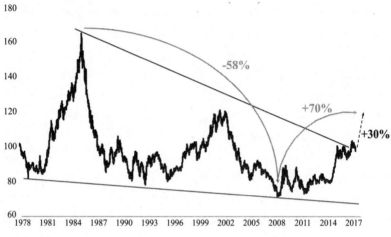

Source: Bloomberg, Dent Research

It was devalued by our issuing so much domestic and foreign debt. But that debt faces massive restructuring in the crisis ahead. Fewer dollars means they're worth more!

The dollar literally bottomed longer-term, at 71, in January 2008 . . . right when the Great Recession started. It's been up to as high as 104 in 2017—a 46 percent gain. Is that a safe haven or what?

I see the dollar going back to its high of 120, maybe higher.

Once there, it'll be back to fair value.

But at levels as low as 97, and potentially as low as 92 in 2017, it's a bargain, and another safe haven sector to put money into.

UUP (the PowerShares DB US Dollar Index Bullish Fund) is the easiest way to bet on the dollar going up . . . or you can find a good dollar bull fund.

Playing a Bear Market

When playing a bear market, the same rules hold: You want to diversify your risks, especially knowing that collapses move even faster than rallies.

You need to decide how much safe cash or near cash you want to hold to sleep at night and to handle financial emergencies, like the loss of your job or your house.

Then decide how much to put into longer-term high-quality bonds, like those 30-year Treasuries and AAA corporates, but I think it's still premature to make this move at the time of this writing, in August 2017.

Then decide how much you want to put into a dollar bull fund or the ETF UUP, which tracks the U.S. dollar versus its six major trading partners.

If you're willing to risk part of your wealth, you can also bet on financial assets going down—from stocks to gold.

Stocks are the one type of financial asset that goes down in either a deflationary crisis, like the 1930s, or an inflationary one, like the 1970s. So shorting stocks is the best way to prosper in the downturn, either way.

But don't leverage this bet. The markets are simply too volatile.

You can short the stock market with no leverage by simply buying an ETF (exchange-traded fund) like the ProShares Short S&P 500 (NYSEArca: SH).

It's an inverse fund on the S&P 500, so if the index goes down 50 percent, you make 50 percent.

The ProShares Ultrashort (NYSEArca: QID) is double short the NASDAQ 100, which is likely to get hit the worst. If you make this play, just do a half share, to avoid that two-times leverage (hold the other half in cash or short-term bonds).

Direxion Daily Small Cap Bear 3X ETF (NYSEArca: TZA) is triple short the Russell 2000, which is also likely to lead on the way down. So buy only a one-third share of this one, to remain without leverage. (That means the money you allocate here should be one-third in TZA and two-thirds in cash, to offset the leverage.)

And unlike the gold bugs, I see gold collapsing. It's an inflation hedge, not a deflation hedge.

If gold rallies back as high as $1,425—on my predicted bear-market rally—then it could easily drop to around $700 within a year.

Your last decision is whether to risk some of your funds betting on gold's downside, for the greatest potential returns.

You can buy DB Gold Double Short ETN (NYSEArca: DZZ)—double short gold—at a half share, to offset the leverage, or just simply short GLD, the ETF that follows gold.

There you have it. How to handle the coming crash.

Next up, let's get you into position for the opportunities ahead so that you're ready when we start to come out the other side, with emerging markets and commodities likely leading the charge. . . .

CHAPTER 16

The Emerging World Boomers

It's not as simple as buying an emerging-market fund or an ETF like EEM (iShares MSCI Emerging Markets). That would be a good strategy, but it's not the best one.

Harry Dent

MY DEMOGRAPHIC RESEARCH makes it crystal clear that emerging countries, outside of China and a few others like Thailand, will dominate demographic growth in the next global boom. But the even more powerful factor is the urbanization process, with the typical emerging country only 50 percent urbanized, as compared with 85 percent in the typical developed country.

In emerging countries, urbanization increases household income as much as three times from its level in rural areas. As people move into the cities, they also climb the social and economic ladder into the middle class.

With the cycles swirling around us for the next several years and the force of revolution reshaping our world, emerging markets are in the best position to come booming out the other side.

That's why investors and businesses should be investing more in emerging countries when this crash likely sees its worst, by early 2020.

My research is unique when it comes to projecting urbanization, GDP per capita gains from it, and demographic workforce growth trends and peaks in emerging countries.

It's not what I'm most known for, but it's the most strategic factor in the next global boom, which emerging countries will dominate.

As a general guideline, those in South and Southeast Asia, from the Philippines to India and Pakistan, have strong demographic growth, urbanization trends, and productivity gains ahead.

This is not the case for China, though.

Latin America has mostly strong demographic growth, but limited continued urbanization and productivity gains.

Much of the Middle East and Africa have not joined the democratic-capitalism party, but those regions otherwise have the most extreme urbanization and demographic potential. One day they'll be the best places to invest, but not yet.

So let's look at who the next boomers will be. . . .

Indonesia: It Doesn't Get Clearer than This

Indonesia is my favorite example of a good, solid emerging country that is urbanizing at high and predictable rates, with consistent GDP per capita gains over time.

Most emerging countries, including Indonesia, have a linear progression of GDP per capita for every 1 percent they gain in their urbanization rate. That was one of my great breakthroughs in my research about a decade ago.

They eventually top out between 80 and 90 percent urban.

The world today is 52 percent urban and rising.

This is the most powerful driver of GDP growth, as urban workers have access to a much broader array of jobs and can specialize much more.

This is what drives productivity, more than just aging into peak spending and income ages, especially because emerging countries don't have as steep a rise in income and spending by age as developed countries do.

Figure 16-1: Indonesia GDP per Capita (PPP) Versus Urbanization

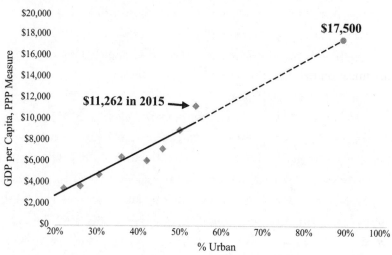

Source: United Nations World Urbanization Prospects, the Conference Board

They don't have as high a proportion of professional, managerial, and technical jobs that accelerate income growth. Construction and agricultural workers don't make that much more as they age.

Here's a chart depicting Indonesia's GDP per capita. . . .

It doesn't get better than this!

The country is 54 percent urban, 2 percent above the global average. It's been urbanizing at a consistent rate on average of 0.92 percent gains annually since 1985, a faster rate than in any emerging country in Asia except China.

That means that over a decade, it will add 9.2 percent of its population to urban areas until the process peaks.

At that rate, it'll take the country about 38 years to become 90 percent urban. That's where it'll likely peak around 2055.

That's almost four decades of productivity gains ahead.

But the most important indicator on this chart is how much India's GDP per capita (based on purchasing power parity, or PPP) grows with urbanization.

There are wide differences in this factor!

The cost of living in Indonesia is much lower than in the United States and most other developed countries. Its actual GDP per capita in 2015, in U.S. dollars, was $3,346. But when adjusted for lower cost of living, it's $11,262.

That's a huge difference.

That puts Indonesia just below the global average of $14,717.

This is important, as the linear correlation between urbanization and GDP per capita does not work nearly as well without the purchasing-power-parity adjustment, and it's more realistic.

Figure 16-1 would project that Indonesia's GDP per capita PPP, at 90 percent urbanization around 2053, would be $17,500. That's 55 percent higher than today!

This would be in addition to its strong population and workforce growth.

That puts Indonesia in the upper ranks of emerging countries, which range from $7,000 in Kenya to $22,000 in Mexico when they reach 90 percent urbanization in the future.

Speaking of Mexico. . . .

Mexico: Mostly Done, but Still a Boomer

Mexico is another example of a consistent urbanization and GDP per capita trend, but, unlike Indonesia, it's close to maturity.

At 81 percent urban, Mexico has a GDP per capita PPP of $18,232. That's higher than Brazil's and on the very high side for Latin America, with Chile higher, at $22,197, followed by Uruguay, at $19,952, and Argentina, at $19,196.

Its nominal GDP per capita in U.S. dollars is just $8,981.

It projects to $22,000 PPP-adjusted at 90 percent urbanization, which is 26 percent higher than in Indonesia. It's been more successful at entering higher-end manufacturing industries, which are 18 percent of GDP.

Figure 16-2: Mexico GDP per Capita (PPP) Versus Urbanization

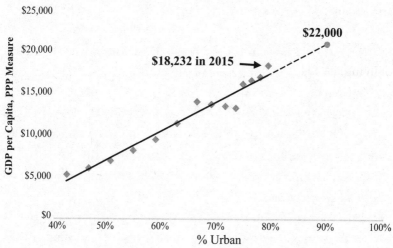

Source: United Nations World Urbanization Prospects, The Conference Board

But its rate of urbanization has been and is now much slower than Indonesia's.

It's been urbanizing at a rate of 0.37 percent per year since 1985. (It started much earlier, which is typical of Latin America.) After hitting 80 percent, it's slowed down, which is also typical of the region. Some countries never get over 75 to 80 percent.

At this rate, Mexico would be fully urbanized, at 90 percent, by 2039. That's just in time for the next Commodity Cycle peak.

It should be at its best between 2036, when the next global boom temporarily peaks, and 2038–40, when the next Commodity Cycle peaks.

Brazil: Like an 87-Year Old, but It Can Still Surprise You

Brazil, the largest country in South America, had a GDP per capita PPP of only $14,535 in 2015, and it's already 87 percent urban, with very little potential for further gains.

From 1985 to 2015, Brazil advanced from 71 to 87 percent urban, at a rate of 0.53 percent per year. It should peak at around 90 percent urban by 2020.

Why would I suggest that you invest in a country that's the equivalent of an 87-year-old in terms of the most powerful life-cycle and growth trend?

Because Brazil will have a positive Commodity Cycle again from the early 2020s forward, as will most other emerging countries, with stronger urbanization and demographic growth trends.

When looking at urbanization and GDP per capita growth, you occasionally get miracles. . . .

Countries like Japan, South Korea, Taiwan, Singapore, and Malaysia saw an S curve, or exponential pattern, of GDP per capita growth instead of a linear path.

Japan transitioned from an emerging to a developed country in three decades: the 1960s, '70s, and '80s.

Korea's baby boom generation followed Japan's by 22 years, and so did its S-curve urbanization cycle, in the 1980s, '90s, and 2000s. No coincidence that Korea's baby boom peaked in 1971, exactly 22 years after Japan's peaked in 1949.

All of these East Asian Tigers now have developed-world standards of living, with GDP per capita PPP ranging from $25,312 in Malaysia to $34,387 in South Korea, $37,872 in Japan, and a whopping $80,192 in Singapore.

The only Latin American country to achieve this is Puerto Rico.

It went from $7,000 in 1985 to $29,000 in 2015, *after* it was already 80 percent urban. I've NEVER seen that before!

What all of these countries have in common is that they transitioned to higher-end manufacturing and financial sectors, with, of course, higher-paying jobs.

Forty-six percent of Puerto Rico's economy is manufacturing, and the majority of that is in pharmaceuticals, biotech, and medical devices. Another 20 percent is in financial!

Only so many countries can do that. Not even China, for the most part, has entered the higher-end manufacturing or finance sectors!

Puerto Rico did that out of its close, territorial status with the United States. Its major exports are mostly to the United States and were launched based on favorable tax policies from the United States for pharma and related industries.

The Demographic Trends Are Very Different

Only in emerging countries are demographic trends second to urbanization, especially where there's a steeper curve on productivity, as in Mexico, Indonesia, China, and India.

This is because developed countries are already urbanized and can thrive on increasing productivity only in the highest-end industries and services.

When I analyze emerging countries, I use workforce growth instead of the 46-to-47-year birth lag for peak spending, because the difference between the incomes of older and younger workers isn't as large in the former. But frankly, using both the 46-year lag and the workforce growth approaches, the projections aren't that different.

In terms of demographic growth ahead, Indonesia's in the middle of the pack for the Southeast Asian countries. It looks good, but it's not as strong as India, and it's nowhere near Kenya, the Middle East, and Africa.

Look at its Spending Wave chart (Figure 16-3).

Indonesia has one of the longest demographic growth trends in Southeast Asia. It doesn't peak until around 2060. But it does plateau after 2045.

That's another plus for Indonesia in the next global boom, from 2023 to 2036.

Cambodia peaks way out into around 2070, with a plateau between 2055 and 2075.

Figure 16-3: Indonesia Workforce Growth

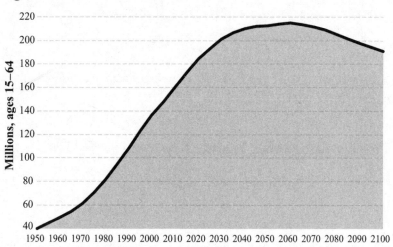

Source: United Nations Population Division

The Philippines peaks latest, around 2080, and it has the strongest demographic growth in the decades ahead.

But would I bet on Cambodia or the Philippines between 2020 and 2035?

I'll take Cambodia! So should you.

The Philippines still has high corruption and stagnant urbanization growth. That's why you see Philippine workers everywhere you travel—they don't have opportunities in their own country.

Then comes Myanmar, peaking around 2050, and Vietnam, with its peak around 2035–40.

The country that has the highest standard of living in Southeast Asia is Thailand, thanks to Bangkok and its burgeoning tourism industry.

Its GDP per capita projects as high as $35,000 at 90 percent urbanization. But its demographics already peaked, in 2015, and turn down sharply ahead, due to its higher urbanization and lower birth rates.

Figure 16-4: Mexico Workforce Growth

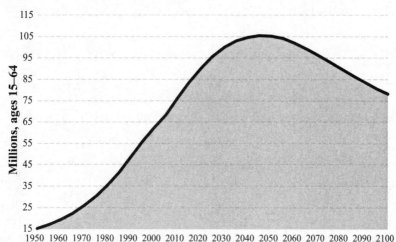

Source: United Nations Population Division

Now let's look at Mexico's demographic trends (above). They're typical of Latin America.

Not only does Mexico have very little urbanization opportunity compared with Indonesia, but its demographic growth peaks earlier as well. Then its demographic trends plateau between 2040 and 2050, before starting to drop off. Hence, Mexico will not look as attractive after 2040, and should be adversely affected by the peak in the U.S. Spending Wave around 2036.

Colombia peaks the earliest, around 2030, with a plateau between 2025 and 2045. That's not good for the country, despite its growing tourism boom since it killed off the drug cartels.

Brazil's peak is next, around 2035.

Argentina's demographic trends peak the latest, around 2065, with a plateau between 2055 and 2075.

In general, Latin America and the Caribbean follow Mexico's demographics, peaking around 2045 and plateauing between 2035 and 2055.

Latin America will have demographics and the 30-year Commodity Cycle in its favor from 2020 to 2040, but not urbanization and the productivity from that.

Still, it'll be a very good place to invest.

Of all the emerging regions and countries, however, Southeast Asia and India have all three of the key cycles working to their advantage, especially urbanization potential and high rates of productivity combined. That makes those areas the ones to invest in.

Here's a table of the key Southeast and South Asian countries, looking at the key components I measure and project.

Not surprisingly, my number-one rating goes to India. Its scale and underinvestment in infrastructure and its urbanization trends give it phenomenal potential. Add to that the first apparently progressive, pro-business government in its history, led by Prime Minister Modi, and India is off the charts in terms of investment potential.

India is the only major emerging country to reach new highs over its 2007 peak because of this.

In fact, India is the next China (unless they just blow it politically).

Figure 16-5: Growth Potential in Emerging Asia

Country	Workforce Growth, 1985–2015	Advancement in Urbanization Rate, 1985–2015	GDP per Capita PPP Growth Rate, 1985–2015	Workforce Growth Projections, 2020–2035	Growth Potential 2020–2035 (Last two columns added)
			Annual Averages		
India	2.18%	0.28%	4.74% (6.11% 2005–2015 and future)	1.01%	7.12%
Myanmar	1.73%	0.33%	5.71%	0.62%	6.33%
Cambodia	2.91%	0.23%	4.06%	1.42%	5.48%
Philippines	2.57%	0.04%	3.20%	1.38%	4.58%
Indonesia	2.03%	0.92%	3.74%	0.76%	4.50%
Vietnam	2.23%	0.47%	4.06%	0.41%	4.47%
Pakistan	2.84%	0.32%	2.05%	1.99%	4.04%
China	1.35%	1.09%	8.94% (4.47% future expected)	-0.54%	3.93%
Thailand	1.43%	0.74%	4.29%	-0.79%	3.51%

Source: Dent Research, United Nations Population Division, Total Economy Database

India's strong demographic growth peaks around 2050 and then plateaus into around 2065. By then it could achieve near peak urbanization as well.

Given its higher projected population growth and scale, it should be the greatest driver of global growth ahead, just as China was from the early 1980s to now.

The country has been slower at urbanization, but that will accelerate. Its productivity from urbanization is already second only to China's since 1985.

Myanmar's growth potential is 6.33 percent. It's the new rising star in Southeast Asia, after the military dictators figured out they could make more money attracting tourists (and not abusing their people in front of them).

Cambodia is next, with a growth potential of 5.48 percent. It has high GDP per capita growth versus urbanization, and it will enjoy the highest demographic growth in Southeast Asia into 2035.

Then comes the Philippines, with growth potential at 5.48 percent. But this will happen only if it starts urbanizing again and the downturn revolutionizes its internal corruption.

Indonesia is in the middle, with growth potential of 4.50 percent. It has scale to its advantage, like India.

Pakistan could be another surprising star if it can change its anti-Western, terrorist-nurturing stance when our Geopolitical Cycle turns back up between 2020 and 2036. It could even rival India one day.

Right now, though, the country has the economic potential to grow at something like 4.0 percent.

China comes in near the bottom, at a still healthy 3.93 percent growth rate, but I maintain that it'll take China more than ten years to work off the excess capacity and debt it has.

Finally, let's look at Latin America for comparison. . . .

The Growth Potential to the South

All these countries have little urbanization and productivity potential, as I explained earlier. That's why, in the fourth column, I've cut
their past productivity rates in half. In columns four and five, I sum
up the productivity and demographic growth trends, for an overall
rating in column six.

Puerto Rico comes out on top thanks to its high productivity
and concentration in manufacturing industries that cater to the aging
U.S. population.

But it has a debt crisis to deal with first. And it needs to stem the
flow of people leaving the country for better jobs in the United States.
That will flatten out or reverse only when the United States has a
bigger depression, between late 2017 and late 2022.

Puerto Rico has been in a decade-long recession and has unemployment rates just above 10 percent. But it still has the highest standard of living in all of Latin America, due to its strong, high-end
exports to the United States.

Figure 16-6: Growth Potential in Latin America and the Caribbean

Country	Workforce Growth 1985–2015	Advancement in Urbanization Rate, 1985–2015	GDP per Capita PPP Growth Rate, 1985–2015	Projected GDP per Capita Growth Rate, 2020–2035 at half of previous	Workforce Growth Projections, 2020–2035	Growth Potential 2020–2035 (Last two columns added)
Annual Averages						
Puerto Rico	0.55%	0.31%	5.39%	2.69%	-0.45%	2.24%
Chile	1.61%	0.23%	4.01%	2.01%	0.18%	2.19%
Peru	2.43%	0.39%	2.10%	1.05%	1.00%	2.05%
Ecuador	2.12%	.042%	1.18%	0.59%	1.20%	1.79%
Uruguay	0.54%	0.27%	3.00%	1.50%	0.17%	1.67%
Argentina	1.38%	0.23%	1.44%	0.72%	0.85%	1.57%
Colombia	2.05%	0.36%	2.27%	1.13%	0.29%	1.42%
Mexico	2.39%	0.34%	0.97%	0.48%	0.90%	1.38%
Brazil	1.93%	0.53%	1.12%	0.56%	0.25%	0.81%

Source: Dent Research, United Nations Population Division, Total Economy Database

Chile comes next, with the highest productivity rates outside of Puerto Rico but one of the lowest demographic growth rates into 2035.

Peru, with modest rates of both productivity and demographic growth, is next.

Ecuador follows, with the highest demographic growth ahead but one of the lower productivity rates.

Uruguay has the lowest demographic growth rates but a very high productivity rate. It seems to be the leading-edge country for expat migrants, with its pristine beaches and unspoiled soil for agriculture.

My friend Doug Bell has been successfully raising money for agricultural investments and exports there.

Argentina has the best city, Buenos Aires, and one of the higher rates of demographic growth, taking the longest to peak—in 2065. But its productivity rates are on the lower side.

Colombia has the worst demographic trends, with a measly 0.29 percent growth rate ahead, but a higher-than-average productivity growth rate thanks to its burgeoning tourism sector.

Surprisingly, Mexico comes in second to last. Its productivity is slowing because its urbanization is low, at 0.48 percent, and its demographic growth is only average for Latin America. That was the biggest surprise to me, given how Mexico has risen as a substantial exporter in recent decades.

The last place I would invest is Brazil. It's maxed out on urbanization, along with productivity on the very low side and low demographic growth potential.

To Summarize...

The best emerging markets after the financial and economic reset ahead are in India and Southeast Asia . . . not China. And the growth rates there look to be substantially stronger than Latin America. So, why not focus in the best emerging markets region: Asia.

The next commodity boom will also lift most emerging countries, beyond these urbanization and demographic factors. We'll look at commodities next.

The next boom will be more and more about emerging countries exporting commodities to one another.

Now that's a trend to invest in!

It will also be about wealthier developed countries investing more in emerging countries, as their own infrastructures won't be expanding much, if at all.

CHAPTER 17

The Next Commodity Stars

There are two commodity-related sectors to put into your portfolio for the next big boom.

Harry Dent

WHILE THE GENERAL 30-YEAR COMMODITIES CYCLE moves like clockwork in the uptrends, it's a little less precise on the downswings as I mentioned earlier.

The tops in 1920, 1949–51, 1980, and 2008–11 were 30 years apart, give or take a year.

But the bottoms were less consistent. The 1920 top took 13 years to bottom, which it did in 1933. The 1951 top took 17 years to bottom. The 1980 peak took 21 years to bottom, although much of that loss happened during the first six years after the peak.

Now, the 2008–11 peak looks close to a bottom in the years ahead.

The first peak, in mid-2008, was driven by energy, industrial metals, and agriculture. The second peak, in early 2011, was in precious metals and some industrial metals, like iron ore and copper.

Oil's and iron ore's respective 80 percent crashes are why I think this cycle could bottom by early 2020 or early 2023 at the latest.

That means a major commodity boom is coming, starting between 2020 and 2023 and peaking around 2038–40. And this one could be

Figure 17-1: 30-Year Commodity Cycle: Greatest Surge Ahead
TR/CC CRB Index (PPI before 1947)

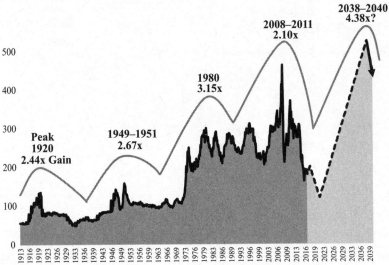

Source: Dent Research, Bloomberg

bigger than anything we've ever seen, inflating as much as 4.8 times. The last major bubble grew only 3.15 times from the late 1960s into 1980.

I always tell the gold bugs who argue that we'll see gold hit $5,000 per ounce that they're right. . . . After they're dead!

The important point to understand about commodities is that they have extreme cycles. That's why the best traders make their money in this sector.

And sudden weather patterns or mining strikes can cause tremendous short-term fluctuations, often exploding like a bomb! Unless you're working with someone who has a proven system, don't trade commodities. You can invest in them, but tread cautiously.

Remember that commodities are all different in their ability to ramp up supply (elasticity) when demand accelerates. It's easier to cultivate more land for crops or livestock in an era of urbanization, but it's not so easy to drill deeper for more oil or unearth more industrial metals like iron ore, coal, lead, nickel, and copper. Pulling uranium and the rare metals out of the ground is even harder.

Also, commodities and the emerging world are intrinsically connected. Where one goes, so goes the other.

As the emerging world dominates growth in the next global boom, it will need more of the basic commodities, from rice and corn to rubber, precious metals, industrial metals, and energy.

The best way to forecast such future needs and appreciation potential is to see how different commodities performed in the last Commodity Cycle boom, from around 2001 into 2008–11.

The last cycle also offers other insights, because it saw the first big surge in emerging countries like China and India. That will prove telling in the next cycle as these countries continue to urbanize and move into middle-class living standards.

Think about it.

How much gold or copper or iron ore is there in the world?

And how much of what *is* there can we reach?

There are always new innovations to find more, but they're often at higher costs. Take the energy sector, for example. . . .

Oil and Natural Gas

The fracking revolution found a way to drill horizontally and free up more oil and natural gas, but even that is not a low-cost innovation. Fracking can't compete with the lowest-cost large, vertical wells in Saudi Arabia and Iraq, but it can compete in the $30–$50 range and higher.

Such an innovation is not as likely to occur for basic industrial metals and precious metals . . . at least not in a hurry.

Fracking is an example of how an innovation can change an industry. It made oil, natural gas, and energy one of the most powerful

Figure 17-2: Oil and Natural Gas Never the Same Again after Fracking
Bloomberg Commodity Sub-Indices (100=1999)

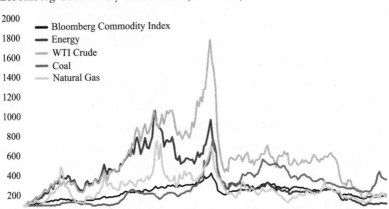

Source: Dent Research, Bloomberg

bubble trends in this past 30-year cycle. But I don't see that happening
in the future.

Fracking puts a lid on oil and natural gas prices, as these wells can
easily be started back up when prices rise high enough.

We won't see sustainable $100 oil again, or if so, it will be only
in a short-term crisis (a larger Middle East war) during the upcoming
worst two years of the 34-year Geopolitical Cycle. Andy also sees
a potential oil crisis in this time frame with his histograms. I think
oil will be in a $20–$60 range for a long time. Hence, this is not the
place to focus for investment returns. Oil will also be fighting electric
cars, which look like a strong long-term trend.

We won't see $14 natural gas again, either.

The trend toward "clean coal" is interesting, and we could see
higher appreciation from coal prices in the next global boom. But
everything in energy will have to compete with the swing producers
in the North American fracking industries that kick in increasingly
when prices get above $50.

Energy and Metals

Here we're looking at three major sectors that have outperformed the TR/CC CRB Index, and it's clear that the metals had the biggest gains.

Energy was clearly the leading sector into mid-2008, and then crude oil crashed 78 percent in 4.5 months. That's the fastest crash I've ever seen from a modern-day bubble burst! Since then, oil and natural gas have become underperformers and have lids on them from the swing capacity of the frackers in North America.

Energy will likely be an underperformer for decades ahead.

Precious metals did well, but not as well as the best industrial metals, like lead and nickel.

The greatest secret is that the rare minerals, like uranium and rhodium, did the best because they're rare! But they're also hard to invest in and extremely volatile.

Adjusted for risk and volatility, for the next global commodity

Figure 17-3: Precious and Industrial Metals Are the Strongest Bloomberg Commodity Sub-Indices (100=1999)

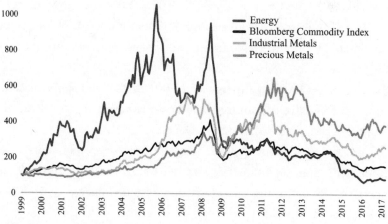

Source: Dent Research, Bloomberg

boom, precious metals and industrial metals look like the best sectors
to concentrate in.

Cement and Agriculture

There are sectors like cement that are clearly critical to growing
infrastructure in emerging countries, but cement's economics make
it a local industry, not an international one.

It doesn't make sense to export cement around the world, because
it has such a high weight/size-to-value ratio!

If you have cement plants, you can invest in the fastest-growing
countries, fine . . . but there's still the same factor of elastic supply.
There's always more sand and water in most places.

And agriculture (food), livestock, and textiles underperformed
and had the lowest gains, respectively, although they still performed
well during that last Commodity Cycle.

Industrial Metals

The industrial metals had some great performers between early 1999
and late 2011.

Iron ore stood out from around 2010, but it doesn't look as good
now, given the longer time frame and higher risk involved in mining it.

Its 1,100 percent gain between 2001 and 2011 tops platinum,
silver, gold, and most commodity sectors, except for rare minerals
like uranium and rhodium (more ahead).

Uranium enjoyed a 19-times gain from November 2001 into
June 2007. But, again, when adjusted for time frame and risk, it
doesn't come out of this cycle looking so good. That's why we'll dig
deeper ahead.

But overall, it's the precious metals that did the best, when
adjusted for risk.

Figure 17-4: Nickel, Lead, Iron Ore, and Tin Are the Strongest in the Metals
Bloomberg Commodity Sub-Indices (100=1999)

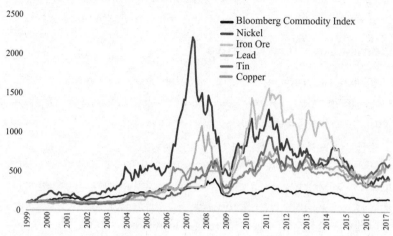

Source: Dent Research, Bloomberg

Note that, of all the precious metals, gold has the highest application in jewelry and monetary backing and investment. Silver follows, then platinum.

Figure 17-5: Platinum and Silver Lead Precious Metals Run into 2011
Bloomberg Commodity Sub-Indices (100=1999)

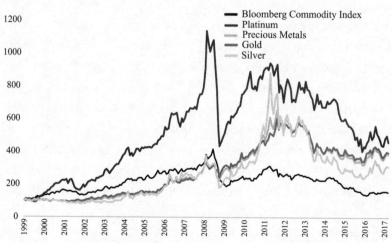

Source: Dent Research, Bloomberg

You can see in the preceding chart that platinum leans the most toward the industrial side, as it peaked in early 2008. When you buy platinum, you're really getting exposure to industrial metals and, to a lesser degree, precious metals.

Gold and silver face strong futures, particularly with Asians' love of wearing them as a show of wealth. China and India rival each other for spending on gold, but Indians spend much more compared with their incomes . . . and they're set to grow much faster than China in the coming decades.

Out of the precious metals, platinum has higher returns, a bit more than silver, which accelerates a good bit faster than gold. But silver has the highest risk and volatility, and gold the lowest. Gold actually has the best risk–adjusted performance.

From these three charts, the commodities that stand out are nickel, lead, iron ore, platinum, silver, gold, and coal.

But we have to adjust for risk and time frame, which I'll do next. This changes the picture.

The Risk Factor in Commodities Is Always High... Even in a Boom

The problem with commodities is that they're the most volatile of investment sectors. This makes it more important to adjust for risk and to combine a number of commodities in your portfolio to offset one another.

As we can see from the previous charts, we had a series of major peaks as early as 2005 in natural gas and as late as 2011 in gold in the broader Commodity Cycle that peaked between mid-2008 and early 2011.

Soybean meal was kicking ass and was still rising into June 2016.

Let me explain the next chart briefly . . .

Figure 17-6: Best Commodities in Last Bubble, into 2008–11

Commodity	Times Gain in Bubble	Average Annual Return, Bottom to Top	Risk Factor, Relative Standard Deviation Bottom to Top	Risk-Adjusted Return Index, Returns/STDEV, Bottom to Top
Lead	13.6 (Sep. 2002–Oct. 2007)	54.2%	0.94	57.9%
WTI Crude	17.7 (Jan. 1999–Jun. 2008)	35.9%	0.65	55.4%
Coal	7.7 (Aug. 2002–Jul. 2008)	43.2%	0.92	46.9%
Platinum	10.8 (Jan. 2001–Feb. 2008)	28.8%	0.62	46.7%
Nickel	22.1 (Oct. 2001–Apr. 2007)	56.0%	1.24	45.2%
Gold	6.6 (Mar. 2001–Aug. 2011)	19.3%	0.56	34.5%
Tin	12.1 (Sep. 2001–Feb. 2011)	29.5%	0.86	34.3%
Rubber	12.7 (Dec. 2001–Feb. 2011)	31.7%	0.95	33.5%
Iron Ore	11.4 (Dec. 2004–Feb. 2011)	47.4%	1.43	33.1%
Uranium	19.2 (Nov. 2001–Jun. 2007)	49.4%	1.65	30.0%
Silver	10.8 (Nov. 2001–Apr. 2011)	30.2%	1.03	29.4%
Copper	7.2 (Oct. 2001–Feb. 2011)	24.6%	0.88	28.0%
Soybean Meal	14.1 (Mar. 2001–Jun. 2016)	21.3%	0.95	22.5%
Vale	21.0 (Mar. 2002–May. 2008)	56.9%	1.20	47.6%
BHP Billiton	9.7 (Mar. 2002–Jun. 2008)	41.0%	0.93	44.2%

Source: Dent Research, Bloomberg

I look at when each commodity started to rise significantly and measure the times gain into when it topped.

The standouts in this table are:

- nickel, at a 22.1-times gain
- uranium, at 19.2-times gain
- crude oil, at 17.7-times gain
- soybean meal, at 14.1-times gain

As you can see, the time frames can range from six to ten years. That's a big difference.

Soybean meal was the outlier, taking 16.25 years to peak.

Commodities with longer bubbles, of eight to ten years, don't have as high an average annual compound return compared with their times gain as do bubbles of five to seven years.

To adjust for time frames in the second column, I calculated that average compound return per year in each bubble. Here the standouts are:

- nickel, at 56.0 percent
- lead, at 54.2 percent
- uranium, at 49.4 percent
- iron ore, at 47.4 percent
- coal, at 43.2 percent

This tells me that industrial metals take it hands down on returns in a bubble! Look to these as we expand into the next commodity bubble.

In the third column, I consider risk.

I first calculated the standard deviation during the bubble boom. Then I put them on an index, with 1.0 being average among all of these commodities. That means that more than 1 is riskier and less than 1 is less risky. The lower numbers are better.

This is where the precious metals shine.

Gold has the lowest volatility, at 0.56. That was in the boom from March 2001 into September 2011. It's also been the least risky in the crashes since 2008 and 2011.

Crude comes next, at 0.65.

Platinum, with its higher returns and industrial-metal leaning, comes in at a surprisingly low index of 0.62.

Silver is a good bit more volatile, at a near average rating of 1.03.

The commodities with the highest volatility include:

- uranium, at a whopping 1.65
- iron ore, at 1.43 (also down near 80 percent after 2011)
- nickel, at 1.24

Finally, I rated all of these commodities, from highest to lowest, by dividing the average annual returns in column two by the risk index in column three. That means that a higher risk index lowers the risk-adjusted return in column four, and a lower one raises it.

The result?

The top five commodities are:

- lead, with a 57.9 percent risk-adjusted annual return
- crude, with 55.4 percent
- coal, with 46.9 percent
- platinum, with 46.7 percent
- nickel, with 45.2 percent

Gold does better than silver, with 34.5 percent. Tin does well, with 34.3 percent, followed by rubber, with 33.5 percent. Silver does well, with 29.4 percent, and copper is right behind, at 28.0 percent.

Soybean meal, copper, silver, and uranium come out on the bottom when adjusted for risk.

Note that many major commodities, from corn to cattle, didn't even make it into this level of analysis for outperformance.

Of these top-performing commodities, you can invest easily only in those with exchange-traded funds or futures contracts.

Only gold, silver, and crude have ETFs large enough to play with good volume. And I don't like oil and much of the energy sectors as much as the metals. The ETFs for platinum, copper, coal, and soybean meal are too small.

Since a lot of metals are not accessible, some of the best, like nickel, lead, and iron ore, aren't even in the futures market. But there is another way to play this top sector: the multinational mining companies that focus on industrial, precious metals, and coal. These include BHP Billiton and Vale.

What to Put in Your Portfolio for the Next Commodity Boom

In short, a good, simple portfolio in metal commodities for the next great commodity boom should include the following three, easily invested stocks or ETFs:

- Gold (GLD)
- Vale (Vale)
- BHP Billiton (BHP)

We're looking at creating some other options to get into the better metals, like lead, nickel, and tin.

Finally, let's look at the gainers and sustainers that will hand you profits in the aging developed world. . . .

CHAPTER 18

The Gainers and the Sustainers

There are only six developed countries that have substantially larger millennial generations, and they're all small.

Harry Dent

WHEN I LOOK AROUND THE WORLD, almost all developed countries have demographic declines over the next decade—although some, like Germany, are declining at more perilous rates than others.

That means that, despite the ongoing efforts by central bankers to keep this bubble going by way of endless stimulus, the outcome is inevitable.

All bubbles pop, and each burst is always bigger than the last.

With debt bulging, revolutionary cycles battering us from every side, and demographic trends growing worse, the financial crisis is going to be nightmarish.

However, looking at the big picture, it's not all bad news. . . .

The Gainers

There are six countries in the developed world with "echo boom" generations larger than the generation of their parents, the baby boomers.

In rough order of demographic strength, they are Israel, Australia, Switzerland, Norway, Sweden, and New Zealand.

The next global boom, between 2020 and 2037, will be dominated by the stronger demographic and urbanization trends in the emerging countries, and these few "winners" in the developed world will also be the best places to invest.

Israel: In the long-term, Israel's demographics are the most favorable. Indeed, they point up for decades ahead, as the country has avoided the steep decline in births that normally accompanies rising wealth and urbanization. Israel is also a leader in technology innovation.

I am strongly in favor of investing in Israel once we get over the current unfavorable geopolitical cycle, sometime around early 2020.

The other five countries do see demographic dips over the next decade but then have echo booms that take them up to new demographic heights.

Australia and New Zealand: After Israel, Australia and New Zealand have the most favorable demographic trends during the downturn

Figure 18-1: Australia Spending Wave
45–49-Year-Olds

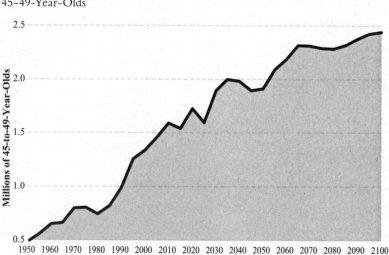

Source: United Nations Population Division

of the next decade. Their trends point up slightly into 2018 and then down modestly into around 2025. After that, they have the strongest demographic surge.

In the near term, Australia and New Zealand will be hit harder than their demographic trends would suggest, because of the inevitable bubble burst in China, as well as their extreme real estate bubbles.

However, the next great boom is likely to be dominated by emerging countries, which are more commodity intensive in their consumption. This may spark the greatest commodity bubble in history, and Australia and New Zealand would be clear beneficiaries.

Switzerland: This is the surprise in Europe, beating our past spending-wave projections. This gain could come only from strong immigration over the past decade, which would make sense, given Switzerland's traditional role as a safe haven from the turmoil throughout Europe and the Middle East.

Norway: The Norwegian economy is a little different, because oil plays such a big part. As a result, its GDP per capita is far greater than ours and exceeds even the total urban and high professional-services economy of Singapore.

The big question for Norway is what role oil will play in its future. If there are major innovations in alternative energy, oil's place may be more questionable. And, certainly, Norway would be hit harder than the other gainers if oil prices are below $30 a barrel over the next several years.

Sweden: This is the other strong country in Scandinavia, with minor downtrends ahead and a larger echo boom to follow. However, it doesn't have the same strong ties to oil prices and exports that Norway does, making it more attractive as an investment.

The Sustainers

The group I call "Sustainers" consists mostly of larger countries, including the United States, Canada, France, the UK, and Denmark, whose echo boom generations are nearly as large as their baby boomer one. As a result, their demographic spending trends point downward over the next decade or so before moving sideways in the decades that follow.

The United States: The USA enjoys the distinct advantage of being the leader in technological innovation. Holding on to that title will be critical for its future, as will its ability to continue attracting immigrants.

Unfortunately, looking at demographics, U.S. immigration is already falling rapidly, and the current administration is not helping the matter.

I forecast this phenomenon 20 years ago, when I saw that immigration, like global trade, falls dramatically during downturns. And it often takes decades to rebound.

If the United States, along with the other Sustainer countries, shuns immigration during the next boom, it will be to its disadvantage, especially because births also fall during downturns.

The U.S. birth rate has been falling since 2007, just as I predicted it would.

Canada: This country is interesting, because, like Australia and New Zealand, it should benefit from strong resource exports. Given what I've already said about the potential for a huge boom in commodity prices, Canada could see some of the strongest trends from the early 2020s through the end of the 2030s. However, the continued commodity bust will hit it harder than the United States in the next several years.

The UK, France, and Denmark: In spite of their economic power, growth in these countries will be hampered by weaker trends across

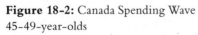

Figure 18-2: Canada Spending Wave
45–49-year-olds

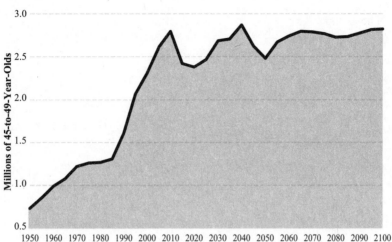

Source: United Nations Population Division

Europe. I consider them to be Sustainers because their demographics will simply move sideways for decades.

The key for these wealthy countries is to attract the best immigrants and technologies. Otherwise, their economies and markets may not see new highs for decades, if ever. As mostly English-speaking countries, the United States, the UK, and Canada enjoy a clear immigration advantage over the other two sustainers. But Australia and New Zealand do best in this category.

But the key point here is that even in these modestly or higher-growth developed countries, the baby boomers or aging sectors will tend to do best, as they had the strongest demographic surges, even in countries that have a larger millennial generation.

Healthcare and wellness, pharmaceuticals and vitamins, biotech and medical devices, cruise ships, and, best of all, funeral homes and nursing homes/assisted living—these are the sectors that will do best in all aging developed countries, and even better in the few that aren't aging as fast.

EPILOGUE

Cycles and Your Life

We're all on a merry-go-round.

Andrew Pancholi and Harry Dent

AS WE'VE SHOWN throughout this book, events repeat as history repeats.

This is a function of mass psychology. It's the behavior of the herd.

But we have our own personal cycles as well.

You'll undoubtedly have heard the maxim "Give me a child until he is seven and I will show you the man."

This has been attributed to not only Aristotle but also Saint Francis Xavier.

There's much truth in this, and, in fact, it is the basis for one of the cycle sets we use. You'll be familiar with it.

It's the seven-year itch.

It's effectively the 28-year and 30-year cycles we've discussed broken down into four parts, each lasting between seven and seven and a half years.

During the first seven years, a child is totally dependent on its parents, particularly the mother.

The next seven years see the father playing a more predominant role while the child moves through puberty and begins maturing.

The third phase sees experimentation and challenges in the

transition of breaking away from parents into individuality. This is particularly so around the ages of 15 to 18, the first half of the third seven-year cycle.

People gain degrees of freedom as they learn to drive and travel, experiment with alcohol and other things, and discover relationships. The transition is usually complete around the age of 21 or 22.

Think about this.

This is the point when many finish college and head out into the real world, taking us into the fourth phase. This is about becoming settled as an adult, having completely cut the apron strings.

The 28-to-30-year point usually sees major life changes take place.

If you were in a relationship that wasn't working out, then you'd find yourself moving on.

Equally, you may decide to take the relationship to a higher level at this point—perhaps a marriage.

If you're already married, this point may see the arrival of a child or a new home or a new city.

Basically, around this time, there's major transition in your life circumstances.

Then the cycle begins its second journey, which continues into the late fifties and into the age of 60.

Again, each segment brings turning points every seven years.

And so it continues.

No one completes his or her fourth 30-year cycle.

But this seven-year cycle doesn't just apply to stages of your life. It fits into everything else as well. . . .

Every seven years from the beginning of something, a degree of unease or change knocks on the door.

You may decide to change careers, or you're promoted seven years after you started that employment.

Within your personal relationships, you may see challenges seven years after you set out together, and then again after 14 to 15 years, and again after 21 to 22 years.

After four of these cycles, larger changes in outlook and life can take place.

When we apply this concept to professions, then we can divide these seven-year sections into development phases.

Consider a highly qualified surgeon or doctor, for example.

On this physician's journey to mastery, it's more than likely that he or she spent the first seven years at medical school, learning all the fundamentals of the profession.

After graduating, our doctor would have worked in hospitals and medical centers, under the guidance of senior doctors, putting into practice everything he or she had learned. This is the second seven-year phase.

Seven years later, they enter the third phase of their career. This is when they reach mastery. They branch out into their own specialist area and surpass in that field. They've done their 10,000 hours.

As they enter the fourth seven-year cycle, they're the undisputed experts and are then in the position to pay it forward by guiding the new doctors who follow behind them.

Another cycle that affects our lives is this next one. . . .

Growth and Renewal

The 12-year cycle is the basis for the 72- and 144-year cycles.

Within our lives, it represents growth periods. We renew or restart an expansive period every 12 years. A dozen years later, you may see a good level of success.

The Populist Movement Cycle, which is timed at 84 years, is interesting . . .

Eighty-four is effectively 12 cycles of seven years each or seven cycles of 12 years each.

Can you see how all this comes together?

The most important point in human life is the halfway zone,

around the age of 40 to 42. This period in our lives is often referred to as the midlife crisis.

Many have reached the top of their game. They feel they're peaking! The kids have left home! They feel unsettled or displaced. It's time to go out and buy that red sports car or a Harley!

There is a real feeling of change in emphasis or direction.

For some, it can represent an entire change in their lives. A lot of it depends on your belief systems, as ultimately, you're in control of your own life and destiny!

This is just a brief overview of how cycles can affect you as a person. There's a lot more to this. Much depends on picking the correct starting points from which the various dances of time unfold.

But always remember one thing: The economy's life cycles are bigger than yours. You need to take into account not only when you'll make major changes or transitions in your education or career or retirement, in business or investments, but also what impact the economic cycles we've talked about in this book has on those decisions.

For example, if you're thinking about retiring and selling your business five years from now, rethink it. The economy's life cycle would suggest you sell that business now, while it's worth much more than it could be five years from now, after the worst crash and financial crisis in history.

If your kids are looking at going to graduate school, then the next few years, when jobs prospects are low, could be a good time to do that.

Even a younger person with a long time frame for investing should be more conservative in his or her asset allocation in this Economic Winter Season crash.

Combine your natural life cycles with the economy's to make the very best decisions for your life, your family, your investments, and your business. That's what we aspire to accomplish for you at Dent Research. For our free newsletter or to get to know us better, simply go to dentresources.com. Also check out markettimingreport.com to follow Andy's work.

This is a fascinating science, and whether we know it or not, we're always partaking in it.

> "The thing that hath been, it is that which shall be; and that which is done is that which shall be done: and there is no new thing under the sun."
>
> —ECCLESIASTES 1:9

ACKNOWLEDGMENTS

My thanks to Teresa van den Barselaar, for another stupendous job of organizing and editing this book, following her work on *The Sale of a Lifetime*.

Thanks to Dave Okenquist, for his dedication to the highest-quality research and his contribution to the eye-opening charts in this book.

Thanks to my patient and ever supportive agent, Susan Golomb at Writers House.

And thanks also to Shannon Sands, publisher of Dent Research; Andrew Pancholi, for his insights and for working with me on this book; David Dittman, for proofreading and fact-checking this book; Megan Johnson, for marketing; Stephanie Gerardot, for publicity; and my business partners at Dent Research: Rodney Johnson and Harry Cornelius.

CHART INDEX

ABOUT HARRY S. DENT, JR.

Raised in Alexandria, Virginia, a place he loved, Harry S. Dent, Jr., was brother to three siblings. His father, Harry S. Dent, Sr., was a strategist and speechwriter for Strom Thurmond, the longest-serving senator in U.S. history.

The family moved to South Carolina when Harry Sr. became chairman of the state Republican Party. He met Richard M. Nixon in that role and became his strategist in the successful 1968 presidential campaign—the Karl Rove to Nixon's George W. Bush. Harry Sr. was the original architect of the "southern strategy."

He used Thurmond to convince the southern states that a vote for third-party candidate Governor George Wallace of Alabama was a vote for Democratic nominee Hubert H. Humphrey, who was President Lyndon Johnson's vice president. After Nixon won the presidency, Harry Sr. worked in the White House as his chief political strategist.

Harry Jr., entered the University of South Carolina in the early 1970s with plans to study economics. But after three short months, he was so disillusioned by the vague and inconclusive state of his would-be profession that he turned his back on it. Instead he threw himself into the burgeoning new science of finance, where identifying and studying demographic, technological, consumer, and many other cycles put him on the path to where he is today. He graduated from USC in the summer of 1975, #1 in his class, with a double major in accounting and finance.

Once out of school, Harry Jr. went to work for Champion International, in its central financial reporting department. There was little to challenge him there, though, and more often than not he'd find himself completing his work after just two hours. Many days were spent reading to while away the time, hiding out in the company's library.

After two years, he went back to school, this time to Harvard, where he received an MBA in 1979. As a Baker Scholar and member of the Century Club, he was in the top 1 percent of his class.

Returning to the business world, Harry worked for Bain & Company from 1979 to 1980. There, he was a business strategy consultant to Fortune 100 companies. While he enjoyed this work, it quickly became evident that he didn't have the patience with the bureaucracy so characteristic of these behemoths. They were totally out of step with the new economy emerging.

So Harry moved to California, where he split his time between consulting for smaller businesses (consumer-oriented companies ranging from $1 million to $20 million) and burying himself in his research.

Malcolm Gladwell argues that 10,000 hours is the magic number of greatness—that is, if you immerse yourself in something for that long, you truly become a master. That's exactly what Harry did during his early years in California, spending the years 1981 to 1989 immersed in his research. By 1988 he was already starting to see results, with breakthrough insights like his Generational Spending Wave.

In September 1989, Harry started the company known today as Dent Research with his first monthly economic newsletter. He self-published his first book, *Our Power to Predict,* in 1989, largely selling it to TEC (The Executive Committee—a global network of small business CEOs), for which he was a top speaker, for $5 per book as a handout.

In between researching and writing, Harry gave speeches, honing his wit and firing his passion. Between 1995 and 2000, he gave at least 1,000 speeches—280 of them in 1998 alone! That same year, his *New York Times* bestseller *The Roaring 2000s* (Simon & Schuster) was published. It sold 700,000 copies domestically (800,000 worldwide) in one year.

Today, he continues to speak, but far less than in those early years. He has appeared on ABC's *Good Morning America,* PBS, CNBC, Fox, and CNN. He's a regular guest on Fox Business. He also hosts the annual Irrational Economic Summit (www.irrationaleconomic summit.com).

Harry's been featured in *Barron's, Investor's Business Daily, Entrepreneur, Fortune, Success, U.S. News & World Report, BusinessWeek, The Wall Street Journal, American Demographics,* and *Omni,* as well as many other publications specific to the regions he visits each year to speak (Australia, India, South Korea, etc.).

And he continues to write, finding it one of several means of getting his important research into the hands of people like you.

His books include *The Great Boom Ahead* (Hyperion), which was published in late 1992. With this book, he stood virtually alone in accurately forecasting the unanticipated boom of the 1990s.

In 1998 and 1999, he followed *The Roaring 2000s* with a second bestseller, *The Roaring 2000s Investor* (Simon & Schuster).

In 2008, he wrote *The Great Depression Ahead* (Free Press), in which he forecast that we'd see a massive market correction and economic turmoil from 2008 to 2013.

Then, in *The Great Crash Ahead* (Free Press), he outlined how ultimately there is nothing the government can do to prevent the inevitable deflationary period inherent in the Economic Winter Season we are currently embroiled in. This inability to change the course of economic events isn't limited to the United States but is endemic across the developed world.

Harry's book *The Demographic Cliff: How to Survive and Prosper During the Great Deflation Ahead* (Portfolio/Penguin, 2015) showed why we're facing a "great deflation" after years of stimulus.

And in his previous book, *The Sale of a Lifetime: How the Great Bubble Burst of 2017–2019 Can Make You Rich* (Portfolio/Penguin, 2016), he presented a detailed analysis of bubbles and the dangers they bring to investors and businessmen. He proved, without a shadow of a doubt, that bubbles are, in fact, NOT black-swan events. He then detailed the "sale of a lifetime" that we'll see as we head into the next decade.

Through his company, Dent Research, he has also published *Spending Waves: The Scientific Key to Predicting Market Behavior for the Next 20 Years* (updated in 2017), an information-packed guide for predicting trends in all key consumer sectors, aimed at any serious marketer, business owner, or investor.

And in 2016, he published the e-book *How to Survive (and Thrive) during the Great Gold Bust Ahead,* in which he finally puts to rest the argument that gold is a savior to all investors. (It's NOT. . . . He's been telling investors to avoid gold in this deflationary period since early 2011!)

Today Harry lives in Puerto Rico, where he uses the research he developed from years of hands-on business experience, and the cycles he analyzes and hones continuously, to offer readers an easy-to-understand view of the economic future through Dent Research publications, including *Boom & Bust, The Leading Edge, Ahead of the Curve* webinars, and the free daily e-letter, *Economy & Markets,* all available at dentresources.com.

To Harry, surviving any market and economic shakeouts, or prospering through any booms, is about collaboration.

You can reach him at economyandmarkets@dentresearch.com.

ABOUT ANDREW PANCHOLI

Andrew Pancholi authors *The Market Timing Report* (www.market timingreport.com), which identifies timing points across key markets well in advance.

He is a general partner and portfolio manager at Fidelis Capital Management (which was named the 2016 Systematic Value Fund of the Year). He and William Copeland (founding partner of legendary Vinik Asset Management) run the Special Situations Fund.

He is also Harry's "go-to" man when it comes to timing markets. Harry met Andy when speaking at an Anthony Robbins Platinum Partnership event in Miami in 2008. It was instant cycle camaraderie, Andy having been an avid student of Harry's work.

He is the mastermind behind the proprietary Cycles Analysis system, which identifies turning points in markets days, weeks, months, and even years ahead of when they occur. Not only is he renowned for his expertise in financial cycles, but his operation forecasts cyclical geopolitical events.

Back in April 2014, Andrew flew across the Atlantic to brief Harry about the imminent collapse of the euro. He gave not only the exact dates but also the price the euro would reach, to within a hand-ful of ticks.

This kind of down-to-the-day forecasting is common practice for Andrew, who accurately timed the collapse of oil and the finan-cial challenges the UK faced six months before Brexit. He also called the commodity bull markets in 2008 and 2010.

Andrew's clients have a significant edge with the information he provides. They are able to enter and exit positions with accurate tim-ing, as well as profit from what the public calls "black swan" events.

He consults for banks and institutions, including some of the largest operations in the world. Several A-list celebrities from film, television, and various arts consult with him on the mathematics of life cycles.

In 2015, he was invited by NYU London to present a TEDx talk on recurring cycles, not only in history and stock markets but also in personal lives.

In October 2016, Andrew spoke alongside Harry and names such as Lacy Hunt and George Gilder at the Irrational Economic Summit in Palm Beach.

In January 2017, he was the subject of an in-depth video, primar-ily for professional portfolio managers, with Real Vision TV, cover-ing the cycles coming into play in 2017 and how they impact equity, commodity, and currency markets.

He is a regular contributor to *Traders World*.

His background includes extensive study in the works of legend-ary trader W. D. Gann, Edward R. Dewey, Elliott Wave, and many other cycles-related subjects. A long-standing friendship developed with Nikki and Cody Jones and her family, who are the owners and custodians of the Gann material. Andrew assisted them in verifying and cataloging the collection (wdgann.com).

He worked with Peter Pich of Gannsoft in the 1990s developing the Ganntrader software, which at the time was one of the most sophis-ticated forecasting programs available. He has spoken at seminars on

Gann trading with Lambert-Gann Educators across the United States and in the UK.

He also speaks about peak performance in trading.

On top of all of that, Andrew is a senior training and standardization captain, flying wide-bodied jets. His duties have included flying heads of state and royalty around the world. He has taken the rigorous safety disciplines used in flying aircraft and applied them to trading and risk. He is a fellow of the Royal Aeronautical Society.

As well as looking at markets, his team has made major advances in earthquake prediction and long-range weather forecasting.

Born in Irvine, Scotland, and having lived in Liverpool and Leeds, he got his BSc (Econ) Honors degree from the University of Hull. He now lives in Surrey, just outside London. With a cultural heritage emanating from India, Andrew has been brought up on cycles from a very young age, encouraged by his academic parents.

His wife, Karen, is from Chicago, and they have a young son and a teenage daughter. They live in a house once occupied by Sir Frank Whittle, inventor of the jet engine.

When he's not studying cycles for work, he relaxes by studying other cycles!

ECONOMY & MARKETS

The FIRST e-Letter of Its Kind!
Expert Economic Forecasting Powered by
Demographic Trends, Purchasing Power, and Cycles Analysis

Harry S. Dent, Jr. and his team at Dent Research believe that knowing what cycles are passing around us and understanding what consumers are going to buy next (or not) is the best way to protect your investment portfolio, maximize your returns, and make smart business and financial decisions.

Each weekday in *Economy & Markets*, Harry and his team share their views on demographic trends, stock market research and trends, the housing market, different economic, market and business cycles, investment and 401(k) strategies, the looming market crash, commodities, and more.

Economy & Markets readers discover:

- When it's time to start profiting from the rise of specific emerging market economies.
- When commodities are likely to peak again.
- When the housing market will turn down again, and how other real estate market trends will change.
- When bonds would be a better investment than stock allocations.
- Exactly what industries and investments will hand you the fastest profits.
- Much more!

Sign up at meetharrydent.com **FREE!**

DENTRESOURCES.COM

Get a Free Report to Prepare for the Revolution
Visit DENTRESOURCES.COM Today

Harry Dent has recruited some of the top financial minds money can buy. Their only interest is making sure readers—like you—get the unbiased, independent economic research and investment recommendations you need to outperform everyone else in the market.

He's been able to assemble one of the most experienced and most talented team of investment experts in the financial industry. DENT-RESOURCES.COM has all the details of this team, including . . .

- An in-house forensic accountant who has perfected a way to identify companies that manipulate their numbers.
- An industry veteran who has designed a simple but deceptively complex strategy to generate steady double-digit returns no matter what the market brings. Because one thing is for certain—baby boomers have money and they are spending it.
- A former financial adviser and trading desk manager who developed a proprietary algorithm to help him analyze important economic data and isolate trades in a segment of the financial markets that most people never consider—Treasury Bond markets.
- And a market technician who has built trading strategies that identify short-term trigger events with remarkable accuracy . . . so you can make money no matter which way the market is moving.
- Plus, details of the proprietary systems and algorithms that each one of these experts has developed and painstakingly tested over decades to help you profit.
- And a **SPECIAL FREE REPORT** to say thank you for reading the research Harry S. Dent, Jr. and his team prepare for you.

Are you ready to seize the day?
Let us show you how.

THE MARKET TIMING REPORT

Mastering Profits

One of the biggest challenges you face as a trader or portfolio manager is knowing when to enter or exit a trade or campaign. You get out too soon and miss out on profits. You stay in too late and see your profits evaporate.

How different would your financial situation be if you could time markets?

If you knew well in advance that a trend was likely to start or end, imagine how powerful that would be to you.

Well, using cycles, we time markets well in advance. Our Profit Finding Oracle system highlights time periods when high probability trend changes can occur. We also use our timeline that highlights market moves weeks, months, and years in advance.

The Market Timing Report . . .

- Focuses on S&P 500, Crude Oil, Gold, EUR, Dollar Index
- Is published monthly
- Provides high probability turning points and probability information
- Is derived from the Cycles Analysis "Profit Finding Oracle" Program
- Is based on seasonality, cycles, and other proprietary methods
- Looks at forthcoming geopolitical cycles and events

Try it now!
Get the edge!
Find out more at www.markettimingreport.com.

Do you need geopolitical strategic information for any business venture?

Do you want to know where your business is in terms of industry cycles?

Is a country you wish to expand your business in about to face major upheaval?

Cycles Analysis provides specialist consultation in these and several other areas.

Contact us with your needs at info@cyclesanalysis.com.